CSR, Sustainability, Ethics & Governance

Series Editors

Samuel O. Idowu, London Metropolitan University, London, UK

René Schmidpeter, M3TRIX Institute of Sustainable Business, Cologne, Germany

In recent years the discussion concerning the relation between business and society has made immense strides. This has in turn led to a broad academic and practical discussion on innovative management concepts, such as Corporate Social Responsibility, Corporate Governance and Sustainability Management. This series offers a comprehensive overview of the latest theoretical and empirical research and provides sound concepts for sustainable business strategies. In order to do so, it combines the insights of leading researchers and thinkers in the fields of management theory and the social sciences – and from all over the world, thus contributing to the interdisciplinary and intercultural discussion on the role of business in society. The underlying intention of this series is to help solve the world's most challenging problems by developing new management concepts that create value for business and society alike. In order to support those managers, researchers and students who are pursuing sustainable business approaches for our common future, the series offers them access to cutting-edge management approaches.

* * *

CSR, Sustainability, Ethics & Governance is accepted by the Norwegian Register for Scientific Journals, Series and Publishers, maintained and operated by the Norwegian Social Science Data Services (NSD)

Noémi També Bearpark

Deconstructing Money Laundering Risk

De-risking, the Risk-based Approach and Risk Communication

Noémi També Bearpark
Luxembourg School of Business
Luxembourg, Luxembourg

ISSN 2196-7075   ISSN 2196-7083   (electronic)
CSR, Sustainability, Ethics & Governance
ISBN 978-3-031-07507-0   ISBN 978-3-031-07508-7   (eBook)
https://doi.org/10.1007/978-3-031-07508-7

© The Editor(s) (if applicable) and The Author(s), under exclusive license to Springer Nature Switzerland AG 2022
This work is subject to copyright. All rights are solely and exclusively licensed by the Publisher, whether the whole or part of the material is concerned, specifically the rights of translation, reprinting, reuse of illustrations, recitation, broadcasting, reproduction on microfilms or in any other physical way, and transmission or information storage and retrieval, electronic adaptation, computer software, or by similar or dissimilar methodology now known or hereafter developed.
The use of general descriptive names, registered names, trademarks, service marks, etc. in this publication does not imply, even in the absence of a specific statement, that such names are exempt from the relevant protective laws and regulations and therefore free for general use.
The publisher, the authors and the editors are safe to assume that the advice and information in this book are believed to be true and accurate at the date of publication. Neither the publisher nor the authors or the editors give a warranty, expressed or implied, with respect to the material contained herein or for any errors or omissions that may have been made. The publisher remains neutral with regard to jurisdictional claims in published maps and institutional affiliations.

This Springer imprint is published by the registered company Springer Nature Switzerland AG
The registered company address is: Gewerbestrasse 11, 6330 Cham, Switzerland

To Dr. Joseph També

Introduction

Over the past 50 years, anti-money laundering (AML) regulations have evolved at an ever-increasing pace, which is indicative of the international community's commitment to tackling the problems of money laundering (ML) and terrorism financing that threaten society on a global scale. Yet, the success and efficiency of current AML efforts remains a controversial topic. There appear to be no effective avenues through which practitioners can assess and evaluate their current AML efforts and initiatives. Furthermore, such efforts are incessantly discredited by the latest ML scandal or terrorist attack reported in the media.

In order to understand the current state of affairs, the author focuses on ML *risk* as opposed to AML legislation, typologies, impact on society, and the industry's initiatives to tackle ML, which represent the primary focus of extant academic AML literature (Ryder, 2012; Unger & Van der Linde, 2013; Levi et al., 2018). Essentially, the author locates her research on the nature of risk, its makeup, attributes, and potentially its function, thus seeking to observe the way that risk practitioners across the AML landscape handle ML risk, given the tools afforded by AML regulation. Furthermore, the current research also explores how initiatives for handling ML risk have impacted ML risk.

However, before exploring these topics further, it is essential to provide a brief overview of the main drivers of the current AML agenda. In short, the basic assumptions are that ML is harmful to society (Unger & Van der Linde, 2013); it affects the integrity of both banking and financial services, prevents the economic development of less developed countries, promotes corruption, and can "weaken the social fabric, collective ethical standards, and, ultimately, the democratic institutions of society" (Asian Development Bank, 2003, p. 6). Furthermore, ML allows criminals to enjoy the proceeds of their crimes and "changes the cost-benefit calculation of criminals" (Unger & Waarden, 2013, p. 399); it involves converting criminal income into assets that cannot be traced back to their illegal origins (Hopton, 2009), breaking the connection between the proceeds of crime and the original crime. ML is generally articulated as comprising three steps: (1) infusing illicitly acquired money into the financial system (placement); (2) performing a number of transactions to disguise the criminal source (layering); and (3) re-investing the now legitimate money in high-value goods (integration) (Hopton, 2009).

Hence, AML initiatives and regulations have developed a set of processes aimed to detect and prevent ML. AML targets the proceeds of illicit activity by identifying banking customers' identities, tracing the origins and destination of their funds, and identifying and reporting transactions that are out of character or, more specifically, *suspicious*. Such AML initiatives are the result of the Financial Action Task Force's (FATF) 40 Recommendations, which have evolved into binding and mandatory international standards for all UN member states and have been endorsed by the G7 and implemented by EU member states into national legislation. Hence, financial institutions such as banks represent the first line of defence against ML within the financial sector. In addition, the 40 Recommendations specify the need for financial institutions to adopt the risk-based approach (RBA) to assess ML risks (Recommendations 14–18, FATF, 2012) and adjust their ML risk controls accordingly. The RBA provides financial institutions with a methodology to map their ML risk exposure by classifying and arranging customers, products, product delivery channels, and geographical risks. To illustrate, Mexico represents a high geographical risk because of cartel wars, corruption, and high levels of narcotics and human trafficking that occur in this jurisdiction. Thus, mapping ML risk exposure involves "recognising the existence of risk(s), undertaking an assessment of the risk(s) and developing strategies to manage and mitigate the identified risks" (FATF, 2007, pp. 2–3).

However, the acceleration of the number of financial institutions involved in ML scandals over the past 10 years raises the question of whether the current AML regime is adequate for fighting ML. Given the high costs of AML compliance, finding an answer to this question is imperative (Yeandle et al., 2005; KPMG, 2014). AML compliance costs an estimated USD83.5 billion annually (LexisNexis, 2017) across France, Germany, Italy, Switzerland, and the Netherlands. There is no robust evidence nor clarity regarding whether or how current AML measures such as the RBA reduce ML or ML risk, and yet, the RBA remains essential to regulatory frameworks and hence AML controls. The extant literature analyses how the RBA delivers the AML agenda (Tavares et al., 2010; Yeandle et al., 2005), with the majority of research focusing on the way the RBA compares to rule-based regimes (Unger & van Waarden, 2013), ML typologies, RBA outputs in terms of data, risk assessments, profiles, and customer due diligence (CDD) performance. However, current research rarely questions whether the existing strategy for combating ML is adequate. There seems to be a deep conviction among practitioners that *breaking risk* into smaller pieces for analysis (e.g. as the RBA) will help reduce risk (Costanzo, 2013; Vettori, 2013). In contrast, however, the author of the current research observes, assesses, and questions the current ML risk assessment process and explores its performance in relation to ML risk governance.

Accordingly, this research reviews the application of the RBA, how it is interpreted, deconstructed, and communicated by key AML stakeholders, and what the unexpected implications of the RBA may be on ML risk. More specifically, it seeks to identify whether the RBA impacts future ML risk and whether this is observable. This book sets out to examine the following issues regarding the risk-based approach:

- What are the ways in which the risk-based approach enables (or disables) AML practitioners to observe and deconstruct ML risks and what are the challenges that they face in applying the risk-based approach?
- In what way does the application of the risk-based approach impact the handling of future/emergent ML risks and what are the broader AML systemic circumstances and challenges of such an impact?

The empirical research was performed as a comparative case study across two financial intelligence units (FIUs), which are national intelligence organisations in charge of receiving, analysing, and disseminating transactions and activities that have been flagged by financial institutions as being suspicious in terms of ML or terrorism financing. The author also conducted complementary interviews with the FATF, regulators, finance practitioners, economic crime bureaus, the US Secret Service, and ML defence lawyers.

Since the author is informed by the interpretivist tradition, this variety provided an enormous scope for investigative depth. As a theoretical foundation, the author applied Luhmann's systems theory and more specifically his risk/danger model. Based on that model, the author created a novel framework that enables the observation of AML stakeholders and their handling of ML risk. The work contributes to the empirical application of systems theory and develops new concepts in extension to Luhmann's systems theory. In terms of the AML domain, the author contributes by identifying enhancements to the current ML risk and intelligence communication framework that may be used to more effectively deliver the AML agenda.

In order to address the above issues, the following book is structured as follows: Chapter 1 provides a general literature review split into three sections. Section 1.1 discusses the problem of ML and provides current estimates of the ML market and methods to assess the effectiveness of AML efforts. Section 1.2 reviews AML legislation and tracks the emergence of the risk narrative in terms of how it has shaped current AML requirements. Finally, Sect. 1.3 introduces risk, the perception of risk, its governance, as well as social theories of risk. Chapter 1 thus aims to contextualise the AML domain and what it aims to confront: ML risk.

Chapter 2 documents the key concepts of Luhmann's system theory as well as his risk/danger model. This chapter provides the foundation for the empirical research and data analysis. Chapter 3 describes the comparative case study and the findings from the empirical research. It provides a description of the empirical settings to offer context for the fieldwork that was performed and concludes with the list of key findings that emerged from the research.

Chapter 4 focuses on the analysis and discussion of these findings, which leads to a set of seven key propositions developed by the author, resulting in six recommendations intended to enhance the current ML risk and intelligence communication framework across primary stakeholders, namely FIUs, regulators, and obliged entities. Chapter 4 also presents the contributions the research makes to theory and the domain. Finally, Chap. 5 provides an overview of the work undertaken and examines the above issues and also presents some research limitations as well as suggestions for future research.

References

Asian Development Bank. (2003). *Manual on countering money laundering and the financing of terrorism*. Accessed Dec 2, 2015. Available online: https://www.unodc.org/tldb/pdf/Asian-bank-guide.pdf

Costanzo, P. (2013). The risk-based approach to anti-money laundering and counter-terrorist financing in international and EU standards: What it is, what it entails. In B. Unger & D. van der Linde (Eds.), *Research handbook on money laundering* (p. 349). Edward Elgar Publishing.

FATF. (2007). *Guidance on the risk-based approach to combating money laundering and terrorist financing*. FATF. Retrieved November 18, 2015, from http://www.fatf-gafi.org/media/fatf/documents/reports/High%20Level%20Principles%20and%20Procedures.pdf

FATF. (2012). *FATF steps up the fight against money laundering and terrorist financing*. FATF. Retrieved October 19, 2015, from http://www.fatf-gafi.org/publications/fatfrecommendations/documents/fatfstepsupthefightagainstmoneylaunderingandterroristfinancing.html

Hopton, D. (2009). *Money laundering: A concise guide for all business* (2nd ed.). Gower Publishing Ltd.

KPMG. (2014). *Global anti money laundering survey*. Retrieved April 8, 2015, from https://assets.kpmg/content/dam/kpmg/pdf/2014/01/global-anti-money-laundering-survey.pdf

Levi, M., Reuter, P., & Halliday, T. (2018). Can the AML system be evaluated without better data? *Crime Law Society Change, 69*, 307–328. Retrieved October 9, 2019, from https://doi.org/10.1007/s10611-017-9757-4

LexisNexis. (2017). *The true cost of anti-money laundering compliance*. Accessed Apr 8, 2018. Available online: https://risk.lexisnexis.com/global/en/insights-resources/research/the-true-cost-of-amlcompliance-european-survey

Ryder, N. (2012). *Money laundering—An endless cycle?* Routledge.

Tavares, C., Thomas, G., & Roudaut, M. (2010). *Money laundering in Europe* (Eurostat methodologies and working papers). Eurostat. Retrieved December 6, 2015, from http://www.apml.gov.rs/REPOSITORY/409_1_ks-ra-10-003-en.pdf

Unger, B., & van Waarden, F. (2013). How to dodge drowning in data? Rule and risk based money laundering compared. In B. Unger & D. Van der Linde (Eds.), *Research handbook on money laundering* (pp. 399–425). Elgar.

Unger, B., & Van der Linde, D. (Eds.). (2013). *Research handbook on money laundering*. Elgar Publishing.

Vettori, B. (2013). Evaluating anti-money laundering policies. In B. Unger & Van der D. Linde (Eds.), *Research handbook on money laundering* (pp. 474–486). Elgar.

Yeandle, M., Mainelli, M., Berendt, A., & Healy, B. (2005) *Anti-money laundering requirements: Costs, benefits and perceptions*. Corporation of London. Retrieved April 7, 2015, from http://www.zyen.com/PDF/AMLR_FULL.pdf

Contents

1 Introduction to Anti-Money Laundering ... 1
  1.1 Section 1: Estimating the Extent of ML and Measuring AML
      Effectiveness ... 1
      Estimating the Extent of ML ... 1
      Assessing the Effectiveness of AML Frameworks ... 4
      Are Fines Adequate Indicators of AML Effectiveness? ... 8
  1.2 Section 2: Legislation and the Emergence of the Risk Narrative ... 10
      International Bodies ... 10
      Regional Initiatives ... 13
  1.3 Section 3: Risk and Governance ... 17
      Defining and Measuring Risk ... 18
      Is Risk Real? ... 24
      The Evolution of the Risk Discourse within Governance and the
      Risk-Based Approach ... 28
      The Risk-Based Approach to ML Risk Governance ... 31
      Why we Need Social Sciences to Understand Risk ... 35
  References ... 36

2 Risk and Luhmann's Systems Theory ... 45
  2.1 Luhmann's System Theory (LST) and Social Systems ... 46
      System, Boundary and Environment ... 47
      Operational Closure, Autopoiesis and Self-Reference ... 50
      Structural Coupling ... 54
      Re-Entry and Observing Systems ... 55
      Double Contingency and Communication ... 58
      Function Systems and Binary Codes ... 59
      Organisations and Decisions ... 64
  2.2 Luhmann's Sociological Theory on Risk ... 73
      Risk Governance and Communication According to Luhmann ... 79
  References ... 84

3	**Case Studies and Empirical Findings**	89
	3.1 Fieldwork and Research	89
	3.2 The SAR Analysis and Escalation Process: Summary	91
	Summary of FIU1's SAR Process	91
	Summary of FIU2's SAR Process	92
	3.3 The SARs Regime	93
	FIUs Develop Competitive Advantages Over Others	102
	3.4 The Risk-Based Approach	108
	Financial Institutions and Their Relationships with AML and ML	108
	The Role of the Regulator	113
	The Illusion of Risk Deconstruction	117
	3.5 Risk Appetite, Intelligence and Re-entry	121
	Risk Appetite and Intelligence	121
	The Re-entry of Risk	127
	3.6 Re-risking: A Consequence of De-risking	133
	De-risking Is Risk Assessment	133
	De-risking: Forcing the Re-entry of the Risk/Danger Distinction onto Other Systems	135
	References	139
4	**Analysis and Discussion**	143
	4.1 Section 1: Extracting Propositions	143
	ML Intelligence: Using Obliged Entities' Risk Profiles	143
	The FIU: Externalising Danger and De-risking	145
	The Inefficiency of the Current SAR Regime: A Communication Issue	151
	The FIU: Boundary Operationalisation and Attempts at Bridging Function Systems	154
	De-risking and the Recursivity of Re-risking	158
	The Important Role of Risk Taker as Risk Bearer	163
	4.2 Section 2: Theoretical and Domain Contributions	169
	Contributions and Recommendations	169
	References	189
5	**Conclusion**	191
	5.1 Propositions' Overview	191
	5.2 Answering Key Issues	192
	5.3 Applicability and Implications for Future Research	195
	References	196

About the Author

Noémi També Bearpark is an Associate Professor at the Luxembourg School of Business and the founder and director of Tambe advisory and consulting, which delivers financial crime prevention, anti-money laundering, counter-terrorist financing, and counter-proliferation finance systems and controls across the banking, non-profit, and public sectors. Her academic research mainly focuses on anti-money laundering where she evaluates risk management and communication across organisations within the private and the public sector. She holds her PhD in Systems Studies from the Centre for Systems Studies, University of Hull, UK.

Abbreviations

AML	Anti-money laundering
BBA	British Bankers' Association
BIS	Bank for International Settements
BSA	Bank Secrecy Act
CDD	Customer due diligence
CFT	Counter finance terrorism
CTR	Currency transaction reports
EBA	European Banking Authority
EC	European Commission
EDD	Enhanced due diligence
EU	Euroepan Union
FATF	Financial Action Task Force
FCA	Financial Conduct Authority (UK regulator)
FI	Financial institution
FINCEN	Financial Crimes Enforcement Network (US Financial Intelligence Unit)
FINTRAC	Financial Transactions and Reports Analysis Centre of Canada (Canadian Financial Intelligence Unit)
FIU	Financial Intelligence Unit
FSA	Financial Services Authority (Regulator)
GDP	Gross domestic product
HIDTA	High Intensity Drug Trafficking Areas
HIFCA	High Intensity Money Laundering and Related Financial Crime Area
IMF	International Monetary Fund
KYC	Know your customers
LEA	Law Enforcement Agency
MiFID	Markets in Financial Instruments Directive
ML	Money laundering
MLRO	Money Laundering Reporting Office

MROS	Money Laundering Reporting Office Switzerland (Swiss Financial Intelligence Unit)
MSB	Money service business
NED	Non-executive director
NRA	National risk assessment
OE	Obliged entity
PEP	Politically exposed person
RBA	Risk-based approach
SAR	Suspicious activity report
ST	Systems theory
STR	Suspicious transaction report
TF	Terrorism financing
UK	United Kingdom
UNODC	United Nations Office on Drugs and Crime
US	United States
VAT	Value-added tax

List of Figures

Fig. 2.1	A typology of systems (Borsch, 2011, p. 20)	47
Fig. 2.2	System, environment and boundary	48
Fig. 2.3	The financial institution as the system	49
Fig. 2.4	The form of distinction (Spencer Brown, 1969)	57
Fig. 2.5	The form of decision and its paradox (Åkerstrøm Anderson, 2001)	65
Fig. 2.6	Deparadoxisation (adapted from Knudsen, 2007)	67
Fig. 2.7	Luhmann's risk model (Luhmann, 1993)	75
Fig. 2.8	De-risking through Luhmann's risk/danger model (Bukola, 2014; Durner & Shetret, 2015; FCA, 2016)	78
Fig. 2.9	The ecology of ML risk (adapted from Hardy & Maguire, 2019)	80
Fig. 2.10	Barclays Bank 2015 fine through Luhmann's risk/danger model (FCA, 2015a, b)	83
Fig. 4.1	The translation of SARs across organisations	147
Fig. 4.2	De-risking and re-risking	160
Fig. 4.3	High-risk/low-risk re-entry [adapted from Åkerstrøm Anderson (2001)]	168
Fig. 4.4	De-risking and ML danger externalisation mechanism	172
Fig. 4.5	Irritation and resonance; de-risking and re-risking	172
Fig. 4.6	Regulator's de-risking decisions	174
Fig. 4.7	Luhmann's risk/danger model	176
Fig. 4.8	Luhmann's extended risk/danger model	176
Fig. 4.9	Luhmann's extended risk/danger model across period t and $t+1$	178
Fig. 4.10	FIUs and the bridging of the economic and legal function systems	180
Fig. 4.11	FIUs' operationalisation of translation codes	181

Fig. 4.12	A suggested model for the sharing of ML intelligence across obliged entities	183
Fig. 4.13	Incentivisation of obliged entities	184
Fig. 4.14	Interorganisational AML communication framework	185
Fig. 4.15	Consolidated framework for ML risk communication	188

List of Tables

Table 1.1	Biases of risk perception (Renn, 1987, p. 54)	21
Table 1.2	The four semantic images of risk in public perception (Renn, 1987, p. 55)	22
Table 2.1	Function systems, function, binary codes and medium (Moeller, 2006; Roth & Schütz, 2015)	63
Table 2.2	Barclays Bank 2015 regulatory fine through LST	71
Table 3.1	List of interviewees	90
Table 3.2	Summary of findings	138
Table 4.1	Summary of propositions	170
Table 4.2	Summary of recommendations mapped against propositions and relevant findings	186

Chapter 1
Introduction to Anti-Money Laundering

This chapter reviews the literature on AML and risk in three sections.

Section 1.1 discusses the money laundering (ML) market while documenting the challenges associated with attempts to evaluate the global extent of ML. Section 1.1 also discusses methodologies that have been devised to assess the effectiveness of current anti-money laundering (AML) efforts.

Section 1.2 describes the key international initiatives established to fight ML along with the main governmental and judicial initiatives and regulations responsible for enforcing and maintaining AML. Global initiatives are reviewed first, followed by regional initiatives.

Section 1.3 addresses the challenges of describing and defining risk. Indeed, although risk has become a term that is increasingly used and banalised, defining it is tricky as it is perceived as either a tangible and real objective idea or as simple subjective attribution, depending on the observer. Section 1.3 also explores the evolution of risk governance and its implications for AML.

1.1 Section 1: Estimating the Extent of ML and Measuring AML Effectiveness

Estimating the Extent of ML

According to Camdessus, the former managing director of the International Monetary Fund (IMF) (Camdessus, 1998), the generally accepted value of the ML market is 2 to 5% of global gross domestic product (GDP). However, it was later clarified that this figure was actually not an IMF estimate but was "based on the slightest effort made by others" (Levi et al., 2018, p. 312). The Walker model, which is further discussed below, suggests that USD 2.85 trillion are laundered globally on an annual basis (Walker, 2007; Unger & van Waarden, 2013). Similarly, a 2011

UNODC report states that "the best estimate for the amount available for laundering through the financial system would be equivalent to 2.7% of global GDP (2.1%–4%) or USD 1.6 trillion in 2009. Still within the IMF 'consensus range', this figure is located towards its lower end" (UNODC, 2011, p. 4). As Demetis explains, "an example that clearly demonstrates the aforementioned problematic nature of estimating the ML market is that of Australia, where estimates range from 1.4% to 47.1% of the GDP" (Demetis, 2010, p. 14). Indeed, when comparing these figures, it is apparent that estimating the ML market is fraught with difficulty. For instance, ML assessment method's robustness and validity are unclear. In addition, the author questions what such estimates actually accomplish.

Estimating ML entails estimating revenues generated through criminal activities as well as expenditure of funds originating from predicate offences. Originally, drug-related offences were the only predicate offences (Ryder, 2012), and as such, estimations of ML only focused on the drug market. Now, predicate offences designate any serious crime including tax fraud and tax evasion as per the European Union's Fourth AML Directive (Council Directive 2015/849 of 20 May, 2015). Furthermore, the definition of serious crime as per the United Nations on Drugs and Crime (UNODC) is so wide that it is difficult to capture all serious crime and thus estimate the size of the ML market. The UNODC defines serious crime as:

> Conduct constituting an offence punishable by a maximum deprivation of liberty of at least four years or a more serious penalty. In other words, according to and for purposes of the Organized Crime Convention, any conduct for which the maximum deprivation of liberty provided by the applicable domestic criminal legislation is of at least four years is considered a serious crime. (UNODC, 2011, p. 1)

Furthermore, as argued by Levi et al. "an increasing number of predicate crimes (such as Grand Corruption and tax evasion)—i.e. crimes that give rise to proceeds that are concealed or otherwise dealt with—are added" (2018, p. 313) to the list of serious crimes. Yet, it is difficult to define what a predicate crime is, evidenced, for example, by Austria who defines "a predicate offence of money laundering only under certain conditions. These conditions include deliberate financial crimes which are punishable by more than 3 years imprisonment" (Nowotny, 2013, p. 149).

In addition to challenges related to defining what a ML offence is, it is also difficult to identify the appropriate methodology for estimating the extent of ML in different countries or globally. Reuter (2013) looks at Walker's work (1995), which develops a model to estimate the extent of ML in Australia. The methodology identifies the main categories of crime, estimating the amount of money generated by these crimes and assessing how the funds are laundered. Walker's study includes the following crime categories: "homicide, robbery and extortion, frauds, thefts, pollution, flora and fauna, environmental offences, drugs, arms trading/trafficking, illegal gambling, stock/equity market fraud, illegal prostitution, illegal immigration, people trafficking, computer crime, terrorism" (Walker, 2007, p. 49), which illustrates the ever-expanding scope of potential ML offences. In order to assess Walker's work, Reuter (2013) focuses on drug sales and fraud.

Although the author seeks to discuss issues in estimation methodologies, detailed accounts of Reuter's critique of Walker's model are not necessary for the current project and will not be provided here. To illustrate Reuter's critique of Walker's work, this section only focuses on the drugs sales category. According to Walker, 83% of revenues from drugs sales are laundered. However, Reuter posits that this figure is too high, since for drugs such as cocaine and heroin, for instance, "most of the mark-up is applied at the bottom of the system" (Reuter, 2013, p. 229) and, as such, the bulk of revenue goes to sellers at the bottom of the food chain. Accordingly, Reuter believes that money is simply spent rather than placed within the financial system, stating: "It is not that I think that John Walker has done his work poorly. Rather I believe that this methodology is fundamentally flawed" (Reuter, 2013, p. 230).

Walker and Unger (2013) similarly criticise Levi and Gold's (1994) methodology. To assess the extent of ML, Levi and Gold analysed data that included suspicious transactions. However, Unger and Walker argue that since, as discussed above, ML involves three main stages (placement, layering, and integration), the same money could pass through many transactions and institutions. "Counting financial transaction data is therefore certain to involve double—or even multiple—counting. Worse, counting suspicious transactions is certain to include large errors both ways ('suspicious' transactions that are actually legitimate and 'legitimate' transactions that are actually criminal" (Walker & Unger, 2013, p. 160). Further examples relating to the difficulty in devising robust methodologies for estimating ML are offered by, for example, Kilmer, Caulkins, and Reuter' study (2010) and the 2007 Home Office-sponsored report by the Matrix Knowledge Group on the illicit drug trade in the UK (1997). Hence, as Levi et al. (2018) explain "as frequently repeated in Mutual Evaluation Reports,[1] there are no credible estimates of the total amount laundered, either globally or nationally" (p. 310).

Estimating the ML market is problematic not only in terms of defining the breadth of what is to be measured but also in terms of how it is to be quantified. Reuter argues that this should not, however, concern society, as "knowing how much money is laundered serves no important policy purpose. It is simply one of those adornments for conversation" (Reuter, 2013, p. 224). He believes that estimating ML volumes is a diversion of attention away from what really matters: combating crime. Similarly, van Duyne argues that:

> Apart from moral considerations, is crime-money really a threat? Not if it has undergone a proper 'whitewashing programme' [...]. In that case it has become part of the GDP and a taxable asset. If not, it is still spent in daily life, becoming 'white' as soon as it is exchanged for taxable articles: generating VAT or sales tax plus income tax for the seller. (van Duyne, 2013, p. 248)

---

[1] Mutual evaluation reports are generated by peer reviews performed by FATF members to assess the implementation of FATF standards on combating ML. Section 1.2 provides further information on FATF and its standards.

However, this argument fails to account for two problems: First, money requiring laundering, stems from a type of criminal activity that will keep occurring as long as it remains profitable. Second, in line with van Duyne's argument above, not all "crime-money" is spent on taxable goods or contributes back to the economy. For instance, funds embezzled by corrupt governments, laundered or not, are not generally spent locally on taxable goods. For instance, according to Transparency International (2019), although USD 268 million hidden in a Deutsche Bank account in Jersey (UK) will now be returned to Nigeria, the country never benefited from any taxes on whatever goods or services purchased by de facto President Abacha with previously embezzled funds. In Nigeria, "the unabashed pillage by senior officials fomented slow growth and declining standards of living. The economic malaise dissipated the middle class, intensified communal tensions, and weakened an already feeble state apparatus" (Lewis, 1999, p. 50). Similarly, in Lebanon when the company Sukleen, acting as a monopoly since the 1990s, thanks to its close ties to Lebanon's corrupt government, was unable to fulfil its waste disposal functions, because it was squandering public funds instead, the threat to public health reached alarming levels. Human Rights Watch issued a report in 2017 stating: "Lebanese authorities' lack of effective action to address widespread open burning of waste and a lack of adequate monitoring or information about the health effects violate Lebanon's obligations under international law" (Human Rights Watch, 2017, p. 8). Thus, van Duyne's arguments that ML buys products that are ultimately taxable (and hence whitewashed) and that ML poses no threat to society are clearly misconstrued and flawed. Therefore, although problematic, further effort should be invested in developing a methodology to evaluate the extent of ML to gauge the magnitude of the threat it poses to the global economy.

A final argument in favour of developing accurate methods for estimating the ML market relates to the high compliance costs faced by the banking industry (estimated in 2018 at USD 270 billion a year [Stuart, 2018]) which leads to losses in profitability and efficiency. This is explored in the following section.

Assessing the Effectiveness of AML Frameworks

Being able to compare the ML market with banking-industry AML costs would hopefully assure the banking industry that the infrastructure they are implementing to fight ML is not only fundamental to preserving the economy, and thus the integrity of the financial sector, but also proportionate to the threat. The financial sector would strongly benefit from an understanding of how their compliance costs compare to the wider ML market and from confirmation that such investments ultimately make a difference and contribute in a meaningful way to AML efforts. As Levi, Reuter and Halliday argue, "the ideal evaluation would take some measures of the target activity, such as the total amount of money laundered, and estimate how much has been reduced by the imposition of AML controls" (2018, p. 310).

However, the difficulty in quantifying the volume of ML "has hampered and still hampers understanding the impact that policies have had on the phenomenon" (Harvey, 2005, p. 339). This invokes the question of whether increases or decreases in the volume of ML indicate the effectiveness of existing AML frameworks (see Sect. 1.2 for a description of the current international model of AML frameworks). However, if such frameworks were to focus on ML volumes "AML agencies would target crimes that generate a high ML volume per investigative unit" (Reuter, 2013, p. 226). Truman and Reuter (2004) "identify five types of crimes (drug dealing, blue collar crime, white collar crime, bribery/corruption and terrorism) that they analyse according to cash intensity, scale of operations, severity of harm and population mostly affected" (Reuter, 2013, p. 226). Therefore, if ML volume is the focus, an AML regime may opt to target white-collar crime; while such a strategy would accomplish little in terms of reducing violent crime, it may substantially decrease the volume of ML. Accordingly, "elevating ML volume as an important construct threatens to distort the functioning of the system from its true purpose, which is reduction of the most serious crimes and global bads" (Reuter, 2013, p. 227).

Reuter's argument is interesting, especially given that it is currently "taken for granted that actions taken against ML and especially the financing of terrorism will have a positive welfare impact, both gross and net of costs" (Levi et al., 2018, p. 309). Reuter's approach to addressing the impact of efforts aimed at addressing ML, however, needs to be put to the test. This would involve developing a methodology that would assess the unit and scale of harm per dollar laundered. Thus, to achieve this, one would have to assess the harm, e.g. per USD 1000 of laundered money, in the context of a comparison of different predicate offences. Reuter develops a taxonomy of predicate crimes that identifies the severity of white-collar crime as modest and terrorism as most severe. While Reuter does not explain how he comes to this conclusion, one might wonder how human trafficking, for example, would compare to Madoff's Ponzi scheme and its repercussions versus the 2015 terrorist attacks in Paris or finally to the Danske Bank ML scandal involving ten Estonian-branch Danske employees.

While Reuter argues that white-collar crime represents a low to modest severity of harm, this position is not reflected, for example, in the statement made by Kilvar Kessler, chair of the Estonian Financial Services Authority in relation to the Danske Bank scandal which was enabled by ten Danske Bank employees within the institution. Kilvar Kessler stated that "serious and large-scale violations of the local rules have been committed in Estonia through the branch of a foreign bank, and this has dealt a serious blow to the transparency, credibility and reputation of the Estonian financial market" (Megaw, 2019), a scandal that may have precipitated the 2019 suicide of Aivar Rehe (head of Danske Bank 2006–2015). In any case, Reuter's approach involves itemising concepts such as mental health, physical suffering, trauma, human life, economic harm, reputation and assigning them an economic value. While economists certainly have developed methodologies enabling them to assign such values (Viscusi & Aldi, 2003; Rojas, 2019), the author believes it should be performed with the express aim of developing a cost-benefit analysis of ML prevention in the context of specific predicate offences, in order to test Reuter's argument that preventing white-collar offences that generate high ML volume accomplishes little in terms of harm reduction.

In addition, the author struggles with the concept of weighing harm per se. There are ethical implications associated with attempts to weigh and measure atrocities of the November 2015 terrorist attacks in Paris against the impact and repercussions of a scheme similar to that of Madoff's Ponzi scheme, for instance. As such, Reuter's harm breakdown methodology is, the author believes, fundamentally flawed.

Unfortunately, traditional methods for estimating AML effectiveness focus primarily on anecdotal evidence, illustrated, for example, by governmental or regulatory press releases that document recent AML efforts. Press releases from the US government, the British regulator or the Danish and Estonian regulators provide no meaningful data relating to AML efforts. Such reports merely detail chronological accounts of banks' failures and the regulators' eventual successes and tend to legitimise the role (or absence) of the regulator in such affairs. Furthermore, although it could be argued that the Paradise and Panama papers released between 2015 and 2017 offer AML data and significantly impacted public opinion, no tangible data related to this scandal has emerged that could help the AML industry measure the effectiveness of AML and anti-corruption efforts.

Levi, Reuter and Halliday argue that "the ideal evaluation would take some measure of the target activity, such as the total amount of money laundered, and estimate how much that has been reduced by the imposition of AML controls" (Levi et al., 2018, p. 310). In the absence of such a measure of the target activity, Levi, Reuter and Halliday have reviewed a set of mutual evaluation reports and the data used to produce them. They note that many of these reports provide little data related to crime proceeds in the relevant countries because "estimates of domestic proceeds of crime are exceedingly difficult to establish" (2018, p. 318). Furthermore, the study looks at official suspicious activity reports and acknowledges that "the problem with process statistics like these is that they are subject to multiple interpretations which can then become a continuing source of tension between country officials and the assessor panels" (Levi et al., 2018, p. 319).

However, some risk practitioners and scholars believe that the number of suspicious activity reports (SARs) filed by financial institutions and sent to financial intelligence units may be a measure of AML effectiveness. For instance, the Swiss financial intelligence unit (called MROS) which analyses data and information relating to ML and terrorism financing has generated interesting information on the nature of the Swiss reporting system. In 2018, the percentage of SARs forwarded by MROS to the prosecuting authorities for further investigation was 65.1% of the analysed 4125 SARs, an increase over 2017 when 64.9% of SARs were forwarded for prosecution (MROS, 2019). Such data can be described as the true positive rate of a SAR (i.e. the percentage of transactions flagged as "suspicious" that remain "suspicious" after review). In the Swiss context, this may be explained by strong customer vetting and monitoring processes in that country, enabling financial institutions and financial intelligence units to have a high true positive rate. Yet, some argue that the Swiss SAR "numbers are prima facie unsatisfactory" (Chaikin, 2009, p. 247) due to the fact that Swiss financial institutions report a very small number of

1.1 Section 1: Estimating the Extent of ML and Measuring AML Effectiveness 7

SARs to MROS, in comparison to the UK, the USA or Australia. While Chaikin argues that jurisdictions have different reporting thresholds, there is no certainty that having a higher or lower reporting threshold automatically indicates the presence of a more efficient AML framework. Hence, the quantity of SARs does not necessarily constitute a satisfactory measure of effective ML prevention. Ultimately, "the lack of qualitative insight into the nature and seriousness of prosecutions is also a major issue" (Levi et al., 2018, p. 320).

To evaluate and determine the effectiveness of the current AML setup, the academic community as well as the industry has sought to develop alternative analyses. Tavares et al. (2010), for instance, argue in favour of a cost-benefit analysis of existing AML schemes. However, "these studies are not without shortcomings related to the impossibility of economically quantifying some crucial yet intangible cost and benefit items" (Vettori, 2013, p. 484). A 2006 study "conducted to determine in economic, competitive and ethical terms the impact of AML regulation on financial operators in Luxembourg concluded that the costs were not negligible" (Krieger quoted in Vettori, 2013, p. 477). However, the conclusions of this 2006 study did not further elaborate on the fact that such cost-benefit analyses may highlight a difficult problem, namely, the relative ineffectiveness of current AML frameworks.

Hence, coming to terms with this issue, in 2013, the FATF published a document entitled *Methodology for Assessing Technical Compliance with FATF Recommendations and Effectiveness of AML/CFT Systems*. This methodology document was published to provide countries guidance as to how to undertake the fourth round of mutual evaluation reports and seeks to:

> assess the adequacy of the implementation of the FATF recommendations and identifies the extent to which a country achieves a defined set of outcomes that are central to a robust AML/CFT system. The focus of the effectiveness assessment is therefore on the extent to which the legal and institutional framework is producing the expected results. (FATF, 2019a, b, p. 4)

This approach to evaluating AML effectiveness focused on objectives and was not limited to blind data gathering disconnected from measuring actual regulatory effectiveness, as previously observed in the FATF's Recommendation 33:

> Countries should maintain comprehensive statistics on matters relevant to the effectiveness and efficiency of their AML/CFT systems. This should include statistics on the STRs received and disseminated; on money laundering and terrorist financing investigations, prosecutions and convictions; on property frozen, seized and confiscated; and on mutual legal assistance or other international requests for cooperation. (FATF, 2012-2019, p. 24)

Thus, as part of Levi, Reuter and Halliday's review of the fourth round of evaluations in different countries, the team focused on available national risk assessments (NRAs) which were required to be performed prior to visits by the FATF evaluation teams. Levi et al. conclude that "what is striking is how little data or analysis of data played in most of the NRAs we reviewed. The reports provided minimal quantitative data. The failure to provide any positive evidence of effectiveness has proven no barrier to the rapid dissemination of the FATF regime to all parts of the globe" (Levi et al., 2018, p. 322–324).

The ineffectiveness of AML systems is punctuated, for example, by the fact that "in 2006, the UK national AML system had only confiscated a total of GBP 46 million criminally acquired assets (that sum is 0.02 per cent of the estimated total cash laundered over the past 10 years), but at a cost of GBP 400 million for the investigations" (Demetis & Angell, 2006, p. 166). Similarly, the United Nations (UN) estimates that "less than 1% of global illicit financial flows are being seized and frozen" (UNODC, 2011, p. 7). Such figures are staggering and indicate "that if 99% of illicit flows (turnover or profits) annually are not confiscated, the cumulative volume of illicit assets must be very high indeed" (Levi et al., 2018, p. 312). Pol argues that "anecdotal successes may not prove policy success, but individual success stories mask the reality of overall policy failure" (2020, p. 76).

In summary, the limited amount of data available for assessing the effectiveness of AML efforts, in conjunction with evidence suggesting that the amount of ML funds confiscated is negligible, is alarming. Furthermore, in recent years, an increasing number of institutions have been publicly named, shamed and fined due to allegations of ML, and details are, of course, made readily available by regulators and, more importantly, the media. Yet, it remains unclear whether such fines indicate strong AML effectiveness and whether they serve a purpose in making a difference in the fight against ML.

Are Fines Adequate Indicators of AML Effectiveness?

In 2013, US politician Elizabeth Warren asked representatives of the US Treasury Department, Federal Reserve and Office of the Comptroller of the Currency: "How many billions of dollars do you have to launder for drug lords, and how many economic sanctions do you have to violate before someone will consider shutting down a financial institution?" (United States Senate, 2013, p. 12). In hindsight, this question has proven to be prescient. Indeed, the ML scandals of 2018 alone would suggest the existence of an endemic ML problem within the financial sector. While the root cause of such scandals may differ—for example, cases involving the Baltic region may use the banking system to launder dirty Russian money, whereas US cases often involve drug money—the commonality among all such cases is a failure of institutional AML frameworks. Such failures lead many observers such as AML practitioners or the media to question the basic ability of institutions to act as first line of defence against ML. Furthermore, the ML scandals of 2018 alone make it difficult to empathise with financial institutions. Examples include UBS (fined USD 15 million), Rabobank (fined USD 369 million), Commonwealth Bank of Australia (fined USD 534 million), US Bancorp (fined USD 613 million), ING (fined USD 900 million), ABLV Bank Latvia (faced Sect. 311 of the US Patriot Act, preventing the bank from opening or maintaining a correspondent account in the USA, leading to liquidity issues which forced the bank to close), Pilatus Bank (which had its license withdrawn by the European Central Bank), Goldman Sachs (involved in the embezzlement of the Malaysian Development Fund), Deutsche Bank (which has "spent more than USD 18 billion over the past decade in fines to settle legal disputes related to financial crimes" [Matussek et al., 2018]) and, finally, Danske Bank, increasingly regarded as the worst money laundering scandal to date.

The above list, however, is not necessarily meaningful or relevant to financial institutions. When such scandals arise, despite press releases or official reports issued by banks such as HSBC, ING or Danske Bank, scandals re-emerge, sometimes involving the very same institutions that were just recently fined—for example, in the case of Deutsche Bank or HSBC. It would seem that imposing fines leads to little change:

> Wachovia Bank agreed to pay USD 160 million in 2010 for allowing drug cartels to use the bank to launder money through Mexican exchange houses. In 2012 ING was fined USD 619 million for providing banking services to US-sanctioned states such as Cuba, Iran, Sudan, and Myanmar. That same year Standard Chartered was fined USD 667 million for illegal dealings with Iran and then, in 2014, was fined an additional USD 300 million for its failure to weed out transactions prone to money laundering. The largest fine to date came in 2012 when HSBC was fined USD 1.92 billion for laundering money for Mexican cartels and al-Qaeda affiliated groups and for hiding prohibited transactions with nations like Iran and Cuba. The U.S. Justice Department agreed to defer prosecution in all cases. (Haugen, 2015)

Furthermore, though the media celebrates such "record fines", these sanctions are tiny in comparisons to banks' profits. In the case of HSBC's fine, for instance, "the sum represents about four weeks' earnings given the bank's pre-tax profits of USD 21.9 billion" (Pratley, 2012). In 2011, HSBC announced it would introduce reforms and new controls; nevertheless, in February 2015, information emerged, indicating that its Swiss private banking subsidiary was enabling tax evasion, a predicate offence. This occurred despite HSBC alleging that it had improved and strengthened its overall framework, suggesting that such investments may have been primarily made to minimise the risks of additional fines rather than to deter individuals from committing predicate offences. In the case of HSBC, "the US authorities defended their decision not to prosecute it for accepting the tainted money of rogue states and drug lords, insisting that a USD 1.9bn fine for a litany of offences was preferable to the 'collateral consequences' of taking the bank to court" (Pratley, 2012). Again, in 2019, HSBC's Swiss private banking arm agreed to pay a EUR 300 million Belgian tax fraud settlement. The prosecutors stated that HSBC was "charged by a prosecutor for serious and organized tax fraud, forgery and falsification of records, money-laundering and illegal use of financial intermediaries" (Guarascio, 2019).

Yet, the financial sector seems to benefit from a certain level of impunity. In 2005 Riggs Bank was fined a total of USD 41 million for "failing to take adequate measures to prevent ML by former Chilean dictator Augusto Pinochet and officials of Equatorial Guinea" (O'Hara, 2005). However, despite presiding US District Judge Ricardo Urbina description of the bank "as a greedy corporate henchman of dictators and their corrupt regimes" (Clabaugh, 2005), none of Riggs Bank's board members were criminally prosecuted. This point reinforces the belief that certain institutions are simply "too big to jail" (Greenwald, 2012). Thus, the amount of financial fines imposed on banking institutions that fail to abide by AML standards and principles does not necessarily indicate the efficiency of AML initiatives. If anything, one would be tempted to believe the opposite. No matter how many fines are issued, the banking sector continues to fail to enforce its AML duties and responsibilities. In addition, the industry and regulators alike have been unable to develop a set of indicators that would inform as to whether the current AML framework is successfully and adequately tackling ML.

Section 1.1 provides an overview of the threat that ML poses to society, outlines some of the challenges that AML practitioners and scholars face in not only defining ML per se but also in estimating its volume, discusses the direct impact this has on attempts at estimating the effectiveness of current AML efforts and addresses the gap in available data. The following section seeks to offer an understanding of the current AML regulatory and legislative framework.

1.2 Section 2: Legislation and the Emergence of the Risk Narrative

AML regulation's rationale is that engaging in criminal enterprises is financially motivated and utilising criminal proceeds depends on the ability to launder them. Hence, laws and regulations have been designed to identify, trace and confiscate crime-related earnings: If crime ceases to be lucrative for criminals, then there will be no reason to engage in criminal activity. International cooperation is fundamental to the fight because of the increasing integration of the financial sector. As stated by Nance, "in the time that it takes local law enforcement to secure permission to act, launderers can send funds through a maze of jurisdictions, moving evidence beyond law enforcement's reach" (Nance, 2018). This is even more relevant for terrorist funds, which, ever since the 2001 terrorist attacks in New York, have become part of the global AML's focus.

The following section presents the key bodies and institutions relevant to AML and its domain, the development of ML regulation and the evolution of the concept of risk and the risk-based approach (RBA), which has become a pillar of international ML prevention.

International Bodies

The Financial Action Task Force
The Financial Action Task Force (FATF) emerged after the 1988 Vienna Convention. Negotiations surrounding the Vienna Convention were long-winded and difficult, but nevertheless became a critical forum for the regulation of ML. While the USA's suggestion of establishing a fact-finding task force was initially met with

resistance, in 1989, all G7 members eventually agreed to it. Initially, it comprised a small team of 11 individuals and focused on managing the proceeds of the drug trade. The FATF quickly evolved, and "in the intervening decades, FATF members have broadened their focus to include transnational crime, terrorism financing, weapons of mass destruction proliferation, and, to a lesser degree, financial exclusion" (Nance, 2018, p. 115). Thus, in addition to becoming "the single most important international body in terms of the formulation of AML policy" (Ryder, 2012, p. 14), FATF members also describe their efforts as "ensuring the more generalized idea of financial integrity" (Nance, 2018). This is encapsulated in the FATF 40 Recommendations (2012a, b) characterised by the UN commission as "standards by which the measures against ML adopted by concerned States should be judged" (Ryder, 2012, p. 20).

The FATF monitors the adoption of AML measures using three tools: mutual evaluation reports (briefly discussed in Sect. 1.1), typology reports and blacklisting. Mutual evaluation reports aim to assess how the state under review implements the 40 Recommendations and is performed by the FATF, the FATF's regional bodies or the World Bank. An unsatisfactory outcome results in closer monitoring. Typology reports aim to identify and discuss the latest information, the latest ML trends and defective AML measures. Finally, the FATF's call for action process (previously called blacklisting) entails identifying countries with weak AML systems, which is then followed by closer and more frequent monitoring. Should countries wish to be removed from the list, they must commit to a reform plan. Countries that are currently on the call for action list are Iran and the Democratic People's Republic of Korea (FATF, 2020).

In 2003, risk was explicitly added into the AML narrative through the FATF's 40 Recommendations, and official guidance on the risk-based approach (RBA) was issued in 2007:

> The general principle of a RBA is that where there are higher risks countries should require financial institutions to take enhanced measures to manage and mitigate those risks, and that correspondingly where the risks are lower (and there is no suspicion of money laundering or terrorist financing) simplified measures may be permitted. (FATF, 2012a, b, p. 29)

The purpose of this guidance was to "support the development of a common understanding of what the RBA involves, outline the high-level principles involved in applying the RBA and indicate good public and private sector practice in the design and implementation of an effective RBA" (FATF, 2007, p. 1).

The RBA was developed in close cooperation with the private sector. Indeed, the RBA guidance goes as far as to state that "after further international consultation with both public and private sectors, this guidance paper was adopted by the FATF at its June 2007 Plenary. This is the first occasion that the FATF has developed guidance using a public-private sector partnership approach" (FATF, 2007, p. 1). Hence, the cooperation required to develop the RBA exemplifies the integration and ever-increasing role of the private sector in the process of regulation and governance. Thus, unsurprisingly, the guidance on the RBA states:

It must be recognized that any reasonably applied controls, including controls implemented as a result of a reasonably implemented risk-based approach will not identify and detect all instances of money laundering or terrorist financing. Therefore, regulators, law enforcement and judicial authorities must take into account and give due consideration to a financial institution's well-reasoned risk-based approach. (FATF, 2007, p. 3)

This statement clearly originates in the private sector and aims to manage regulatory expectations in relation to the implementation of an RBA. Ultimately it also highlights the fact that the private sector acknowledges and anticipates the fact that ML risk cannot be fully mitigated and that the private sector expects regulators to establish their own level of appetite when it comes to ML risk. This is a topic that arose during the empirical research and is explored and discussed further in Sect. 1.3 as well as in Chaps. 4 and 5.

The United Nations
The key legislative instrument that triggered international AML legislation was the United Nations' 1988 Vienna Convention. Although only focusing on drug-related predicate offences, it targeted ML and recognised it as a criminal offence. It marked "a fundamental switch away from targeting the manufacturing of illicit narcotic substances towards attacking the financial incentives of organised crime and criminal activities" (Ryder, 2012, p. 12).

Subsequently, the Palermo Convention was signed and widened ML activities to all serious offences, not just drug-related proceeds. Demetis qualifies this extension as "the major contribution of the convention" (Demetis, 2010, pp. 22–23). "Countries were required to apply the offence of ML to a broad range of predicate offences, including all serious offences as well as offences of participation in an organised criminal group, corruption, and obstruction to justice" (Png cited in Ryder, 2012, p. 12).

The Basel Committee on Banking Supervision
In 1988, the Basel Committee on Banking Supervision (in charge of supervising the banking sector) published its *Statement on Prevention of Criminal Use of the Banking System for the Purpose of ML*, providing guidance for banks. Furthermore, in 2001, it published its *Customer Due Diligence for Banks*: "Based on existing international standards, national supervisors are expected to set out supervisory practice governing banks' KYC programmes" (Bank for International Settlements, 2011, p. 3). The KYC principles issued by the Basel Committee represent "a critical component in the overall effective management of banking risks and not just AML" (Demetis, 2010, p. 23) and "help to protect banks' reputation and the integrity of the banking system by reducing the likelihood of banks becoming a vehicle for or a victim of financial crime and suffering consequential reputational damage" (Ryder, 2012, p. 18).

The Basel Committee ensures the overall integrity and stability of the banking system through supervision. Hence, rather than ML or tax fraud risk, the Basel Committee on Banking Regulation targets integrity risk, defined as: "being affected by the improper, unethical conduct of the organisation, its employees or management in contravention of legislation and regulation and the standards set by society or by the institution itself" (Simonova, 2011, p. 348). Simonova further highlights that "the risk of reputation loss, financial loss and/or other loss arising from preventive or repressive action by the competent authorities in response to the (unwitting) involvement in ML by customers, intermediaries or the institution's own staff" (Simonova, 2011, p. 348) is a subset of integrity risk.

This is very much aligned with FATF's objectives, which aim to "to set standards and promote effective implementation of legal, regulatory and operational measures for combating money laundering, terrorist financing and other related threats to the integrity of the international financial system" (FATF, 2019a, b, p. 6).

Regional Initiatives

The United States

US AML policy predates international AML measures. It has therefore been argued that US policy drives the FATF's agenda as well as the UN's. Indeed, Simmons argues that "the United States is 'hegemonic' in finance in the sense that it is costlier to alter its preferred regulatory innovation than to try to change the policies of the rest of the world" (2001, p. 595). Drezner, on the other hand, argues that the USA has worked alongside the European Union and that the two were therefore "able to cajole, coerce, and enforce a global anti-money laundering standard into existence" (2007, p. 145). Regardless, the author believes it is important to provide an overview of the US's AML regime because it is the first country to have criminalised ML in 1986, and more importantly, US ML legislation grants the USA extensive extraterritorial jurisdiction for the crime of ML. Furthermore, US institutions were the first to coin the term "risk-based" in the context of AML and combatting the financing of terrorism (CFT).

The Bank Secrecy Act of 1970 (BSA) gave birth to AML policy. Its aim was to combat organised crime and minimise potential abuse of the banking infrastructure. The BSA implemented "record-keeping and reporting requirements to ensure the existence of adequate audit trails of source, volume, and movement of monetary instruments" (FINCEN, n.d.). Former assistant secretary of the US Treasury for Enforcement and Operations, Eugene T. Rossides, famously stated:

> Our overall aim is to build a system to combat organized crime and white-collar crime and to deter and prevent the use of secret foreign bank accounts for tax fraud and their use to screen from view a wide variety of criminally related financial activities, and to conceal and cleanse criminal wealth. (United States Senate Committee, 1970)

The subsequent ML Control Act in 1986 made ML a federal crime and prohibited the breakdown of currency transactions into smaller amounts. This was to prevent avoidance of currency transaction reporting (CTR) requirements for sums over USD 10,000. Furthermore, it prescribed financial sanctions for BSA violations. Finally, under the ML Control Act, banks had to implement procedures to reinforce compliance with the BSA's reporting and record-keeping requirements.

The Annunzio-Wylie Money Laundering Act of 1992 enhanced the BSA, increasing fines for BSA violations, "introducing suspicious activity reports (SARs) and requiring verification and record keeping for wire transfers" (FINCEN, n.d.). The following ML and Financial Crimes Strategy Act (1998) identified and defined "high-risk entities" and emphasised the need to concentrate resources in areas with increased ML, financial crime and drug trafficking by introducing the:

> High Intensity Money Laundering and Related Financial Crime Area (HIFCA) and High Intensity Drug Trafficking Areas (HIDTA). HIFCAs may be defined geographically or they can also be created to address ML in an industry sector, a financial institution, or group of financial institutions. These high risk areas aim to concentrate law enforcement efforts at the federal, state, and local levels in high intensity money laundering zones. (FINCEN, n.d.)

Additional evidence of the evolution towards an RBA is the Uniting and Strengthening America by Providing Appropriate Tools Required to Intercept and Obstruct Terrorism Act of 2001 (US Patriot Act). It was signed following the 2001 terrorist attacks in New York and is relevant to financial institutions both within and outside the USA. It changed reporting requirements, criminalised tax fraud and imposed further requirements in relation to customer identification procedures. Section 312 of the US Patriot Act states:

> Each financial institution that establishes, maintains, administers, or manages a private banking account or a correspondent account in the United States for a non-United States person, including a foreign individual visiting the United States, or a representative of a non-United States person shall establish appropriate, specific, and, where necessary, enhanced, due diligence policies, procedures, and controls that are reasonably designed to detect and report instances of money laundering through those accounts. (US Patriot Act, 2001, s. 312)

The FATF's Guidance on the RBA to Combating ML and TF (June 2007) clearly echoes the above citation. Indeed, the US Patriot Act requires financial institutions to apply due diligence, and if a customer is evaluated as representing a higher ML risk, they need to perform an enhanced review of the account or customer. Hence, Section 312 requires "the implementation of risk based policies, procedures and controls designed to detect and report known or suspected ML activity" (Young cited in Ryder, 2012, p. 46).

In 2004, William Fox, then director of the Financial Crimes Enforcement Network (FINCEN, i.e. the US financial intelligence unit, the institution in charge of receiving, analysing and disseminating CTRs and SARs) stated: "our approach to this regulatory regime is risk-based not rule based. We believe strongly that compliance must be risk-based in order to fairly and effectively regulate the panorama of industries represented under the BSA umbrella" (Fox, 2004a, b). This approach has been reinforced by the application and enforcement of the BSA whose examination manual was described on June 30, 2005, as follows: "The BSA/AML Examination Manual emphasizes a banking organization's responsibility to establish and implement *risk-based* policies, procedures, and processes to comply with the BSA and safeguard its operations from ML and TF" (Federal Reserve Board, 2005a, b).

The European Union

In 1990, the Council of Europe Convention on Laundering, Search, Seizure and Confiscation of the Proceeds from Crime and on the Financing of Terrorism was implemented. It introduced the First ML Directive (1991) where "the European Commission and the member states agreed to prohibit, instead of criminalize, money laundering at the EU level" (Borlini & Montanaro, 1991, p. 1030). It also aimed to align respective member states' national legislation to the requirements that had been set out in the Vienna and Palermo Conventions.

The Second AML Directive was created in 2001 to enhance existing provisions under the First Directive. Influenced by the FATF's 40 Recommendations, the Second Directive "lengthened the list of predicate offences for which suspicious transaction reports were compulsory from just drug trafficking offences to all serious criminal offences" (Ryder, 2012, p. 14). The Third AML Directive (2006) extended existing legislation to nonfinancial businesses and professions and, more importantly, adopted the FATF's enhanced standards issued in 2003. It defined the RBA regarding the customer due diligence (CDD) for banks, whether simplified or enhanced. In addition, the Third AML Directive required the monitoring of financial institutions' relationships with businesses, ensuring alignment between business risk profiles and actual activities. Together with the requirement to create a financial intelligence unit (FIU) in each member state, tax fraud was also included, reflecting an alignment to the US Patriot Act.

In February 2015, the European Commission introduced the Fourth AML Directive (becoming law on June 26, 2017), which aimed to reflect the FATF's updated recommendations (of 2012) and focused on the following: "enhanced RBA, expanded focus on politically exposed persons (PEPs) and beneficial ownership, introduction of tax crimes as a predicate offence, harmonised sanctions regimes and new requirements relating to cash payments and gambling services providers" (Council Directive 2015/849 of May 20, 2015).

Each member state assesses the *level of risk* within their respective jurisdictions and "implement commensurate measures to mitigate such risks" (European Banking Authority, 2017, p. 43). Also, the commission is required to "identify high-risk third countries with strategic deficiencies in their anti-money laundering and countering terrorist financing regimes that pose significant threats" (European Commission, 2020a, b). In addition, there were enhancements to customer due diligence (CDD) processes and procedures, requiring obliged entities to determine when simplified or enhanced CDD measures were to be applied and to justify the underlying rationale. The reader should note that obliged entities encompass "credit and financial institutions, auditors, external accountants, notaries, legal professionals, trust, company services providers, estate agents, gambling services providers and high-value goods traders" (European Commission, 2019a, b, p. 6). As such, "the requirements of implementing an RBA had changed. Although some might say that it became more flexible, many would argue that the Fourth Directive made the process more complicated" (Hanley-Giersch, 2015, p. 75).

In addition, the Fourth Directive also states that enhanced CDD is always required when transactions involve PEPs whether foreign or, for the first time, domestic. This is because "it is recognised that many PEPs are in positions that potentially can be abused for the purpose of committing ML offences and related predicate offences, including corruption and bribery" (FATF, 2013, p. 3). In addition, the Fourth Directive maintains the threshold for beneficial ownership (shareholding above 25%) but obligates businesses to keep records verifying beneficial owners' identities. Prior to the Fourth Directive, there was an informal framework for cooperation between FIUs. The Fourth Directive states: "Member States should in particular ensure that their FIUs exchange information freely, spontaneously or upon request, with third-country FIUs" (Council Directive 2015/849 of May 20, 2015, Article 58). Finally, the Fourth Directive required member states to hold obliged entities liable for regulatory breaches, determining levels of sanctions and conditions of application.

In July 2016, the European Commission presented a proposal to amend the Fourth AML Directive adopted by the European Parliament as the Fifth AML Directive. The European Commission released a statement explaining that "the proposal was presented by the Commission in the wake of terrorist attacks and the revelation of the Panama Papers scandal, and is part of the Commission's action plan to strengthen the fight against terrorist financing" (European Commission, 2018). Some of the key aspects of the Fifth AML Directive include enhanced powers for financial intelligence units, stricter due diligence processes for financial flows from and to high-risk countries, the regulation of cryptocurrencies and prepaid cards and enhanced access to central registries and beneficial ownership registers (Directive (EU) 2018/843). Member states were required to implement the Fifth AML Directive into national law by January 2020.

In November 2018, the European Parliament published yet another directive, namely, the Sixth AML Directive (Council Directive 2018/1673, 2018a, b), implemented into national law by December 2020 and adopted by June 2021. The key changes include but are not limited to the harmonisation of 22 predicate offences including counterfeiting, environmental crimes, self-laundering, new ML offences (aiding, abetting and attempting to commit ML), extending criminal liability to legal persons (such as companies or incorporated partnerships) and individuals holding a certain role or responsibility on their behalf, enhanced punitive measures for legal persons and individuals and better cross-border cooperation when member states each have jurisdiction over an offence.

In addition, in May 2020 the European Commission published an action plan for ML and TF prevention built on six pillars: "effective implementation of effective rule, a single EU rulebook, EU level supervision, support and cooperation mechanism for FIUs, better use of information to enforce criminal law, a stronger EU in the world" (European Commission, 2020a, b, p. 3). This was followed by the publication of a set of legislative proposals in July 2021that aim to facilitate effective and consistent AML and CFT through the establishment of a single European rulebook, an EU-level supervisory authority and crypto asset regulation. The EU's new

Anti-Money Laundering Authority (AMLA) is expected to be in place by 2024, supervising large financial institutions and coordinating national ML authorities.

The close succession of the Fourth, Fifth and Sixth AML Directives are an indication of how ML and terrorism financing risks are putting pressure on governments and regulators alike as well as how the EU is strengthening the AML and CFT framework further. For instance, the European Commission (EC) has issued:

> an upgraded mandate for the European Banking Authority, new provisions that will apply to cash controls starting from June 2021, amendments to the Capital Requirements Directive (CRDV), new rules on access to financial information by law enforcement authorities and a harmonised definition of offences and sanctions related to money laundering. In addition, the EU established a new comprehensive whistle-blower protection regime, to be transposed by December 2021, which complements existing rules on whistle-blower protection in the 4AMLD. The new regime will strengthen the ability of national and EU authorities to prevent, detect and address breaches to, amongst other, anti-money laundering and countering the financing of terrorism rules. (European Commission, 2020a, b, pp. 1-2)

However, bearing in mind that obliged entities are also required to implement other regulatory requirements pertaining to the financial sector such as the Payments Services Directive, the updated Markets in Financial Instruments Directive (MiFID II) and the General Data Protection Regulation (GDPR), obliged entities are under tremendous pressure requiring regulators to avoid knee jerk reactions.

Section 1.2 provides an overview of AML's legislative and regulatory context along with the key regulatory bodies in charge of oversight and governance. The following section moves towards understanding ML through the prism of risk.

1.3 Section 3: Risk and Governance

Sections 1.1 and 1.2 discuss threats posed by ML as well as the legislative and regulatory framework in place to protect society from such threats. Section 1.3 aims to explore assumptions made in relation to defining risk. The purpose is to widen the observation and hence the understanding of risk as a concept but also as a discipline. Hence, Sect. 1.3 aims to develop an understanding of risk and to clarify perceptions of risk among experts as well as other key stakeholders (such as members of society). Finally, Sect. 1.3 concludes with an overview of the evolution of risk and the development of increased societal awareness of and sensitivity to risk. As such, this section will lay a robust foundation on which to build a theory capable of guiding the description, analysis and deconstruction of risk handling in the domain of ML governance within the financial sector.

Defining and Measuring Risk

Discussing "risk" raises the immediate problem that it may mean different things to different people (Fischhoff et al., 1984). There is no common understanding of or, hence, definition of the concept of risk neither among specialists, scientists nor laypeople. As argued by Beck, this may be due to the fact that any given risk definition is a power game. Indeed, "the inequalities of definition enable powerful actors to maximize risks for 'others' and minimize risks for 'themselves'" (Jabareen, 2015, p. 22). This is "especially true for world risk society where Western governments or powerful economic actors define risks for others. Not all actors really benefit from the reflexivity of risk only those with real scope to define their own risks" (Beck, 2006, p. 333). In addition, one problematic dimension of this issue concerns the selection of relevant risks: "Once again, discipline-specific research can reveal that this is not a matter of chance but that demonstrable social factors control the selection process" (Luhmann, 1993a, p. 4). Thus, not only do risks "reinforce many societal, political, and economic structures" (Russell & Babrow, 2011, p. 244); they are also preselected in "conformity with or in breach of prevailing opinion" (Luhmann, 1993a, p. 3). An illustration of this problem of risk selection can be seen in the issues identified by politics or the media and discussed in public forums. For example, different countries report on different risks. Likewise, within the same society, different social groups, for instance, will prioritise different risks. For example, in the UK, a social movement called Extinction Rebellion focuses on climate change as the primary risk facing the UK, whereas a social movement labelled by the British media as "remainers" targets potential economic, political and social risks associated with leaving the EU as paramount. Likewise, the threat posed by the COVID-19 pandemic has been reported by some media as a plot to control citizens, warning against the risk of wearing masks and accepting tracking and tracing mechanisms (Evstatieva, 2020), while others have discussed COVID-19 as a risk to global health.

The word *risk* can be traced to the emerging insurance industry originating in the maritime sector of twelfth-century Europe (Luhmann, 1993a; Voss, 2005). The review of early contracts regulating "who is to bear a loss in the event of [a risk] occurrence" (Luhmann, 1993a, p. 10) indicates that "losses became increasingly associated with human decisions, as opposed to nature, God, or providence" (Luhmann, 1993a, p. xxviii; Beck, 1986). Currently, it is safe to say that risk is an interdisciplinary concept that relates to individuals' expectations in relation to an event and its outcome which may be more or less certain—or uncertain (Zinn, 2008). In the words of Renn, risk is "the possibility that human actions or events lead to consequences that have an impact on what humans value" (Renn, 1987, p. 51).

Vasvari (2015) cites a key ingredient of risk as the element of probable uncertainty (in the sense of something that is "likely to be the case") and the "first component of uncertainty is the identification and justification of probabilities linked to specific adverse effects or distribution of effects" (Klinke et al., 2002, p. 1079). It is important to note, however, that there is no homogenous definition of uncertainty and that different individuals will define uncertainty differently as, for example, "incertitude, variability, indeterminacy, ignorance, lack of knowledge" (Klinke et al., 2002, p. 1074). Hence, this brings us to the fundamental yet uncomfortable question of whether risk is an objective or subjective state and, thus, whether risk is subject to different perceptions by different observers. This is discussed in Sect. 3.2.

Risk also involves a distinct temporal aspect—specifically, the consideration of the future outcome and individual impacts of a given risk. Thus, as a concept, risk hinges on expectations driven by *perception*, ability or willingness to *manage* (un)-certain outcomes and *appetite or aversion* to potential impacts. Vasvari (2015) identifies a number of approaches to capturing, or defining, the nature of risk: technical, economic, psychological and sociological. The author focuses here on the first three approaches, and Chap. 2 explores the sociology of risk.

Technical and Economic Approaches
From the perspective of technical and economic approaches, objective measures of harm associated with uncertain events can be measured. Accordingly, technical approaches define risk "as a probability construct: the perceived likelihood that a particular event will lead to certain consequences" (Russell & Babrow, 2011, p. 244). Indeed, risk is traditionally seen as the probability and magnitude of a loss, disaster or other undesirable event. First, the probability that the event will occur is assessed, and, subsequently, the magnitude of the loss triggered by the event is quantified on the basis of, for example, financial losses or the number of lives lost. As such, such an approach seems to be strongly influenced by utilitarian economics in that a potentially undesirable outcome is weighed against the potential return/utility of the decision generating the outcome versus the return/utility of *not* making a decision at all. Accordingly, the assessment of risk is based on the expected utility of outcomes associated with the risks taken.

It is only natural to wonder who performs such risk-measuring exercises. In the field of AML and concerning broader financial risks such as market or credit risks, the answer is an expert group of risk assessors. However, should the particular utility desired by such experts be taken as paramount to the overall utility of society? Clearly, the selection of an uncertain utility associated with a decision made by experts should "reflect society's values rather than those of any single interest" (Fischhoff et al., 1984, p. 128). However, it is essential that other stakeholders, such as the general public or the government, have some power to champion general societal utility over that of designated experts should the two not coincide. For instance, *The Independent* reported that the Bank of England estimated that the 2008 credit crisis cost the UK a total of GBP 7.4 trillion in terms of lost output and estimated that major UK banks received GBP 50 billion in taxpayer-funded support (O'Grady, 2010). It is indeed questionable whether such bailouts justified the cost to society (Block, 2010), whether British and/or US taxpayers were appropriately involved in the decision-making process and, finally, whether the greater social utility had been assessed alongside that of the wider financial sector, bearing in mind that financial distress would have inevitably impacted society's overall utility.

The same questions emerge when financial institutions such as HSBC or ING become involved in serious cases of ML, only to face the relatively minor repercussions of fines and a public rap on the knuckles. Indeed, the ING criminal investigation report by the National Office for Serious Fraud in the Netherlands indicates that ING has been identified by the Financial Stability Board as being a systemic institution, "essential to the financial system and hence to the functioning of the economy and society" (Openbaar Ministerie, 2018, p. 3). Yet, ING has been involved in the recent past in two serious cases of regulatory violations. In 2012, ING was charged with facilitating billions of dollars' worth of transactions for Cuban and Iranian customers, constituting serious economic sanctions violations. At the time, ING had agreed to pay USD 619 million in fines. Similarly, in 2018, ING admitted that criminals had been using the bank to launder dirty money and agreed to pay USD 900 million in fines. Clearly, fines in cases such as these do not appear to encourage institutions to tighten their internal AML controls, despite the impact of their money laundering crimes on society. ING's actions have single-handedly weakened the sanctions regulatory regime by facilitating large transactions on behalf of Iranian and Cuban clients and enabling rampant corruption in foreign jurisdictions. In another case, Russian telecommunications company VimpelCom sent tens of millions of dollars' worth of bribes via its ING accounts to a "company owned by Gulnara Karimova, the daughter of then-president of Uzbekistan Islam Karimov" (Racz, 2018). As such, one must question whose utility the Dutch prosecution office maximised in its settlement with ING and would society as a whole agree with this decision.

While in reference to the 2008 credit crisis, it has been argued that "since it is the people [...] who are affected by the potential harm of technologies or other risk-inducing activities, it should be their prerogative to determine the level of risk that they judge tolerable for themselves and their community" (Klinke et al., 2002, p. 1073), such an approach has certain weaknesses. For example, is the public truly capable of assessing risks, or is the public perception of risk subjective, irrational and uneducated? Indeed, social media coverage may be capable of influencing and possibly misguiding public perceptions. For example, in February 2018, the US government indicted 13 Russian nationals for having interfered with the 2016 US presidential election through social media propaganda. "The indictment, brought by the office of special counsel Robert Mueller, represents the most direct allegation to date of illegal Russian meddling during the election. It claims that Russians created bogus Internet postings, posed online as American political activists and fraudulently purchased advertisements—all with the goal of swaying political opinion during the bitterly contested race" (Tucker, 2018). Furthermore, in March 2018, allegations emerged that Facebook, the largest social media platform, with over 2 billion monthly users as of April 2019 (according to *Business Insider*), had enabled the targeting of voters in the 2016 US presidential election. It is believed that the social platform mismanaged a serious data breach allowing Cambridge Analytica Political Global, the political data company working on Trump's presidential campaign, to harvest the data of up to 87 million users (Badshah, 2018). Michael Turnbull, Cambridge Analytica's managing director, has stated the

Table 1.1 Biases of risk perception (Renn, 1987, p. 54)

Biases	Description
Availability	Events that come to people's mind immediately are rated as more probable than events that are less mentally available
Anchoring effect	Probabilities are adjusted to cognitive routines or to the perceived significance of the information
Representativeness	Unique events experienced in person or associated with properties of an event are preferred over information on probabilities or relative frequencies when people make predictions or inferences about probabilities

following: "Our job is to understand what are those really deep-seated, underlying fears you didn't know that was a fear until you saw something that just evoked that reaction from you. And our job is to drop the bucket further down the well than anyone else to understand deep-seated, underlying fears" (Carisimo, 2018). Thus the following quote is particularly appropriate:

> People are irredeemably irrational, vulnerable to manipulation by sensational mass media and radical environmental groups. And therefore, it follows that the right way to deal with the public vis-à-vis risk is not to deal with the public vis-à-vis risk. Ignore people if you can, mis-lead them if you must, lie to them in extremis, but for heaven's sake don't level with them because they will screw it up. (Sandmann, 1989, p. 3)

What Sandmann argues is that ignorance or misperceptions should not drive risk assessments and hence risk management.

Nevertheless, a number of scholars believe that individuals' judgements, instincts and informed and misinformed perceptions of risk are legitimate components of risk assessment. As such, there is widespread belief that perception should feed into risk assessments and management processes. This would not be problematic if public assessments of risk matched that of experts, but a number of studies have identified gaps between what experts and the general public evaluate as risky (Slovic, 1987; Renn, 1998). This suggests that if there is a misalignment, one should at least attempt to understand the root cause of this misalignment.

Psychological Approaches and Risk Perception
Researchers looking at individuals' opinions, judgements and perceptions of risk have demonstrated that, in contrast to technical and economic approaches to risk, individuals' evaluations are not driven by rational assessments of likely outcomes or expected utility, because individuals are biased by a number of factors when evaluating the probability of an event and hence its associated risk or reward (Slovic, 1987; Renn, 1987, 1990, 1998; Klinke et al., 2002; Kahneman, 2011). Such factors are not necessarily rational and are strongly influenced by initial impressions or biases, as indicated in Table 1.1.

Thus, while Table 1.1 demonstrates that rationality is often not the primary factor individuals use to form risk perceptions, what emerges is that "experience of and familiarity with the context provide additional information to calibrate individual judgements, particularly for nontrivial decisions" (Renn, 1987, p. 54). Furthermore,

Table 1.2 The four semantic images of risk in public perception (Renn, 1987, p. 55)

Pending danger (sword of Damocles)	Artificial risk source Large catastrophic potential Inequitable risk-benefit distribution Perception of randomness as a threat
Slow killers (Pandora's box)	(artificial) ingredient in food, water or air Delayed effects, non-catastrophic Contingent on information rather than experience Quest for deterministic risk management Strong incentive for blame
Cost-benefit ratio (Athena's scale)	Confined to monetary gains and losses Orientation towards variance of distribution rather than expected value Asymmetry between risks and gains Dominance of probabilistic thinking
Avocational thrill (Hercules image)	Personal control over degree of risk Personal skills necessary to master danger Voluntary activity Non-catastrophic consequences

as indicated above, individuals do not necessarily adjust their risk perceptions in light of new or challenging information. As Renn argues, this problem applies to expert individuals as well, who also may be similarly attached to initial impressions and express high levels of confidence in their quantitative judgements and underestimate remaining uncertainties when performing their own risk assessments (Renn, 1998). In sum, even the "technical" approaches discussed above are highly subjective (Keynes, 1921; Renn, 1992 and Vasvari, 2015): the result of such assessments relies on perceived probability, ignorance and "degrees of our belief in the future" (Vasvari, 2015, p. 32). Thus, while attitudes towards risk and perception of risk are, of course, driven by the availability of information, they are also strongly impacted by the personal biases, cognitive ability and limitations of individual experts and laypersons alike. For instance, a private banker based in Moldavia and dealing with Russian money and customers on a daily basis will evaluate ML risks associated with the latter differently to a private banker based in a jurisdiction with limited dealings with Russian funds.

Another element raised by Renn (1987) is that of semantic context. Indeed, the meaning of risk will vary depending on the context in which the term is employed. Thus, regarding the assessment of risks, Renn identifies four semantic images.

Table 1.2 highlights the fact that risk perception is context dependent and driven by key characteristics or properties of the actual risk such as "dread, personal control, familiarity with risk, the perception of equitable sharing of both benefits and risks and potential for blame" (Renn, 1990, p. 3). This is what Hardy and Maguire (2019) call a discursive perspective where a risk object, the entity posing a risk, is constructed from conceptual elements: "an object deemed to 'pose' risk, a putative harm and a linkage alleging some form of causation between the object and the harm" (Hilgartner, 1992, p. 40).

In summary, risk is more than the product of probabilities and impact. It encapsulates individual values, perceived occurrences and the wider social context, including perceptions of blame, inequities and confidence in government and institutions (Beck, 1986; Douglas & Wildavsky, 1982; Luhmann, 1993a, b). "Perhaps the most important message is that there is wisdom as well as error in public attitudes and perceptions. Laypeople's conceptualisation of risk is much richer than that of the experts and reflects legitimate concerns that are typically omitted from expert risk assessments" (Slovic, 1987, p. 285). Sandmann states that risk equals hazard and outrage (Sandmann, 1989), and while at this stage such a definition may not support the understanding of how risk assessments should be performed, it certainly indicates that perception should be treated as a potential component essential to making adequate risk assessments and developing effective management processes.

One thing that Slovic, however, fails to acknowledge is the fact that experts may actually express through their technical risk assessments, their concerns, or *outrage* as Sandmann would say. Indeed, technical assessments performed by risk analysts can be overridden, enabling analysts to use heuristic techniques often influenced by "gut instinct", or sensitivity to a particular topic or ethics, when assessing certain risks associated with a particular event. For instance, a suspicious activity report involving the defrauding of a frail old lady may trigger an emotion in an ML risk analyst who will therefore tweak the risk-scoring tool to assign a greater overall risk score to that case than to a similar case involving a younger individual, who is financially educated and manages his or her own company and whom the analyst would thus perceive to be less vulnerable.

Before concluding this section on defining and measuring risk through models or heuristic methods, the author wishes to briefly discuss a 2019 report issued by the Basel Institute on Governance, which assessed the risk of money laundering and terrorist financing around the globe. This report is worth considering because it demonstrates weaknesses of so-called objective risk assessment tools. The methodology of the report involved the development of a "conceptual framework that captures the multidimensionality of the data and categorises the indicators into five domains identified as key to ML/TF risks" (Basel Institute on Governance, 2019, p. 28). More specifically, the institute considered data such as the FATF mutual evaluation reports and other reports and indices published by the World Bank, the US State Department, Transparency International and others. Surprisingly, Estonia, the jurisdiction marred by the biggest ML scandal to date, was ranked among the 125 countries whose scores were calculated as representing the least ML risk. The arguments proposed by the institute were that Estonia's 2014 FATF mutual evaluation report by Moneyval (defined on their website as a committee of experts on the evaluation of AML measures and the financing of terrorism) indicated good performance. Another argument suggested was that "the Basel AML Index measures the *risk* of money laundering, not the actual amount of money laundering" (Basel Institute on Governance, 2019). This argument exemplifies the difficulty associated with defining risk. Indeed, many AML practitioners would argue that the amount of ML in a jurisdiction is most certainly a fundamental indicator of ML risk within that jurisdiction. The Basel Institute on Governance, however, appears to believe that confirmed ML activity (as was the case for Estonia through the Estonian branch of Danske Bank) is separate from ML *risk* itself. Interestingly, the methodology of this report uses a technical approach relying on the work performed by AML experts. Nevertheless, the results of their analysis were surprising, to say the least, since they did not reflect the risks flourishing in the Estonian jurisdiction that led to the damages later observed in the Estonian Jurisdiction that will no doubt lead to further observable damages in 2020 and 2021.

Is Risk Real?

The preceding section examines different approaches used to assess risk. To address the ontology of risk, it would be accurate to say that technical and economic approaches to estimating risk are aligned with what one may call a realist tradition: estimates of risk "constitute true representations of observable hazards that can and will affect people as predicted by the calculated results regardless of the beliefs or convictions of the analysts involved" (Klinke et al., 2002, p. 1073). However, constructivists disagree with the above statement. They believe that risk assessments are mental constructions. The *real* world cannot be known by any cognitive system, as each cognitive system is restricted by its own mode of observation, which constructs its own reality. Hence, "such quantifying processes lead to what Luhmann terms 'scientization,' a method through which humans mistakenly identify social constructions as naturally occurring phenomena" (Russell & Babrow, 2011, p. 244). As observers, individuals build or construct narratives through which risk emerges, which is not "a measurable feature of material reality" (Russell & Babrow, 2011, p. 244) but a social construction.

Russell and Brabow argue that human beings create and rely upon narrative construction and communication to guide "both their interpretations and enactments of meaning in embodied experience" (Russell & Babrow, 2011. p. 241):

> We actively piece together concepts, characters, values and motives, and themes and plots to create coherent frames for interpreting and speaking about lived experience. In summary, histories, in general, are developed through exclusionary processes for depicting reality. (Russell & Babrow, 2011. p. 241)

Hence, the key task at this point is to remove all ambiguities relating to the nature, essence and, hence, the ontology of risk. Is risk independent of human cognition, or is its existence dependent on an observer whose knowledge of the world may also be a construct? If so, which observers are qualified to make that judgement, and, ultimately, can such a judgement be made in the first place? This section focuses on the manner in which risk comes to be recognised and perceived from an epistemological and ontological perspective. Indeed, there is an unquestionable paradox that emerges when considering the reality of risk. There are unequivocal and, what one would call, *real* or tangible hazards and threats out there. However, the perception or understanding of such threats is inevitably distorted and/or limited

1.3 Section 3: Risk and Governance

by one's own and possibly unique understanding and perception of the world. Indeed, the wide spectrum of how risk as a concept is defined—or, as seen in the previous section, assessed—is engrained in the way one perceives the epistemology and ontology of risk.

For example, one could question when ML risk becomes risk. What is the tipping point that makes ML risk observable? Could it be argued that ML is intrinsically risky to the financial sector or does it become risk only when identified and publicised through regulators' press releases and other media, i.e. once it is observed? The Danske case illustrates the relevance of such questions. Indeed, it has now been documented that the Estonian branch of Danske Bank, which laundered EUR 200 billion of dirty Russian and Azeri money, may have been implicated in ML as early as 2007. Between 2007 and 2015 (when both Estonian and Danish regulators were aware of serious AML failings according to the 2018 Bruun and Hjejle report), it is fair to say that such activities had not (yet) translated into what the Basel Institute on Governance would call risk. Neither the Danish nor the Estonian regulators had thoroughly followed up on their investigations into Danske's Estonian branch despite being aware of serious AML issues. Based on the above facts, one could thus assume that risk was observable in 2015 when Danske Bank was asked by the Estonian regulator to exit all its non-resident customers. Subsequently, in 2017, the consequences and damages associated with the ML risk that Danske Bank had accepted emerged. Information concerning the EUR 200 billion that were laundered was made public; Estonia's reputation was ruined; Aivar Rehe, who led Danske Bank from 2006 till 2015, committed suicide; Estonia banned Danske Bank from the country; and a network of other banks such as Swedbank and Deutsche Bank were similarly contaminated by the Danske scandal. What is striking, however, is that none of this would have happened had the information not been known. Thus, one cannot help but wonder whether ML risk is the likelihood of an institution being used for ML purposes or whether ML risk is the likelihood of knowledge and observation of ML becoming public. Perhaps risk hinges on information or on that "bit of information which makes a difference" (Bateson, 1972, p. 315). As stated by van Koningsveld, "Money Laundering—'you don't see it until you understand it'" (2013, p. 435).

However, there are unambiguous events: plane crashes happen, nuclear disasters occur, and financial crises are real. Although such events are what Searle would qualify as "brute facts" (Searle, 1995) as one could not deny that a plane crash has taken place, individuals' immediate experience, interpretations, or perceptions are likely to differ. Rosa et al. (2014) state that "there can never be an isomorphism between the world and its states and our understanding of it. Since we can never have perfect knowledge of the world—even an independent world—all of our knowledge is always socially shaped and mediated. In that restricted sense, all knowledge is socially constructed" (p. 15). That which supports overlaps in individual understandings of the world and individuals' knowledge is what Searle calls collective intentionality. He states:

> the central span on the bridge from physics to society is collective intentionality, and the decisive movement on that bridge in the creation of social reality is the collective intentional imposition of function on entities that cannot perform these functions without that imposition. (Searle, 1995, p. 41)

Thus, it is necessary to explore the coexistence between socially defined perceptions of risk and the brutal reality of risk. To approach this challenge, the following section explores the premise of constructivism and the notion of a realist world independent of human cognition.

Under the assumption that knowledge and reality are social constructs, the notion of risk is also socially constructed. As such, the financial crisis of 2008 would also be a construct, generated by a subjective process and eventually leading to a collective judgement. Developing an understanding of this process necessitates identifying precisely what triggers the subjective and collective judgement processes, how such triggers are generated, the source of the momentum for collective judgement and the origins of the concept of financial crisis itself. Understanding social constructs, in general, necessitates a genealogical focus: social constructions are generated by social constructs, which, in turn, are also generated by social constructs. Indeed, the 2008 financial crisis was driven by a number of concepts that feed on social constructs; for example, money, subprime loans, collaterised debt obligations, misguided credit ratings, low interest rates and the belief that risk can be banished from society (The Economist, 2013). However, one might naturally wonder what original event or trigger initiated the first social construct. Indeed, if one dispenses with the notion of an external, objective reality, it is indeed difficult to identify what might drive the selection of one version of "reality" over another. Answering such essential philosophical questions is decidedly outside the scope of this work; nevertheless, this line of questioning is fruitful, since it helps to articulate the nature of reality. If there truly exists a state of reality that is independent of all observers and attributed meaning, then that would imply that meaning itself is based on subjective, individual or collective constructs, rather than on some essential, objective element of "reality".

For instance, Hilgartner (1992) and Hardy and Maguire (2019) argue that organisations translate risk. Risks are "translated into problems of organisational control systems" (Power, 2004a, b, p. 4) that are easier to understand for the institution expected to handle them (Hardy & Maguire, 2019), thus facilitating the implementation of risk management measures. This also supports the decision-making process in the redistribution of risk responsibility and accountability. For instance, the risk-based approach (RBA), endorsed by the Fourth AML Directive, essentially translates ML risk into risks that financial institutions are more familiar with. This approach consists in identifying the supposed components of ML risk and listing them as subrisks that obliged entities understand:

> Member States shall ensure that obliged entities take appropriate steps to identify and assess the risks of money laundering and terrorist financing, taking into account risk factors including those relating to their customers, countries or geographic areas, products, services, transactions or delivery channels. Those steps shall be proportionate to the nature and size of the obliged entities. (Article 8)

Shifting to the opposite end of the spectrum, it is also important to consider the possibility of a reality completely independent of human cognition. Doing so would require the identification of some signal confirming ontological realism. Rosa et al. (2014), for example, select gravity as a clear signal that represents "constraints" imposed by a world that is out there, independent of human cognition and agency. Although the constraints that manifest in the phenomenon of gravity may be interpreted differently (e.g. Newtonian gravity versus Einstein's concept of gravity), gravity is "real", and no individual can expect to float should they step off a cliff (on this planet, in any case). As such, gravity transcends all cultural boundaries, and all earthly subjects would experience falling off a cliff in a similar way (i.e. they would all "fall"). Accordingly, in a world of ontological realism, risks are real, and risk narratives are not primarily based on personal experience or self-referential cognition; rather they emerge from objective events that are simple outcomes and not substantially altered by different subjective interpretations.

However, as discussed in Sect. 3.1, it is important to remember that while risk may be considered by some to be an objective state of the world, the process of assessing risk is always observer dependent; thus the assessment of risk, in any case, translates the notion of an ontologically real risk into a constructed reality. Indeed, there are three fundamental elements common to nearly all definitions of risk (Rosa et al., 2014): first the notion that there is a state of reality that will lead to a potential outcome and second the fact that there always is an element of uncertainty associated with that outcome and, finally, that there is an uncertain impact associated with that uncertain outcome. The above discussion reviewing approaches to defining and assessing risk explores technological and economic methods and suggests that even the concept of probabilities can be seen as a subjective human invention (Keynes, 1921). Yet, while this constructed concept of probability is generally labelled as "normative" by observers and is applied to capture uncertainty, uncertainty can nevertheless never be wholly removed, because uncertainty is, simply, a constant feature of the world from the human perspective, despite all efforts to remove uncertainty through risk management frameworks. Yet, so-called normative or "objective" methodologies have become fundamental to how risk is perceived, assessed and managed by the private sector and governmental bodies (Enterprise Risk Management or International Risk Governance Frameworks are examples of normative governance programmes). Thus, it can be argued that while risk may or may not be ontologically real, uncertainty constitutes a key component of risk governance, defined by Lim as the way "various actors, rules, conventions, processes, and mechanisms are involved in collecting, analysing, and communicating risk information and the decisions taken to manage risks" (Lim, 2011, p. 14).

As such, the elements of risk governance involve recognising risk, determining the probability of it materialising and making a decision as to how best to manage it. These elements are the product of definitively constructed processes: Is there a risk and do others perceive it as such? Does this risk have a high or low likelihood of materialising and how low or high is the impact likely to be should it materialise? Is the decision to act proportional to the risk identified? Each of these questions relates to the means of acquiring knowledge and is clearly within an epistemological realm of inquiry.

More specifically, risk exists because of three conditions: there is a particular situation, there is an uncertain outcome associated with that situation, and there is a potential and uncertain impact associated with the outcome. Hence, risk involves a triad of conditions. This triad can also be used to describe the Danske Bank's ML activities: there is ML at Danske Bank (whether observed or not), the ML will lead to uncertain outcomes (it may be uncovered, lead to regulatory sanctions and result into reputational damage), and these outcomes will have uncertain impacts (the sanctions may be more or less severe or the Danske Bank brand may be more or less impacted).

To conclude this exploration of the epistemological and ontological spectrum of risk, the author briefly discusses the epistemology and ontology that grounds the theoretical basis developed in Chap. 2, which can be summarised by Luhmann's following quote: "There is an external world [...] but we have no direct contact with it" (Luhmann, 1990, p. 64). This is because contact can only be observer relative and subject to cognitive bias. More specifically, this project generally adopts the epistemology of constructivism: indeed, ML offences represent, at first glance, an objective concept, if such a thing exists. Nevertheless, they are dependent on legislation (a definitively social construct) that serves to both expand and specifically define what actions constitute predicate offences while also adjusting their meaning and customising them within different national contexts. While, from an ontological perspective, then, the research subscribes to a realist stance based on the conviction that a reality outside of human cognition and interpretation does exist, this reality does not entail meaning, as meaning only arises when an observer interacts with reality; as such, "reality" will have different meanings for different individual observers.

The following section provides an overview of the evolution of risk and how the private sector and academia appear to increasingly use risk in their discourses similarly to the way regulation and legislation characterise risk, as discussed in Sect. 1.2. In doing so, this section offers tools and reference points for navigating Chap. 2, which details the theoretical framework of this research.

The Evolution of the Risk Discourse within Governance and the Risk-Based Approach

The mid-1980s witnessed the start of a series of crises initiating erosion in the trust that individuals had placed in experts, practitioners and technology in general. Such crises included environmental crises (e.g. Chernobyl, 1986; the Exxon Valdez Oil leak, 1989), health-related crises (e.g. the AIDS and the COVID-19 pandemics) as well as an almost continuous stream of financial and regulatory crises (Black Tuesday, 1986; the collapse of the fraudulent and poorly regulated Bank of Credit and Commerce International, 1991; the Maxwell pension plundering scandal, 1992; the Enron accounting scandal, 2001; the subprime crisis, 2008; the European sovereign debt crisis, 2009; the HSBC ML scandal, 2015; the Russian and Azeri Laundromat, 2016–2017; the Paradise and Panama Papers, 2016–2017; the Danske Bank ML scandal, 2017–2020; the Wirecard fraud, 2020). Ultimately, these crises threw into doubt the "rationality" of scientists, the expertise of quantitative analysts, the ethics of bankers and the reliability of the political elite. Therefore, the small potential risk of a major catastrophe became no longer socially acceptable and no longer justifiable by the entities that the public had grown to mistrust. Such entities are increasingly perceived as posing a *risk* to social integrity. "The feeling of insecurity has become one of society's main concerns and one of the key drivers of its self-observation" (Le Bouter, 2014, p. 33, author's translation). As Wildavsky argues: "The richest, longest lived, best protected, most resourceful civilisation, with the highest degree of insight into its own technology, is on its way to becoming the most frightened" (Wildavsky, 1979, p. 32).

In 1986, in the midst of many such crises, two key sociological books on risk emerged: Beck's *Risk Society* (1986) and Luhmann's *Ecological Communication* (1986). Their respective success reflected the public's awareness of the ever-increasing emergence of risks, despite the reassuring risk assessments offered by the technocratic elite. More than 60,000 copies of Beck's publication were sold, and Luhmann's work was reprinted a number of times despite Luhmann's generally acknowledged inaccessibility (Rosa et al., 2014). The social theories articulated by Beck and Luhmann clearly reflected the current public intuition and judgement: "Their arguments resonated with a population disgusted with the seemingly unshakeable beliefs of the technological elite" (Rosa et al., 2014, p. 36). Hence, given the public's growing awareness of risks, disenchantment and resistance to innovation at the time (Zinn, 2008), experts were forced to identify and develop further frameworks to justify their decision-making processes and regulating authority in order to secure public acceptance.

Overlapping the erosion of the public's trust in the elite, a strong deregulatory narrative emerged, hinging on allegations of overregulation, inflexibility, high regulatory costs and inefficiencies (Hutter, 2005). In the UK, this trend culminated in the 1994 Deregulation and Contracting Out Act and the implementation of a Deregulation Task Office. In the USA, such institutional reforms were launched by Reagan's "regulatory relief" in 1984. Hood (1991) calls this trend a "new public management" that aims to "slow down or reverse government growth, shift administration towards privatisation, develop automation" (Hood, 1991, p. 3). Hence this new pressure made it necessary for regulators to demonstrate and justify how they managed their operations and resources effectively and efficiently (Hood, 1991), relying on the adoption of private sector practices, which were widely seen as the gold standard: "Generally there was an emphasis upon adopting private sector styles of management and an almost unthinkable acceptance that private sector practices were the benchmark against which to assess public sector activities" (Hutter, 2005, p. 2).

Hutter argues that in recent years there has been a "rapid development of a risk industry" and that "risk has become a new lens through which to view the world", supported by a "strong regulatory rhetoric, centring on alleged over-regulation, legalism, inflexibility and an alleged absence of attention being paid to the costs of regulation" (Hutter, 2005, p. 1). Hence, in 1992, in response to a recent series of UK financial scandals and a growing trend towards the adoption of risk management practices, *The Financial Aspects of Corporate Governance Report* (also known as the Cadbury Report) was published. The purpose of this report was to improve internal control mechanisms, financial reporting quality and corporate governance (Spira & Page, 2003). This was followed by the Hampel report (1998) and, finally, the Turnbull report (1999):

> In Britain, the adoption of risk management in government is clearly related to the influence of corporate codes notably the Turnbull Report. The Turnbull Report is identified as especially significant as a voluntary code which adopts a *risk based approach* to designing, operating and maintaining a sound system of control in business financial management. (Hutter, 2005, p. 2)

Similarly, in the USA, the Enron scandal prompted the Sarbanes-Oxley Act (2002), which aimed to legislate new compliance, accounting, auditing and corporate management standards. In addition, as a consequence of the global financial crisis, also known as the subprime crisis, the Basel Committee for Banking Supervision, a key player in global financial regulation (comprising prudential supervisors, central banks representatives and financial regulators) produced *The Principles for Enhancing Corporate Governance* (Basel Committee on Banking Supervision, 2010) which were subsequently revised in 2014. This report identifies principles of board governance, risk management and internal controls stating the importance of "independent risk and control functions, for which the board provides effective oversight" (Basel Committee on Banking Supervision, Principle 1, 2010). It also states that a company's management board should, among many things, approve and oversee "the implementation of the bank's overall risk strategy, including its risk tolerance/appetite" (Basel Committee on Banking Supervision, Principle 22, 2010).

Finally, financial regulators across the world began developing an RBA to regulation. Indeed, the UK Financial Services Authority (FSA), rebranded as the Financial Conduct Authority (FCA) following the subprime crisis, the Canadian Office of the Superintendent of Financial Institutions and the Australian Prudential Regulation Authority were all proponents of risk-based methods. Not only was the adoption of an RBA triggered by public and political pressure; it was also a function of internal pressures relating to their statutory remits. Black (2004) identifies three driving factors for such pressure: internal restructuration (each of the above regulators were created as a response to a crisis), a feel that the tools at hand were not adequate for efficient regulatory supervision and the need to manage the public's expectations "that financial regulators could not, and should not, be expected to prevent all financial failures" (Black, 2004, p. 48). Similarly, as discussed in Chap. 1, Sect. 1.2, in 2003, risk was explicitly added into the AML discourse through the

FATF's 40 Recommendations, and FATF official guidance on the RBA was issued in 2007 and developed in close cooperation with the private sector.

The Risk-Based Approach to ML Risk Governance

The RBA is central to the FATF 40 Recommendations, which all institutions must uphold and apply. Not only do the 40 Recommendations enable financial institutions to identify and assess ML risks posed by clients and potential clients, but they also support financial institutions in identifying and applying the necessary measures to manage such risks and prevent or limit potential future damages to the financial sector associated with such risks. As documented in the FATF official guidance on the RBA:

> There are no universally accepted methodologies that prescribe the nature and extent of a risk-based approach. However, an effective risk-based approach does involve identifying and categorizing money laundering risks and establishing reasonable controls based on risks identified. (FATF, 2007, p. 2)

The RBA aims to support financial institutions by allowing them to customise their exposure to ML risks. There are key steps to the implementation of the RBA. The first step involves identifying the inherent risks faced by a financial institution, mostly underpinned by the institution's geographical location, the products offered, the channels of delivery and customer base, etc. This allows the institution to assess and set its tolerance to such risks. Risk tolerance or appetite is generally part of the institutional culture. Then, risk-reduction measures and key controls are identified or created to fit with the inherent risks and the actual risk tolerance of the institution. This process allows an institution to evaluate its residual risks and implement its RBA to managing its ML risk by delegating the necessary resources, monitoring and oversight to higher-risk areas.

The introduction of the RBA and the development of the Fourth AML Directive led to an increase in regulatory expectations. Obliged entities are required to document and provide a detailed rationale for applying an RBA. Indeed, the Fourth AML Directive explains that "obliged entities shall ascertain that the business relationship or the transaction presents a lower degree of risk" (Article 15) if simplified due diligence is to be applied. The directive goes further and explains that these guidelines must be issued "on the risk factors to be taken into consideration and the measures to be taken in situations where simplified customer due diligence measures are appropriate" (Article 16) and explains that "when assessing the risks of money laundering and terrorist financing relating to types of customers, geographic areas particular products, services, transactions or delivery channels, Member States and obliged entities shall take into account at least the factors of potentially lower risk situations set out in Annex II" (Article 16). Finally, the Fourth AML Directive states that:

when dealing with natural persons or legal entities established in the third countries identified by the Commission as high-risk third countries, as well as in other cases of higher risk that are identified by Member States or obliged entities, Member States shall require obliged entities to apply enhanced customer due diligence measures to manage and mitigate those risks appropriately. (...) When assessing the risks of money laundering and terrorist financing, Member States and obliged entities shall take into account at least the factors of potentially higher-risk situations set out in Annex III. (Article 18)

Articles 16 and 17 and Annex II and III of the Fourth AML Directive clearly articulate that, despite the reservations expressed by the AML community, the European Commission's expectations in relation to obliged entities' ML prevention responsibilities are not only growing but are also becoming more complex.

Unlike rules-based regulation, Pieth and Aiolfi (2003) explain that the RBA "utilizes the professional know-how, experience and also the differentiated approach of financial institutions to understand financial transactions and the often complex financial structures on which they are predicated" (p. 15). In addition, Ross and Hannan (2007) explain that the RBA enables "AML efforts to be proportionate to the risks involved, provides a basis for reducing the flow of reports in a way that favours meaningful intelligence and provides greater flexibility and sensitivity in responding to complex problems" (p. 107). They argue, furthermore, that the RBA approach "transfers responsibility from regulatory institutions to financial institutions" (p. 108).

As a consequence of the RBA, the responsibility for risk governance has therefore moved towards non-governmental actors and, specifically, towards the business sector. Power (1997) describes this phenomenon as a move from a risk society (Beck, 1986) to an audit society. Governance mechanisms in an audit society reside with the regulated, as opposed to the regulator, and rely on the former's financial and human capital. As such, regulated institutions are expected to be transparent in order to justify their decision-making processes, not only to the disenchanted public, but to the regulator as well. This is performed "via systems of layered influences, chains of control practices in which each 'link' controls the next. In short, an explicit regulatory style is emerging which can be characterised by the idea of 'control of control'" (Power, 1997, p. 3), a strapline inspired, no doubt, by Foucault's "conduct of conduct" (1991).

However, the potential problem with this regulatory style is that it can become associated with an emerging dichotomy between the actual codified regulation that is the RBA and the regulator's actual expectations of how obliged entities are expected to implement it. This was identified as a potential issue at the outset of the RBA, and a statement about the matter, perhaps not unlike a disclaimer, was inserted into the 2007 guidance on the RBA: "regulators, law enforcement and judicial authorities must take into account and give due consideration to a financial institution's well-reasoned risk-based approach" (FATF, 2007, p. 3). This statement aims to mitigate the consequences of potential misalignments between the way the RBA may be interpreted by regulatory bodies and the private sector. For instance, in 2013 "over 140 UK-based remittance companies were surprised to receive a notice from Barclays Bank indicating they had been reviewed according to its new risk-based eligibility criteria and, as a result, the bank would no longer be doing business with them" (Ramachandran et al., 2018, p. 238). Barclays Bank had applied the RBA and, as a consequence, had terminated all business relationships with money services businesses (MSBs) by 2014. In the USA as well, regulators, noticing MSBs' increasing struggle to maintain banking relationships, described this phenomenon as the result of a "misperception of the requirements of the Bank Secrecy Act, and the erroneous view that money services businesses present a uniform and unacceptable high risk of money laundering" (Ramachandran et al., 2018, p. 240). This issue of misalignment between supervisory authorities and the private sector is clearly documented by the British Bankers Association (BBA), which stated in its 2015 response to the "Cutting Red Tape" review of the UK's AML regime (a review led by the Department for Business, Energy and Industrial Strategy):

> the FCA statement in 2015 on "de-risking" in the view of the BBA membership rather confused a number of issues and was seen by some to undermine the flexibility that would properly be afforded to banks to adopt a risk-based approach. The banking industry would therefore welcome discussions to promote a closer common understanding with the FCA on the practical application of the Risk Based approach. (BBA, 2015, p. 5)

The BBA further states:

> While the FCA and the banking industry are in agreement at strategic policy level that a risk-based approach to financial crime is most effective, there can be differences of view on the practical application. (BBA, 2015, p. 5)

Ross and Hannan (2007) clearly document that this is the main weakness of the RBA. Unlike a rules-based regime, the RBA requires risk to be "conceptualised and analysed in much more concrete terms than in the past" (p. 113). Essentially risk and its key attributes need to be understood, and the RBA simply does not provide the tools to achieve this.

> A key challenge for criminology is to move from seeing money laundering and terrorist financing as consisting of generic or archetypal cases, to understanding them as dynamic and purposeful activities that are informed by distinctive bodies of knowledge, expertise and practice. (Ross & Hannan, 2007, p. 113)

Demetis and Angell (2007) go further in their criticism of the RBA stating the following:

> In proposing levels of risk they are implying that risk can be quantified, but without explicitly stating how. With no yardstick, such quantification can only come from qualitative mechanisms that will somehow distinguish between high and low risk. Any such assignment of probabilities or numerological representations to risk is problematic. As it posits an epistemological anomaly: that risk can be represented by something that lies somewhere in the "grey area" between quantitative and qualitative analysis. (p. 422)

The phenomenon of de-risking is particularly illustrative of the way the RBA fails to understand risk's systemic nature. De-risking is currently defined as "the phenomenon of financial institutions terminating or restricting business relationships with clients or categories of clients to avoid, rather than manage, risk in line with the FATF's risk-based approach" (FATF, 2014a, b, para. 1). It has had unfortunate repercussions such as "reducing the flow of remittance to developing countries"

(Ramachandran et al., 2018, p. 250) and making such flows less transparent by being pushed into Hawala networks which are not easily regulated. Furthermore, correspondent banking relationships have declined resulting in banks losing access to the global banking network thus "hamper(ing) global trade" (Ramachandran et al., 2018, p. 257).

Although there are a number of drivers of de-risking (declining client profitability, increased compliance costs, increased regulatory and reputational risks), one of de-risking's key driver is the application of the RBA. The FATF has encouraged institutions to develop risk assessment tools, identify high-risk clients and implement initiatives to mitigate high risks. Annex III of the Fourth AML Directive goes as far as to list correspondent banks and money transfer businesses as high-risk clients. The ever-increasing focus on AML and CFT along with a risk-based regulatory environment has essentially developed a culture that can only aspire to de-risking (Rose, 2019). And yet, the FATF and supervisory authorities assume that de-risking is risk avoidance instead of risk governance. They fail to see that the majority of financial institutions that terminate certain relationships aim to reduce the complexity they face after having assessed through the RBA that ML risk is a composite of many elements and parameters that are interdependent. This is discussed further in Sect. 2.2 and Chaps. 4 and 5.

Another weakness of the RBA is how it fails to capture the differences in risks faced by financial institutions and regulators and the dynamic feedback loop between those risks, again highlighting the wider issue raised by Ross and Hannan (2007) and Demetis and Angell (2007) on the "complexity of representing risk" (p. 426). Certainly, both institutions are required to manage and minimise ML risks through the RBA. However, while financial institutions must focus on managing regulatory risk (defined as risk of changes to regulation or misalignment of regulatory interpretation), regulators face another kind of risk, namely, the risk of losing their credibility. For instance, Black and Baldwin highlight the challenges faced by regulators when applying the RBA:

> Risk-based regulators have to address a number of issues including: the risks they will identify as requiring attention; the indicators and methods they will use to assess those risks; where they will prioritise their attention and where they will not. They will also have to decide how the implementation of the risk-based framework will be managed; how it will be justified and communicated both internally and externally; how they will respond to changes and, ultimately, what level of risk or failure they are prepared to accept. (2012, p. 2)

Hence, should ML scandals arise, regulatory bodies need to be able to justify their previous and current decisions as well as actions in order to preserve their credibility. Press releases and reports issued by the Estonian and Danish regulators in the aftermath of the Danske Bank scandal, for example, certainly offer an excellent illustration of this point.

In response to the Danish regulator's 2019 report on the Danske Bank supervision, the Estonian regulator stated: "we welcome the clear indication now given by our Danish colleagues that Finantsinspektsioon of Estonia should firmly take the lead in supervising the Danske Bank in Estonia, clarity that we have been waiting for from Danish regulator for some years" (Finantsinpektsioon, 2019). In addition, to avoid any confusion as to where responsibility and liability lie in relation to the scandal, the Estonian regulator added: "Danske Bank failed in its governance. The Danish Financial Supervisory Authority was and is responsible for supervising the governance of Danske Bank, including its branches. Finantsinspektsioon stands ready to take over supervision of Danske Bank as whole" (Finantsinpektsioon, 2019). This statement was made in reference to the Danish regulator's comment indicating that the Estonian regulator was responsible of Danske Bank in Estonia. More specifically, the Danish report stated that "as the host country supervisor, the EFSA (Estonian regulator) is responsible for the AML supervision of the Estonian branch" (Finanstilsynet, 2019, p. 2).

In sum, it could be argued that while the RBA is not a tool that can mitigate regulatory risk faced by obliged entities, it can support regulators in their attempts to mitigate credibility risk. Thus, a regulator could claim that any misstep on the part of regulated entities concerns a misalignment in the interpretation and application of the RBA rather than a regulator's error. Indeed, the regulator needs "a systematic basis for making regulatory assessments that it could produce to defend its actions and decisions, particularly decisions not to act" (Black, 2004, p. 48). The RBA may have evolved into such a tool for regulators. However, if the RBA is, indeed, used as a negotiation tool for allocating accountability (Gephart Jr., 1993) and a systematic basis for defending regulators' actions, this will only aggravate regulatory risks faced by the private sector, thus possibly destabilising the current AML framework.

The previous section discusses the evolution of risk as a part of the regulatory discourse and investigates the expansion of risk-based regulation, leading to the adoption of the RBA in the field of ML prevention and the rationale for risk-based regulation versus a rules-based approach. In addition, it discusses the RBA's failure to understand risk's complex nature as illustrated by de-risking. Furthermore, this section explores the dichotomy between the actual codified regulation that is the RBA and the regulator's actual expectations of how obliged entities are expected to implement it. While the difference in applications of the RBA may be the result of differing interpretations of the RBA, the contrast may also be the result of the distinct risks faced by regulators and obliged entities, namely, credibility risks and regulatory risks, respectively. This will be further explored in the findings and discussion chapters (Chaps. 4 and 5).

Why we Need Social Sciences to Understand Risk

Risks are identified, assessed, communicated and managed by human beings and organisations comprising numerous individuals. When things go wrong—for example, when an institution such as HSBC, Deutsche Bank or Danske Bank is fined for facilitating the money laundering of Mexican cartels, oligarchs or corrupt heads of state—it is not due to one individual's mistake. Rather, as famously stated by Merton, such outcomes are "unanticipated consequences of purposive social action" (Merton, 1936). Accordingly, the following chapter will identify a theoretical framework to support the exploration of how risk is understood, discussed and, more importantly, *observed* by the organisations in charge of AML. As argued by Jasanoff, "risk is culturally embedded in texture and meaning that vary from one social group to another. Trying to assess risk is therefore necessarily a social and political exercise" (Jasanoff, 1999, p. 150).

The following chapter introduces the reader to Luhmann's systems theory, as it is the tool that will be used to observe risk in the domain of AML and will explore the central concepts of Luhmann's systems theory (1995a, b) and also introduce Luhmann's sociological theory of risk (Luhmann, 1993a). In addition, the author will contrast Luhmann's system theory with Foucault's concept of governmentality (1991), Becks's notion of risk society (1986) and Douglas's cultural theory of risk (Douglas, 1966; Douglas & Wildavsky, 1982). The following chapter will also explore other theoretical frameworks, such as the principal/agent model, transaction cost theory and institutionalism, which have been used in the AML literature. This is in order to justify why Luhmann's system theory is the most relevant and applicable theory for understanding the analysis of risk deconstruction in the ML and AML domains.

References

Badshah, N. (2018, September 21). Facebook to contact 87 million users affected by data breach *The guardian.* [Online] Accessed Nov 4, 2019, from https://www.theguardian.com/technology/2018/apr/08/facebook-to-contact-the-87-million-users-affected-by-data-breach

Bank for International Settlements. (2011). *Principles for the sound management of operational risk.* Accessed Oct 5, 2019, from https://www.bis.org/publ/bcbs195.pdf

Basel Committee on Banking Supervision. (2010). *Principles for enhancing corporate governance.* Accessed Apr 23, 2020. Available online: https://www.bis.org/publ/bcbs176.pdf

Basel Institute on Governance. (2019). *Basel AML Index* (8th ed.). Accessed Oct 25, 2019. Available online: https://www.baselgovernance.org/sites/default/files/2019-10/Basel%20AML%20Index%208%20edition.pdf

Bateson, G. (1972). *Steps to an ecology of mind: Collected essays in anthropology, psychiatry, evolution, and epistemology (Chandler publications for health sciences).* Jason Aronson.

Beck, U. (1986). *Risk Society.* Sage Publication Ltd.

Beck, U. (2006). Living in the world risk society. *Economy and Society, 35*(3), 329–345.

Black, J. (2004). *The development of risk-based regulation in Financial Services: Canada, the UK and Australia,* ESRC Centre for the Analysis of Risk and Regulation, London School of Economics. Accessed Oct 15, 2018, from https://www.researchgate.net/profile/Julia_Black/publication/268395436_The_Development_of_Risk_Based_Regulation_in_Financial_Services_Canada_the_UK_and_Australia_A_Research_Report/links/54d5c60b0cf24647580 83251/The-Development-of-Risk-Based-Regulation-in-Financial-Services-Canada-the-UK-and-Australia-A-Research-Report.pdf

Block, C. D. (2010). Measuring the true cost of government bailout. *Washington University Law Review, 88*(1), 149–228.

Borlini, L., & Montanaro, F. (1991). The evolution of the EU law against criminal finance: The "hardening" of FATF standards within the EU. *Georgetown Journal of International Law, 48,* 1009–1062.

References

British Bankers Association. (2015). *BBA response to cutting red tape review–effectiveness of the UK's AML regime.* Accessed Oct 27, 2019, from https://www.bba.org.uk/policy/bba-consultation-responses/bba-response-to-cutting-red-tape-review-effectiveness-of-the-uks-aml-regime/

Camdessus, M. (1998, February 10). Money laundering: The importance of international countermeasures–Address by Michel Camdessus. *Plenary meeting of the financial action task force.* Paris. Accessed Dec 17, 2015, from https://www.imf.org/external/np/speeches/1998/021098.htm

Carisimo, J. (2018, March 19). Cambridge Analytica CEO Alexander Nix describes "shadow" election tactics. *CBS News* [Online]. Accessed May 14, 2018, from https://www.cbsnews.com/news/cambridge-analytica-ceo-alexander-nix-data-firm-describes-shadow-election-tactics-2018-03-19/

Chaikin, D. (2009). How effective are suspicious transaction reporting systems? *Journal of Money Laundering Control, 12*(3), 238–253.

Clabaugh, J. (2005, March 29). Judge: Riggs was 'henchman of dictators'. *Washington Business Journal* [Online]. Accessed Sep 29, 2015, from http://www.bizjournals.com/washington/stories/2005/03/28/daily13.html

Council Directive (EC). (2015). 2015/849/EC of 20 May 2015 *on the prevention of the use of the financial system for the purposes of money laundering or terrorist financing.* Accessed Aug 8, 2015, from https://op.europa.eu/en/publication-detail/-/publication/0bff31ef-0b49-11e5-8817-01aa75ed71a1

Council Directive (EC). (2018a). *2018/843EC of 30 May 2018 amending Directive (EU) 2015/849 on the prevention of the use of the financial system for the purposes of money laundering or terrorist financing, and amending Directives 2009/138/EC and 2013/36/EU.* Accessed Jun 1, 2018, from https://eur-lex.europa.eu/legal-content/EN/TXT/?uri=CELEX%3A32018L0843

Council Directive (EC). (2018b). 2018/1673*EC of 23 October 2018 amending Directive (EU) 2015/849 on combating money laundering by criminal law.* Accessed Dec 1, 2018, from https://eur-lex.europa.eu/legal-content/EN/TXT/?uri=uriserv:OJ.L_.2018.284.01.0022.01.ENG

Demetis, D., & Angell, I. (2006). AML related technologies: A systemic risk. *Journal of Money Laundering Control, 9*(2), 157–172.

Demetis, D., & Angell, I. (2007). The risk-based approach to AML: Representation, paradox and the 3rd directive. *Journal of Money Laundering control, 10*(4), 412–428.

Demetis, D. (2010). *Technology and anti-money laundering: A systems theory and risk-based approach.* Edward Elgar.

Douglas, M., & Wildavsky, A. (1982). *Risk and culture. An essay on the selection of technological and environmental dangers.* University of California Press.

Douglas, M. (1966). *Purity and danger, an analysis of conceptions of pollution and taboo.* Routledge.

Drezner, D. (2007). *All politics is global: Explaining international regulatory regimes.* Princeton.

European Banking Authority. (2017, September 26). *Final Report: Guidelines on internal governance under Directive 2013/36/EU.* Accessed Jun 16, 2018, from https://eba.europa.eu/sites/default/documents/files/documents/10180/1972987/eb859955-614a-4afb-bdcd-aaa664994889/Final%20Guidelines%20on%20Internal%20Governance%20%28EBA-GL-2017-11%29.pdf?retry=1

European Commission. (2018, April 19). *Joint Statement on the adoption by the European Parliament of the 5th anti-money laundering Directive.* [Joint statement]. Accessed Apr 23, 2018, from https://ec.europa.eu/commission/presscorner/detail/en/STATEMENT_18_3429

European Commission. (2019a). *Report from the commission to the European Parliament and the Council on the assessment of the risk of money laundering and terrorist financing affecting the internal market and relating to cross-border activities.* (24 July, COM (2019) 370 Final). Accessed Aug 3, 2020, from https://ec.europa.eu/info/sites/info/files/supranational_risk_

assessment_of_the_money_laundering_and_terrorist_financing_risks_affecting_the_union_-_annex.pdf

European Commission. (2019b). *Report from the commission to the European Parliament and the Council: assessing the framework for cooperation between Financial Intelligence Units.* (24 July, COM (2019) 370 Final). Accessed July 18, 2020, from https://ec.europa.eu/info/sites/info/files/report_assessing_the_framework_for_financial_intelligence_units_fius_cooperation_with_third_countries_and_obstacles_and_opportunities_to_enhance_cooperation_between_financial_intelligence_units_with.pdf

European Commission. (2020a, May 7). *Communication from the Commission on an action plan for a comprehensive Union policy on preventing money laundering and terrorist financing.* Accessed Sep 4, 2020, from https://ec.europa.eu/finance/docs/law/200507-anti-money-laundering-terrorism-financing-action-plan_en.pdf

European Commission. (2020b, May 20). *Questions and answers–Commission steps up fight against money laundering and terrorism financing.* Accessed Aug 20, 2020, from https://ec.europa.eu/commission/presscorner/detail/en/qanda_20_821

Evstatieva, M. (2020, July 10). Anatomy of a Covid-19 conspiracy theory. *npr* [Online]. Accessed Sep 10, 2020, from https://www.npr.org/2020/07/10/889037310/anatomy-of-a-covid-19-conspiracy-theory?t=1599723673262

FATF. (2007). *Guidance on the risk-based approach to combating money laundering and terrorist financing.* FATF. Accessed Nov 18, 2015, from http://www.fatf-gafi.org/media/fatf/documents/reports/High%20Level%20Principles%20and%20Procedures.pdf

FATF. (2012a). *FATF steps up the fight against money laundering and terrorist financing.* FATF. Accessed Oct 19, 2015, from http://www.fatf-gafi.org/publications/fatfrecommendations/documents/fatfstepsupthefightagainstmoneylaunderingandterroristfinancing.html

FATF. (2013). *Politically exposed persons (recommendations 12 and 22).* FATF. Accessed Sep 8, 2018, from https://www.fatf-gafi.org/media/fatf/documents/recommendations/Guidance-PEP-Rec12-22.pdf

FATF. (2014a). *Guidance for a risk based approach: The banking sector.* Accessed Jun 2, 2015, from http://www.fatf-gafi.org/media/fatf/documents/reports/Risk-Based-Approach-Banking-Sector.pdf. : FATF.

FATF. (2014b, October 23). *"FATF clarifies risk-based approach: Case-by-case, not wholesale de-risking"*, conclusion from FATF Plenary on 22 October, Paris. Accessed Sep 2, 2020, from https://www.fatfgafi.org/documents/documents/rba-and-de-risking.html

FATF. (2012b-2019). *International standards on combating money laundering and the financing of Terrorism & Proliferation, FATF.* FATF. Accessed Oct 19, 2019, from https://www.fatf-gafi.org/media/fatf/documents/recommendations/pdfs/FATF%20Recommendations%202012.pdf.

FATF. (2019a). *Methodology for assessing technical compliance with FATF recommendations and effectiveness of AML/CFT systems.* FATF. Accessed Feb 12, 2019, from http://www.fatf-gafi.org/media/fatf/documents/methodology/FATF%20Methodology%2022%20Feb%202013.pdf

FATF. (2019b, February 21). *Public statement-February 2020. Press release.* Accessed Sep 10, 2020, from http://www.fatf-gafi.org/publications/high-risk-and-other-monitored-jurisdictions/documents/call-for-action-february-2020.html

FATF. (2020, October 18). *Public statement-October 2019. Press release.* Accessed Feb 12, 2020, from http://www.fatf-gafi.org/publications/high-risk-and-other-monitored-jurisdictions/documents/public-statement-october-2019.html

Federal Reserve Board. (2005a, June 30). *Bank secrecy Act/AML (BSA/AML) Examination manual* [Joint press release]. Accessed May 15, 2018, from https://www.federalreserve.gov/boarddocs/press/bcreg/2005/20050630/default.htm

Federal Reserve Board. (2005b). *Agencies release bank secrecy act/anti-money laundering examination manual.* (Joint press release, 30 June). Accessed Nov 27, 2015, from http://www.federalreserve.gov/boarddocs/press/bcreg/2005/20050630/default.htm

Finanstilsynet. (2019). *Report on the Danish FSA's supervision of Danske Bank as regards the Estonia case.* Accessed Nov 2, 2019, from https://www.dfsa.dk/~/media/Nyhedscenter/2019/

References

Report_on_the_Danish_FSAs_supervision_of_Danske-Bank_as_regards_the_Estonia_case-pdf.pdf?la=en

Finantsinspektsioon (2019). *Response to the report on the Danish FSA's supervision of Danske Bank*. Accessed Nov 2, 2019, from https://www.fi.ee/en/news/response-report-danish-fsas-supervision-danske-bank

FINCEN. (n.d.). *History of anti-money laundering laws*. Accessed Nov 11, 2015, from https://www.fincen.gov/statutes_regs/bsa/

Fischhoff, B., Watson, S. R., & Hope, C. (1984). Defining risk. *Policy Sciences, 17*, 123–129.

Fox, W. J. (2004a). *Speech for women in housing and finance*. Accessed Nov 18, 2015, from https://www.fincen.gov/news_room/speech/html/20040225.html

Foucault, M. (1991). Governmentality. In G. Burchell, C. Gordon, & P. Miller (Eds.), *The foucault effect, studies in governmentality* (pp. 87–104). Harvester/Wheatsheaf.

Fox, W. (2004b). *Women in housing and finance*, FINCEN, Accessed from https://www.fincen.gov/news/speeches/william-j-fox-director-financial-crimes-enforcement-network-1

Gephart, R. P., Jr. (1993). The textual approach; risk and blame in disaster sensemaking. *Academy of Management, 36*(6), 1465–1514.

Greenwald, G. (2012, December 12). *HSBC, too big to jail, is the new poster child for US two-tiered justice system. The guardian* [Online]. Accessed Oct 9, 2015, from http://www.theguardian.com/commentisfree/2012/dec/12/hsbc-prosecution-fine-money-laundering

Guarascio, F. (2019). HSBC agrees to 300 mln euro settlement of Belgian tax fraud case: Prosecutors. *Reuters* 6 August [Online]. Accessed Oct 20, 2019, from https://www.reuters.com/article/us-hsbc-belgium-moneylaundering/hsbc-agrees-to-300-mln-euro-settlement-of-belgian-tax-fraud-case-prosecutors-idUSKCN1UW0Y0

Hanley-Giersch J. (2015). *The Fourth EU AML/CFT Directive: A holistic risk based approach*. ACAMS. Accessed Nov 4, 2016, from http://www.berlinrisk.com/Media/Downloads/BR_8_2_9_The%20Fourth%20EU%20AML%20Directive_A%20Holistic%20RBA%20Approach.pdf

Hardy, C., & Maguire, S. (2019). Organizations, risk translations and the ecology of risks: The discursive construction of a novel risk. Academy of management. Accessed Mar 4, 2020, from https://www.researchgate.net/publication/332824257_Organizations_Risk_Translations_and_the_Ecology_of_Risks_The_Discursive_Construction_of_a_Novel_Risk

Harvey, J. (2005). An evaluation of money laundering policies. *Journal of Money Laundering Control, 8*(4), 339–345.

Haugen, A. (2015, May 19). More than sanctions: Criminally prosecute big banks for money laundering. *International Affairs Review*. [Online] Accessed Oct 14, 2015, from https://iar-gwu.org/2015/05/19/more-than-sanctions-criminally-prosecute-big-banks-for-money-laundering/

Hilgartner, S. (1992). The social construction of risk objects: Or, how to pry open networks of risk. In J. F. Short Jr. & L. Clarke (Eds.), *Organizations, uncertainties, and risk* (pp. 39–51). Westview Press.

Hood, C. (1991). A public management for all seasons. *Public Administration, 69*, 3–19.

Human Rights Watch. (2017). *As if you're inhaling your death: The health risks of burning waste in Lebanon*. Accessed Oct 16, 2019, from https://www.hrw.org/sites/default/files/report_pdf/lebanon1117_web_1.pdf

Hutter, B. M. (2005). *The attractions of risk-based regulation: Accounting for the emergence of risk ideas in regulation*. ESRC Centre for Analysis of Risk and Regulation. Accessed Aug 16, 2016, from http://www.lse.ac.uk/accounting/CARR/pdf/DPs/Disspaper33.pdf

Jabareen, Y. (2015). *The risk city: Cities countering climate change: Emerging planning theories and practices around the world*. Dordrecht Springer.

Jasanoff, S. (1999). The Songlines of risk. *Environmental values, 8*(2), 135–152.

Kahneman, D. (2011). *Thinking fast and slow*. Farrar, Straus and Giroux.

Keynes, J. M. (1921). *A treatise on probability*. Macmillan.

Kilmer, B., Caulkins, J., Bond, B., & Reuter, P. (2010). *Reducing drug trafficking revenues and violence in Mexico: Would legalizing marijuana in California help?* Rand.

Klinke, A., Renn, O., & O. (2002). A new approach to risk evaluation and management: Risk-based, precaution-based and discourse-based management. *Risk Analysis, 22*(6), 1071–1094.

Le Bouter, F. (2014). La sociologie constructiviste du risque de Niklas Luhmann. *Communications & Organisation, 45*, 33–48.

Levi, M., & Gold, M. (1994). *Money laundering in the UK: An appraisal of suspicion-based reporting*. Police Foundation.

Levi, M., Reuter, P., & Halliday, T. (2018). Can the AML system be evaluated without better data? *Crime Law Society Change, 69*, 307–328. Accessed Oct 9, 2019, from. https://doi.org/10.1007/s10611-017-9757-4

Lewis P. (1999) Nigeria's economy: Opportunity and challenge, *issue: A journal of opinion*, 27 (1), 50–53.

Lim, W.-K. (2011). Understanding risk governance: Introducing sociological neoinstitutionalism and foucauldian governmentality for further theorizing. *International Journal of Disaster Risk Science, 2*(3), 11–20.

Luhmann, N. (1990). The cognitive program of constructivism and a reality that remains unknown. In W. Krohn (Ed.), *Selforganization: Portrait of a scientific revolution* (pp. 64–85). Kluwer.

Luhmann, N. (1993a). *Risk: A sociological theory*. Transaction Publishers.

Luhmann, N. (1993b). Observing re-entries. *Graduate Faculty Philosophy Journal, 16*(2), 485–498.

Luhmann, N. (1995a). *Social systems*. Stanford University Press.

Luhmann, N. (1995b). The paradox of observing systems. *Cultural Critique, 31*, 37–55.

Matrix Knowledge Group. (2007). *The illicit drug trade in the United Kingdom*. Home Office. Accessed Oct 20, 2019, from (https://www.drugsandalcohol.ie/6375/1/3923-4186.pdf

Matussek, K., Comfort, N., & Arons, S. (2018, November 29). Deutsche Bank offices in Germany raided by authorities over alleged money laundering. *The San Diego Union-Tribune* [Online]. Accessed Feb 10, 2019, from https://www.sandiegouniontribune.com/business/la-fi-deutsche-bank-raid-20181129-story.html?00000168-c155-df9b-adfc-cb55faa70000-p=10

Merton, R. K. (1936). The unanticipated consequences of purposive social action. *American. Sociological Review, 1*(6), 894–904.

Megaw, N. (2019, Febryary 19). Estonian scandal forces Danske out of the Baltics and Russia. *The financial time* [Online]. Accessed Sep 16, 2019, from https://www.ft.com/content/a6881938-344c-11e9-bd3a-8b2a211d90d5

MROS. (2019). *Annual Report 2018, Département fédéral de justice et police Office fédéral de la police (fedpol)*. Accessed Oct 20, 2019, from https://www.fedpol.admin.ch/dam/data/fedpol/kriminalitaet/geldwaescherei/jabe/jb-mros-2018-e.pdf

Nance, M. T. (2018). The regime that FATF built: An introduction to the financial action task force. *Crime Law Society Change, 69*, 109–129. Accessed Oct 20, 2019, from. https://doi.org/10.1007/s10611-017-9748-5

Nowotny, E. (2013). The role of small states for financial market integrity: Austria. In B. Unger & D. van der Linde (Eds.), *Research handbook on money laundering* (pp. 148–158). Edward Elgar.

O'Grady, S. (2010, March 31). Credit crisis cost the nation £167.3 trn, says the Bank of England, *The independent* [Online]. Accessed Mar 12, 2018, from https://www.independent.co.uk/news/business/news/credit-crisis-cost-the-nation-1637trn-says-bank-of-england-1931569.html

O'Hara, T. (2005, Janauary 28). *Risggs bank agrees to guilty plean fine. Washington Post*, [Online] Accessed Mar 2, 2015, from https://www.globalpolicy.org/component/content/article/172/30280.html

Openbaar Ministerie. (2018). *Investigation Houston: Criminal investigation into ING Bank N.V., statements of facts and conclusions of the Netherlands*. Public Prosecution Service. Accessed Feb 12, 2019, from http://robscholtemuseum.nl/wp-content/uploads/2020/01/Netherlands-National-Office-Serious-Fraud-Environmental-Crime-Asset-Confiscation-National-Office-Houston-Criminal-Investigation-into-ING-Bank-N.V.-Statement-of-Facts-and-Conclusions.pdf

References

Pratley, N. (2012, December 11). HSBC fine: What does it take for a bank to get prosecuted? *The guardian,* [Online] Accessed Oct 14, 2015, from http://www.theguardian.com/business/nils-pratley-on-finance/2012/dec/11/hsbc-money-laundering-fine

Tucker, E. (2018, Feburary 16). *Mueller probe indicts 13 Russian nationals for meddling in 2016 ellections. PBS* [Online]. Accessed Mar 16, 2018, from https://www.pbs.org/newshour/politics/mueller-probe-indicts-13-russian-nationals-for-meddling-in-2016-elections

Pieth, M., & Aiolfi, G. (2003). *Anti-money laundering: Levelling the playing field.* Basel Institute of Governance.

Pol, R. (2020). Anti-money laundering: The world's least effective policy experiment? Together we can fix it. *Policy design and practice, 3*(1), 73–94.

Power, M. (1997). From risk society to audit society. *Soziale System, 1,* 3–21. Accessed Aug 5, 2018, from https://www.soziale-systeme.ch/leseproben/power.htm

Power, M. (2004a). The risk Management of Everything. *The journal of risk science, 5*(3), 58–65.

Power, M. (2004b). *The risk management of everything: Rethinking the politics of uncertainty.* Demos.

Ramachandran, V., Collin, C., Juden, M., & Walker, C. (2018). De-risking: An unintended consequence of AML/CFT regulation. In J. Gurulé (Ed.), *The Palgrave handbook of criminal and terrorism financing law* (Vol. 1). Springer International Publishing AG.

Racz, T. (2018, September 12). ING CFO resigns in Netherlands Money Laundering scandal. *OCCRP,* [Online] Accessed oct 25, 2019, from https://www.occrp.org/en/27-ccwatch/cc-watch-briefs/8573-ing-cfo-resigns-in-netherlands-money-laundering-scandal

Renn, O. (1987, October). Evaluation of risk communication: Concepts, strategies, and guidelines in managing environmental risks; *APCA International Speciality Conference* Washington D.C., APCA, 99-127.

Renn, O. (1990). *Risk perception and risk management: A review. Part 1, Centre for Environment.* Technology and Development.

Renn, O. (1992). Concepts of risk: A classification. In S. Krimsky & D. Golding (Eds.), *Social theories of risk* (pp. 53–79). Praeger.

Renn, O. (1998). Risk perception for risk management. *Reliability Engineering and System Safety, 59,* 49–62.

Reuter, P. (2013). Are estimates of the volume of money laundering either feasible or useful? In B. Unger & D. Van der Linde (Eds.), *Research handbook on money laundering* (1st ed., pp. 224–231). Edward Elgar.

Rojas, M. (Ed.). (2019). *The economics of happinee: How the Easterlin paradox transformed our understanding of Well-being and progres.* Springer.

Rosa, E., McRight, A., & Renn, O. (2014). *The risk society revisited: Social theory and risk governance.* Temple University Press.

Rose, K. J. (2019). *De-risking or re-contracting the way around money laundering risks,* (Copenhagen Business School, CBS Law Research Paper No. 19–37). Accessed Sep 2, 2020, from https://papers.ssrn.com/sol3/papers.cfm?abstract_id=3474298

Ross, S., & Hannan, M. (2007). Money laundering regulation and risk-based decision-making. *Journal of Money Laundering Control., 10*(1), 106–115.

Russell, L. D., & Babrow, S. (2011). Risk in the making: Narrative, problematic integration, and the social construction of risk. *Communication Theory, 21,* 239–260.

Ryder, N. (2012). *Money laundering–an endless cycle?* Routledge.

Sandmann, P. M. (1989). Hazard versus outrage. A conceptual frame for describing public perception of risk. In H. Jungermann, R. E. Kasperson, & P. M. Wiedemann (Eds.), *Risk communication* (pp. 163–168). Nuclear Research Center.

Searle, J. R. (1995). *The construction of social reality.* Penguin Books.

Simonova, A. (2011). The risk-based approach to anti-money laundering: Problems and solutions. *Journal of Money Laundering Control, 14*(4), 346–358.

Slovic, P. (1987). Perception of risk. *Science, 236*(4799), 280–285.

Stuart, B. (2018 November 7). The cost of compliance. *International banker*. [Online] Accessed Dec 6, 2018, from https://internationalbanker.com/technology/the-cost-of-compliance/

Spira, L. F., & Page, M. (2003). Risk management: The reinvention of internal control and the changing role of internal audit. *Accounting, Auditing & Accountability Journal, 16*, 640–661.

Tavares, C., Thomas, G., & Roudaut, M. (2010). Money laundering in Europe, (Eurostat methodologies and working papers). Eurostat. Accessed Dec 6, 2015, from http://www.apml.gov.rs/REPOSITORY/409_1_ks-ra-10-003-en.pdf

Transparency International. (2019). *25 corruption scandals that shook the world*. Accessed Feb 10, 2020, from https://www.transparency.org/news/feature/25_corruption_scandals

Truman, E., & Reuter, P. (2004). *Chasing dirty money: The fight against anti-money laundering*. Peterson Institute for International Economics.

The Economist. (2013, September 7). The origins of the financial crisis. *The economist* [Online]. Accessed Sep 10, 2015, from https://www.economist.com/schools-brief/2013/09/07/crash-course

Unger, B., & van Waarden, F. (2013). How to dodge drowning in data? Rule and risk based money laundering compared. In B. Unger & D. Van der Linde (Eds.), *Research handbook on money laundering* (pp. 399–425). Elgar Publishing.

United Nations Office on Drugs and Crime (UNODC). (2011). *Estimating illicit financial flows resulting from drug trafficking and other transnational organized crimes*. Accessed Dec 12, 2015, from https://www.unodc.org/documents/data-and-analysis/Studies/Illicit_financial_flows_2011_web.pdf

United States. (2001). *The USA PATRIOT Act: Preserving life and liberty: Uniting and strengthening America by providing appropriate tools required to intercept and obstruct terrorism*. [Washington, D.C: U.S. Dept. of Justice]. Accessed Sep 14, 2016, from http://purl.access.gpo.gov/GPO/LPS39935

United States Senate. (2013). *Patterns of abuse: Assessing bank secrecy act compliance and enforcement. Hearing before the committee on banking, housing, and Urban Affairs, first session*. U.S. Government Printing Office. Accessed Oct 2, 2015, from https://www.govinfo.gov/content/pkg/CHRG-113shrg80662/html/CHRG-113shrg80662.htm

United States Senate Committee. (1970). *Senate Hearing on Foreign Bank Secrecy*. Accessed Oct 25, 2019. Available online: https://www.govinfo.gov/content/pkg/GPO-CRECB-1970-pt26/pdf/GPO-CRECB-1970-pt26-6-1.pdf

Van Duyne, P. (2013). Crime-money and financial conduct. In B. Unger & D. Van der Linde (Eds.), *Research handbook on money laundering* (pp. 232–249). Elgar Publishing.

Van Koningsveld, J. (2013). Money laundering–'you don't see it until you understand it': Rethinking the stages of the money laundering process to make enforcement more effective. In B. Unger & D. Van der Linde (Eds.), *Research handbook on money laundering* (pp. 435–451). Elgar Publishing.

Vasvari, T. (2015). Risk, risk perception, Rism management–a review of the literature. *Public Finance Quarterly, 1*, 29–48.

Vettori, B. (2013). Evaluating anti-money laundering policies. In B. Unger & D. Van der Linde (Eds.), *Research handbook on money laundering* (pp. 474–486). Elgar Publishing.

Viscusi, W. K., & Aldi, J. E. (2003). *The value of statistical life: A critical review of market estimates throughout the world. (National Bureau of economic research working paper no. 9487)*. National Bureau of Economic Research. Accessed Oct 18, 2019, from https://www.nber.org/papers/w9487.pdf

Voss, M. (2005, January 29–29). Towards a reopening of risk societies: A contribution to the debate on risk and danger. *Learning about Risk, Launch Conference ESRC, Social contexts and Responses to Risk*. Canterbury. Accessed Nov 11, 2015, from http://www.kent.ac.uk/scarr/events/finalpapers/martin%20voss.pdf

Walker, J. (1995). *Estimates of the extent of money laundering in and through Australia*. Australian transaction Report and Analysis Centre. John Walker Consulting Services. Accessed Jan

11, 2020, from https://ccv-secondant.nl/fileadmin/w/secondant_nl/platform/artikelen_2018/Austrac_1995_Estimates_report.pdf

Walker, J. (2007). *The extent of money laundering in and through Australia in 2004*. RMIT University.

Walker, J., & Unger, B. (2013). Measuring global money laundering: The "Walker gravity model". In B. Unger & D. Van der Linde (Eds.), *Research handbook on money laundering* (pp. 159–171). Elgar Publishing.

Wildavsky, A. (1979). Views: No risk is the highest risk of all: A leading political scientist postulates that an overcautious attitude toward new technological developments may paralyze scientific Endeavour and end up leaving us less safe than we were before. *American Scientist, 67*(1), 32–37.

Zinn, J. O. (Ed.). (2008). *Social theories of risk and uncertainty: An introduction*. Blackwell Publishing.

Chapter 2
Risk and Luhmann's Systems Theory

Luhmann's extensive work on society provides a wide paradigm and framework for the analysis of money laundering (ML) risk and anti-money laundering (AML) as a domain. Both constitute interdisciplinary research domains that draw from different fields such as law, economics, organisation theory and sociology and thus require a broad theoretical perspective that facilitates communication across all relevant branches of research. Luhmann's systems theory provides such a framework. His research aims to "grasp the complexity of the entire world" (Borsch, 2011, p. 1) and provides an overarching vision of society. Indeed, Luhmann has written about a wide array of topics including love (1998), law (2004), the environment (1989), the mass media (2000a), art (2000b), religion (2000c), organisations (2003, 2018) and, of course, risk (1993). In sum, Luhmann "has developed a comprehensive theory with flexible networks of interrelated concepts that can be combined in many different ways and can be used to describe the most diverse social phenomena" (Holmström, 2007, p. 255).

Section 2.1 introduces Luhmann's system theory (LST) and discusses and defines the key founding blocks that will articulate Luhmann's vision of society for the reader. Section 2.2 explores Luhmann's social theory on risk and explores its application to the AML domain and to the topic of ML risk. The final section of this chapter, Section 3, describes the key components of some of the major social theories on risk, including *risk society* (Beck, 1986), *governmentality* (Foucault, 1991) and *cultural theory* (Douglas & Wildavsky, 1982), as well as other sociological and economic theories such as institutionalism and agent-principal theory. The author critically evaluates these theories vis-à-vis LST and Luhmann's risk/danger model in order to identify the gaps in these theories, which thus demonstrates how and why Luhmann's risk theory is the most pertinent and useful theoretical framework for this research on ML risk and the AML domain.

© The Author(s), under exclusive license to Springer Nature Switzerland AG 2022
N. També Bearpark, *Deconstructing Money Laundering Risk*, CSR, Sustainability, Ethics & Governance, https://doi.org/10.1007/978-3-031-07508-7_2

2.1 Luhmann's System Theory (LST) and Social Systems

Niklas Luhmann (1927–1998) is recognised as one of the most important German social theorists of his generation. Although opposed to the Nazi regime, he was forcefully conscripted into the German Luftwaffe at the age of 15 and was later captured by the American army at the age of 17. This exposed him to the treatment of war prisoners and made him realise that notions of what is good or bad are extremely nuanced when applied to political regimes. This, no doubt, influenced Luhmann's strong belief that systems are ultimately amoral. Following World War II, Luhmann became a legal expert in public administration and earned a scholarship from Harvard's Graduate School for Public Administration, where he began working with Talcott Parsons. He started exploring the functionalism advocated by Parsons and published a number of papers on the subject (Luhmann, 1962). Eventually, Luhmann moved away from Parsons' functionalism. Indeed, while Parsons argues that human action is central to any system and "defined and mediated in terms of a system of culturally structured and shared symbols" (Parsons, 1951, p. 6), Luhmann states that a system does not start with structure, but is "communicatively established through the ability of individuals to regularly repeat certain behaviour in unison" (Murphy, 1982, p. 299). After leaving public administration, Luhmann accepted a position at the Academy for Administrative Sciences (Speyer, Germany); he later worked at the Centre for Social Research (Dortmund, Germany) and, finally, at Bielefeld University (Bielefeld, Germany) as a professor, where he remained until his death in 1998.

When researching Luhmann, one thing that is particularly striking is the number of references made to the "inaccessibility" of his work (Borsch, 2011; Rosa et al., 2014). Messner goes as far as to state that "Luhmann's complex theory is complicated by a string of conceptual and semantic barriers as well as the hurdles of Luhmann's habitually ironic, sometimes authoritative, and sometimes counter intuitive style" (Messner, 2014, p. 313). Although Luhmann's writing style certainly contributes to the inaccessibility cited by Borsch, the complexity of Luhmann's work is certainly amplified by his theoretical framework, which is based on a multiplicity of disciplines, including biology (Maturana & Varela, 1980), mathematics (Spencer Brown, 1969), sociology (Parsons, 1951) and cybernetics (Ashby, 1956; Von Bertalanffy, 1968). Indeed, "Luhmann sees the nucleus of cybernetic thought in the notion that a system whose operations are oriented on the fulfilment of certain purposes will orient its behaviour on a constant feedback from the environment and can therefore cope with a high, unknown level of complexity" (Pateau, 2013, p. 79). However, as argued by Borsch, it is precisely this multidisciplinary approach that allowed Luhmann to successfully "rethink" modern sociology and develop a grand theory potentially capable of grasping society in its globality.

Luhmann states that some key assumptions of sociology are that "society consists of concrete human-beings and relations between human-beings" and "society is consequently constituted, or at least integrated, by consensus between human-beings, correspondence of their opinions, and complementary of their goal

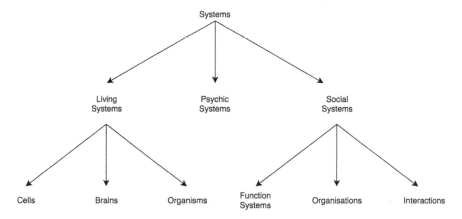

Fig. 2.1 A typology of systems (Borsch, 2011, p. 20)

definitions" (Luhmann cited in Moeller, 2006, p. 229). While Luhmann does not reject the existence of human beings, or psychic systems as he calls them, he does not believe that society should be analysed based on the assumption that it is a large group of individuals bound together by a social contract (e.g. in line with Hobbes and Rousseau). Instead, Luhmann believes that society should be studied by observing and understanding systems in relation to their respective environments.

Luhmann differentiates between three types of systems: living, psychic and social systems. Living systems are biological systems such as cells, bodies or the brain, which Moeller (2006) refers to as *systems of life*. Psychic systems are systems of consciousness or minds. Finally, social systems are what Luhmann calls systems of communication. He divides social systems into three subtypes of systems: societies, organisations and interactions. Interactions encompass meetings, concerts, conferences or Internet chat rooms, for instance. It is important to note that interactional systems are ultimately communication between a set of individuals. Organisational systems (which will be explored further below) refer to institutions such as companies, universities, banks or trade unions. Finally, societies (also referred to as *function systems)* constitute the third social system. Social systems are summarised in Fig. 2.1.

Function systems represent the core of Luhmann's systems theory and will be thoroughly described and discussed. However, first, it is necessary to introduce the key concepts defining systems as such.

System, Boundary and Environment

Luhmann introduces his book *Social Systems* (1995a) with: "the following considerations assume that there are systems. Thus they do not begin with epistemological doubt" (Luhmann, 1995a, b, p. 12). Quite simply, Luhmann sees the world cut in

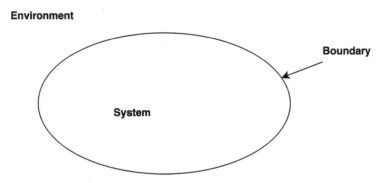

Fig. 2.2 System, environment and boundary

two, divided between systems and their environments. His sociology thus involves a number of implications about how society operates and evolves.

A system is distinct from its environment, and since the environment is not a system, it does not have the same capabilities as the system (Luhmann, 1995a). Furthermore, a system cannot exist without being separated from its environment. If the distinction between a system and its environment is not made, "if everything blends into everything else and no clear boundaries can be established, then no system exists" (Borsch, 2011, p. 21). Thus, for any given system, the system is "nothing but the difference to its environment" (Luhmann, 2002, p. 66).

For Luhmann, systems have their own functions, and system formation is the key feature of modern society. As such, the *system* is Luhmann's essential starting point and the starting point of any systems theoretical analysis. However, the function of the system is, simply, that of differentiation (or distinction) between system and environment for the purpose of minimising the complexity of the environment. Indeed, "the social world comprises enormous complexity which social systems each, in their own way, reduce" (Borsch, 2011, p. 7).

The following diagram conceptualises the system and its environment:

The system is represented (in Fig. 2.2) by the circular shape. The system is differentiated from the environment located outside of the boundary of the system, by the boundary of the system. In addition, the system cannot exist without an environment from which it can separate itself. Systems "only exist to the extent that they are able to differentiate themselves from their environment" (Borsch, 2011, p. 21). In addition, there is no universal environment within which all systems coexist. Rather, each system has its own environment, and each system is part of another system's environment. Indeed, as stated by Luhmann, the environment "is different from every system, because every system excludes only itself from its environment" (Luhmann, 1995a, p. 17).

Furthermore, each system can also encompass multiple subsystems that replicate the system/environment distinction within themselves. This is what Luhmann calls re-entry and will be addressed in detail below. The difference between system and

2.1 Luhmann's System Theory (LST) and Social Systems

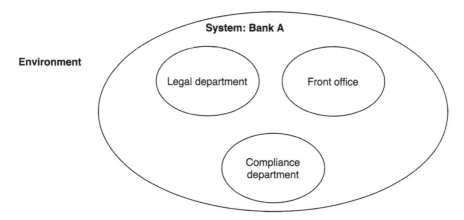

Fig. 2.3 The financial institution as the system

environment can only be delineated by the *observing entity* marking the boundaries between system and environment.

Therefore, "the definition of a system, indeed any definition for that matter, is above all an act of choice and an observer-relative act. The observer is crucial in the construction of any system" (Demetis, 2010. p. 42). Depending on what the observer is focusing on, a system can be a human organism, a society, a financial institution or a financial intelligence unit, among countless other entities. It can be anything the observer conceives of as a system.

Figure 2.3 illustrates Bank A as a system, differentiated from its environment and containing departments that have their own respective objectives and functions. The subsystems are represented in Fig. 2.3 as the legal department, the front office and the compliance department. This is for illustrative purposes only and is in no way an exhaustive list of a financial institution's subsystems. However, in Fig. 2.3 it can be seen that if the system's perspective changes to the compliance department's perspective, for example, the system becomes the compliance department itself, and the environment becomes everything external to the compliance department in undifferentiated form (i.e. where legal department and front office become part of the compliance department's environment). However, while the front office and legal departments are part of the compliance department's environment, these three entities are also related to each other as distinct systems. Thus, it is important that we do not confuse the system/environment relationship with the intrasystem relationship. Indeed, the relationship between all subsystems within a system (i.e. the financial institution) allows the system to exist. The financial institution, as a system, thrives on the feedback of and interaction between each of its subsystems, ensuring its very survival and maintenance. The system ultimately has:

> A higher reflective power than the whole, which encompasses system *and* environment, because the system alone knows about the degrees of freedom it eliminates. And it knows the reasons for eliminating them. (Baecker, 2001, p. 61)

The dynamic relationship between systems will be explored below in the discussion of structural coupling and interpenetration.

In summary, while the environment is more complex than the system because it has more options, variety and degrees of freedom, the system compensates for its "inferiority" by exploiting its contingency (i.e. by eliminating or introducing degrees of freedom). For instance, referring back to Fig. 2.3, in the case of the financial institution, if the ruling government were to announce further economic and financial sanctions against Russia, the system might decide to no longer bank with Russian nationals in order to avoid sanction breaches and regulatory fines. Such behaviour enables the system to survive:

> Intelligence starts where an entity is able to take its own lack of knowledge into account and to search for the knowledge it lacks in other entities which presumably are in a better position to bring forth the knowledge sought. Intelligence begins where one is able to substitute the knowledge of others for one's own non-knowledge. That, too, presupposes being distinct from an environment, which becomes the search space for the lacked knowledge. (Baecker, 2001, p. 62)

Such system/environment differentiation, or systemic differentiation, automatically defines a boundary from which systems can observe their environments and themselves. The boundary is ontologically ambiguous because it is part of both the system and the environment, but it is ultimately an operative concept: "nothing but the type and concretion of its operations which individualise the system. It is the form of the system whose other side thus becomes the environment" (Luhmann, 1997, p. 76). While communication across the boundary is greatly expanded on (Luhmann, 1989, 1995a; Borsch, 2011), the concept of boundary itself remains surprisingly unexplored. As Luhmann states "for a (scientific) observer, where the boundaries lie may still remain analytically unclear, but this does not justify viewing the bounding of systems as a purely analytical determination" (Luhmann, 1995a, b, p. 30). Midgley and Pinzón provide an insight into what boundaries may be, explaining that "boundaries define the limits of knowledge that is regarded as pertinent" (Midgley & Pinzón, 2011, p. 1545).

Now that the system, the system/environment distinction and the boundary have been discussed, the author moves to a discussion of the internal organisation of systems, which Luhmann articulates through his concepts of operational closure, autopoiesis and self-reference.

Operational Closure, Autopoiesis and Self-Reference

"A system is an entity whose elements are related to one another in a certain manner" (Kneer & Nassehi, 1993, p. 17–18). Luhmann posits that consciousness is the operation that maintains the elements of *psychic systems,* life is the operation that maintains the elements of *living systems*, and, finally, communication is the operation that maintains the elements of *social systems*. The boundaries of these systems prevent them from importing or exporting operations outside of themselves.

Although a system can certainly be affected by other systems, no system can replace its operations with the operations of another system. As Borsh (2011) explains, "my thoughts remain my thoughts and cannot be suddenly fused with the thoughts of another person, although we may communicate about our thoughts" (p. 28). Similarly, a social system or an organisation (as per Fig. 2.2 above) cannot import operations used by a living system (e.g. the immune system or the venous system) or that of another social system or organisation. For instance, a bank cannot use the same operations as a court of justice or the Catholic Church. This is because these organisations are based on specialised communication relying on a different kind of operation: e.g. court judgements, payments and transfers or sacraments and rites, respectively. Thus, a legal judgement is not equivalent to a sacrament, just as a sacrament is not equivalent to a banking operation. This is explored in further detail below in the subsection "function system".

In sum, systems cannot use operations that do not belong to them. A system is, by definition, *operatively closed* and thus cannot "cross its own boundary" (Borsch, 2011, p. 23). However, operational closure does not mean that systems are hermetical vis-à-vis other systems or their environment. Operational closure does not entail that "the system has at its disposal all the causes that are necessary for self-production" (Luhmann, 2005, p. 57). A living system, for instance, will require food and water in order to sustain itself, but it is this very living system that metabolises the food or the water into energy. On its own, food or water is not energy. Thus, systems require what Luhmann calls materiality continuum, the "external material conditions of possibility for social systems" (Borsch, 2011, p. 23). The system remains embedded in its environment and cannot *be* without its environment. Ultimately, it is the system's *operational closure* that paradoxically enables the system to be open. As stated by Luhmann "the system is open to its environment *because* of its operational closure" (Luhmann, 2002, p. 93). Indeed, operational closure produces the system's boundary, which not only enables the emergence of the system in the first place by delineating it, but also allows systems to perceive of and interact with their environment as a separate entity, thus enabling system differentiation. For instance, in the case of a bank system, its operational closure allows the bank to look past its own boundary and reflect on events in its larger environment.

Since the system is operatively closed, this means that it can only reproduce its structures and operations through its own operations. Yet, if the system is "located on one side and the environment on the other, how is this difference maintained, reproduced and subjected to evolutionary change?" (Pateau, 2013, p. 85). Luhmann's answer to that question is explained through the concept of *autopoiesis* (Greek: *autos* = self, *poiein* = to produce), which means self-production. Autopoietic systems "are systems that are defined as unities, as networks of productions of components, that recursively, through their interactions, generate and realize the network that produces them and constitute, in the space in which they exist, the boundaries of the network as components that participate in the realization of the network" (Maturana, 1981, p. 21).

Originally, autopoiesis referred to biological living systems that produce themselves using their own elements: "a living cell, for example, reproduces its own molecules, such as lipids, proteins, and so on" (Varela et al., 1974, p. 188). Luhmann borrowed this concept from Maturana and Varela (1974; 1981) and applied it to social systems. Autopoiesis occurs when a system's elements are produced and reproduced by the system's closed network of its own components and operations, i.e. communication and consciousness for social and psychic systems, respectively. Thus, Luhmann posits that systems are autopoietic and "produce and reproduce their own basic operations, i.e. communications" (Borsch, 2011, p. 27).

For example, as an autopoietic system, the psychic system only connects to its own thoughts and ideas:

> Thus, one thought within the system can only connect to another thought within that same system and not immediately to the thought of another psychic system. In order to transport thoughts from one psychic system to another, one needs communication to occur between at least two psychic systems present to each other. The psychic systems constitute a kind of—fuel, in that they supply the communicative process with thought material that must be—transcribed by communication. (Maurer, 2010, p. 6)

In addition to operational closure and autopoiesis, Luhmann adds the concept of self-reference. Every system is self-referential which is to be expected if systems are not only operationally closed but also reproduce their own operations, preconditioned by the differentiation, and thus separation, between system and environment. Hence, to summarise, autopoietic social systems produce and reproduce their own internal operations on the basis of communication (discussed further below). Although the environment can influence the system through irritation (also called resonance), there is no causality: "how the system (or the sub-system) changes primarily depends on the properties, the state of the system, its respective structure and the system's internal references" (Pateau, 2013, p. 87). As such, the system's behaviour is completely self-referential. The system processes events that occur in the environment by relating them to its own internal conditions, criteria and range of operations. Finally, social systems are in constant renewal; Luhmann argues that communication is an event that disappears the moment it occurs. As such, the continuous reproduction of operations is key to the survival of an autopoietic system.

To illustrate, consider the case of financial intelligence units. A financial intelligence unit (FIU) is defined by the Egmont group as "a national centre for the receipt and analysis of suspicious activity reports" (Egmont Group, 2019). An FIU is an organisation and thus, according to Luhmann, a social system. Therefore, communication constitutes its essential operation (as opposed to life for living systems or consciousness for psychic systems). Because they are social systems, FIUs are operationally closed. No other institution can cross the boundary of an FIU and, for example, perform the analysis of SARs submitted to the FIU. However, since no system is hermetic vis-à-vis its environment, the FIU needs SARs to fulfil its purpose of analysing them and thus to exist. While obliged entities identify suspicious transactions and send SARs to the FIU, only the FIU can perform the actual analysis of SARs. Thus, the FIU unit is supplied with SARs and incoming ML intelligence by its environment but the tools for actual analysis are kept within the system of the

FIU. Within its own boundary, the FIU is able to keep past and present ML intelligence and SARs in a suspended state, which enables the FIU to autoproduce the elements needed to perform its function of analysis, thus maintaining its existence as a system.

Before describing other characteristics of Luhmann's social systems, it is important to note that in 2008 Maturana stated that his discordance with Luhmann's application of autopoiesis was that it "left out human beings" (von Heiseler, 2008). However, the author contests the belief that Luhmann ignores psychic systems. Indeed, Luhmann recognises that such systems are necessary to the environment of social systems but simply rejects the fact that individuals' understandings and observations of society provide a thorough and complete observation of society. "One does not locate society *inside* individuals but *between* them. Society exists only when individuals communicate. The limits of society are established by the limits of communication. All that is not communicated remains outside of society" (Lee, 2000, p. 322). In addition, assuming it were possible for a psychic system to provide a complete societal observation, one wonders which of the 7.8 billion psychic systems (as of September 2020) currently on planet Earth could offer such a robust analysis of society and how an observer would go about selecting such a gifted psychic system. To Luhmann, society cannot be reduced to a collection of individuals with their own consciousness, which simply cannot be observed; rather, society occurs in the boundaries *between* systems.

Another criticism is whether "autopoiesis, as originally defined, can be applied to social systems" (Mingers, 2002, p. 278). Again, Luhmann does not attempt to construct a world where nonphysical systems display the exact same attributes and components of physical ones. Instead, Luhmann's theory examines whether social systems are aligned with the behaviour of autopoietic and self-referential systems and explores the implications of such features.

However, a final criticism that the author would levy is the problem that the concept of self-reference and autopoiesis seem to converge within Luhmann's writing. Indeed, Luhmann seems to distinguish between autopoiesis and self-reference in name alone. Generally speaking, a key difference between them is that an autopoietic system is inevitably self-referential, while a self-referential system is not necessarily autopoietic. The classic example demonstrating this distinction involves a smart thermostat with a sensor and a switch. The sensor assesses the temperature of a room and turns the heat on or off, depending on the temperature setting. The thermostat is self-referential but not autopoietic. Its elements have been produced by an engineer, and its goal of maintaining a room at a certain temperature has been set by a homeowner. Furthermore, its function is to create something other than itself. Hence, this system is not autopoietic but *allopoietic* (allo = other). However, Luhmann's definition of a self-referential system seems identical to an autopoietic system, as illustrated by the following quote:

> One can call a system self-referential if it itself constitutes the elements that compose it as functional unities and runs reference to this self-constitution through all the relations among these elements, continuously reproducing its self-constitution in this way. (Luhmann, 1995a, p. 33)

Structural Coupling

Although an autopoietic system is operatively closed, it remains embedded in its environment and has some connection to it. This is what Luhmann calls "structural coupling": "The result of structural coupling is an autonomous and strictly bounded system, that has nevertheless been shaped extensively by its interactions with its environment over time, just as the environment has been shaped by its interactions with the system" (Quick, 2003, para. 18). Luhmann developed this concept to analyse how two social systems influence or irritate one another. Systems react to one another, not in terms of a mutual input-output model or a relationship but as coevolution: each system includes the other system in its environment, observing environmental events or the "noise" of the other according to its own terms and as contributions to its self-reproduction.

For example, both the ML and AML domains are constructed through complex interactions between them: the structural coupling that exists between ML and AML transforms each system's respective configurations. For example, in 2016, a carbon-trading fraud trial took place in France (Mazoue, 2016). The EU Emissions Trading Scheme, designed to combat greenhouse emissions, was exploited by a criminal gang. EU member states set a cap on the amount of carbon that could be produced and granted carbon production allowance or permits that could be traded among companies. Hence if Company A did not use its full pollution allowance, it could sell its remaining permits to Company B, allowing Company B to exceed its own allowance. Between 2008 and 2010, criminals purchased carbon emission permits outside of the EU, which were thus exempt from the EU value-added tax (VAT). Frontmen acting as brokers within the EU sold those allowances back to the EU with VAT added and pocketed the difference (INTERPOL, 2013). This scheme cost the EU five billion euros in lost revenue.

The above case illustrates how criminals structurally adapted their criminal processes in response to the EU Emissions Trading Scheme, thereby creating their own "innovative" scheme to commit fraud. According to the systems theoretical model, new ML typologies provide stimuli that encourage the AML framework to expand and create further irritations that, in turn, will encourage money launderers to become even more resourceful in their criminal endeavours, thus creating even further ML typologies, which will in turn be identified and acted upon by the AML framework, again creating further irritations. This is what Luhmann calls the coevolution of different systems. The reality of such coevolution is acknowledged by the Financial Action Task Force on Money Laundering, which states the following in its typologies report relating to alternative remittance and currency service providers:

> Clearly, laundering through money remittance and currency exchange providers poses a number of regulatory and enforcement challenges. At the same time, it was observed that there is low detection of money laundering in comparison to the size of the industry as a whole. The absence or lax implementation of AML/CFT standards and adequate related policies provide opportunities, which are being exploited by money launderers and other criminals. These issues will likely require further investigation together and updating

research, not only to continue the development of a better understanding of specific money laundering and terrorist financing risks in the money remittance and currency exchange sector but also to ensure that regulatory responses are proportionate and effective. (FATF, 2010, P. 7)

In summary, while operational closure prevents a system from affecting operations in its environment and vice versa, there is nonetheless a coevolution of system and environment in the form of structural coupling, which refers not to a causal relationship between system and environment but to the (co)dependency of a system on its environment. There is thus a coevolution of systems "whereby each includes the other in its environment, interpreting the outputs of the other in its own terms on a continuous basis" (King & Thornhill, 2003, p. 33). Consequently, while structural coupling does not automatically entail communication (discussed further below), it can "cause irritations, surprises and noise in the system" (Francot-Timmermans, 2008, p. 86).

Re-Entry and Observing Systems

Another element of LST is that of re-entry. Essentially, re-entry describes self-observation, i.e. the re-entry of distinction into a distinction. Self-observation entails the observation of one's own observations, which is essentially impossible. Re-entry, however, enables indirect self-observation by allowing a system to re-enter the system/environment distinction within the distinction itself, namely, its own boundary. In order to be able to organise relationships with its internal components, to maintain the distinction between system and environment and thus to observe its environment and itself, the system needs to internalise this system/environment distinction by shifting the locus of observation; this is what Luhmann calls the *re-entry* of the distinction:

> We can conceive of systemic differentiation as the reduplication of the difference between system and environment within systems. Differentiation is the reflexive form of system building. It repeats the same mechanism, using it to amplify its own results. In differentiated systems, we will find two kinds of environment: the outer environment common to all subsystems and the special internal environment for each subsystem. This conception implies that each subsystem reconstructs and, in a sense, is again the whole system in the special form of a difference between system and environment. Differentiation performs the reproduction of the system in itself, multiplying specialized versions of its own identity by splitting it into internal systems and environments; it is not simply decomposition into smaller chunks but, in fact, a process of growth by internal disjunction. (Luhmann, 1977, p. 31)

Hence, by distinguishing itself from the environment, the system has to be able to refer to itself in a continuous manner (Luhmann, 1983). The implication of such *self-reference* is that the re-entry of the system/environment distinction into the existing system/environment distinction of the system is necessary for the system to be able to reflect upon itself. Re-entry enables the system to observe itself and to observe its environment thus creating the distinction between *self-reference* and other reference. Thus, Luhmannian systems theory recognises and acknowledges that psychic systems are not the only entities capable of reflection: nonliving systems can reflect upon themselves as well. One example, for instance, is the case of a financial institution mandating its internal audit function to monitor, audit and perform quality assurance of its own operations. In addition, the case described above of the FIU performing the SAR analysis offers a perfect illustration of re-entry. Incoming SARs provide the stimulus allowing the FIU to re-enter itself. More specifically, new incoming SARs need to be evaluated in the context of previously analysed SARs. Thus, there is a re-entry of the new SAR analysis into the previous one that enables the FIU to observe its own operations through performing its own operations (i.e. the SAR analysis).

For Luhmann, observation is the key concept that makes distinction possible at all. Indeed, the understanding of the world is performed through observation. The environment does not and cannot speak about itself: systems observe their environments and apply their own distinctions to it. Hence, the ontology of the environment, its *reality*, only exists through the lens of particular systems that have been defined through an observer's observation, and "an observer can no longer observe reality without taking into account its very observation as a generating element of reality" (Moeller, 2006, p. 71). However, to make an observation, to define *some thing*, an observer must make a two-sided distinction: what is being observed must be separated from what is not observed. "Such operations are the start of all perception and recognition" (Moeller, 2006, p. 71). Luhmann bases his theory of observation on Spencer-Brown's calculus of form and theory, which seeks to explain the foundation of how knowledge is formed. In this context, Spencer-Brown describes any observation as an operation of differentiation (Spencer Brown, 1969): between what is and what is not or, as he states, between the marked and the unmarked state. This is the act of distinction.

Spencer-Brown understands observation to be the key to any unit of analysis; however, the focus is not the object being observed but the actual act of observation (i.e. how does the observer observe and how does she or he select what is being observed). An observation has two elements: a distinction (between what is and what is not) and an indication (that formally illustrates what is). The observer applies a distinction that enables him or her to divide a space into two. The observer subsequently indicates the space that will be observed, moving the other space aside. As Spencer-Brown would say, "drawing a distinction severs an unmarked space to construct a form with a marked and unmarked side" (Luhmann, 1993, p. 769). This is Spencer-Brown's form of the distinction. Thus, "in contrast to the common use of the term, form does not refer merely to the marked state. The form of something is not sufficiently described by the defined—the marked state—but the unmarked state is a constitutive part of it. The marked side cannot exist without its unmarked side" (Seidl, 2004, p. 22), or put differently, the system cannot exist without an environment, from which the system has been demarcated by an observer.

Fig. 2.4 The form of distinction (Spencer Brown, 1969)

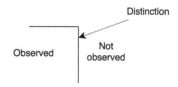

Figure 2.4 shows the side that is being actively observed (the marked state) and the other possibilities that have been actively excluded by the observer (the unmarked state).

Thus, Luhmann's key distinction is expressed as follows:

$$\overline{\text{System}} \,|\, \text{Environment,}$$

where system is the marked state and environment the unmarked state. "Form refers to the unity of the distinction between observed and unobserved" (Åkerstrøm Anderson, 2001, p. 7). However, in addition to splitting the world into the marked and the unmarked, the very act of observation divides and defines the observer as well as the observed:

> Every researcher who wants to study an object of research has to choose (implicitly or explicitly) a way of observing his/her object. The problem for the researcher is that the distinction chosen for one's observation usually blinds out all other possibilities of observation. One is not aware that it is the choice of distinction rather than what is being distinguished that produces the observation. (Seidl & Becker, 2006, p. 13)

However, the form as a whole with both its sides (the inside/marked and the outside/unmarked sides) can only be seen from above, from a standpoint that engulfs both the marked and unmarked space. This refers to yet another order of observation: what von Foerster calls a second-order observation (von Foerster, 1981). Indeed, while first-order observation is not aware of the distinction it makes during observation, second-order observation "is an observation of the distinction implicitly used in the first-order observation" (Luhmann, 1993, p. 227). The second-order observer observes the first-order observation and sees the unmarked side previously defined by the first observer. Essentially, the second-order observer draws a new distinction that contains the former distinction (the marked and the unmarked state) of the first-order observer in the *marked* space of the second-order observation. The second-order observer sees the blind spot that the first-order observer cannot see, but, in turn, creates a new blind spot by drawing his or her own new distinction. As Borsch (2011) points out, "in the moment something is observed, the observer is not able to see what form of distinction he or she employs" (p. 58).

Luhmann borrows and builds on the tradition of second-order observation (called second-order cybernetics) developed by Von Foerster (1974), Von Glasersfeld (1991) and Pask (1969) and aims to study the observations of other systems and examine the blind spots that such observations entail. Second-order cybernetics, however, "does not attempt to [...] clear away all the blind spots, it rather attempts to integrate them into a new theory, [...] at taking them seriously as a condition of systemic reality and complexity" (Moeller, 2006, p. 75). Furthermore, second-order cybernetics aims to "know which distinctions guide the observations of the observed observers and to find out if any stable objects emerge when these observations are recursively applied to their own results" (Luhmann, 2002, p. 99). Hence, as an observer, one can never directly access ontological *reality*. The observer observes others and based on this exercise decides which observations will be selected and which will be used to dissociate his or her understandings and interpretations. However, not all observing is of the second-order nature. As Luhmann says, "even if knowledge were to carry a warning that it was open to doubt, it would still have to be used as a foundation, as a starting point" (Luhmann, 2000a, p. 1), Indeed, academic research, for instance, is based on observations made by scholars whose own observations have already been identified as "knowledge". However (as further discussed in Chap. 3), since knowledge is constructed through distinctions and, as such, is ultimately an observer-dependent construction, there is no "reality" that is free of knowledge, since all reality is constructed by knowledge.

Double Contingency and Communication

Another key building block of Luhmann's systems theory is that of communication, which has already been introduced above. On a practical level, communication occurs between two entities, systems or psychic systems. The receiving entity is tasked with understanding and can only do so based on its own perception of the received message, using its own structure of reality which is contingent on its own logic. Thus, the receiving entity's perception is based on a synthesis of *information, utterance and understanding*. Information is the selection (made by the sender) of what will be uttered. Utterance is the selection of how communication is conveyed. Finally, understanding is how the receiver interprets the utterance. More precisely, understanding refers to what the receiver grasps from the previous communicative operation and how she or he perceives the output. This third step of the process is fundamental to successful communication: it is not about what the sender wants to convey; it is about what the receiver understands, i.e. the understood *meaning*. To illustrate, in the context of the AML domain, information is the selection of the transaction that is flagged as suspicious; utterance is the SAR sent to the FIU. Finally, understanding is what the FIU has grasped from the SAR and the FIU's interpretation of it. Accordingly, "*understanding* merely informs about how *information* and *utterance* are distinguished from one another in a given situation" (Pateau, 2013, p. 95), and communication ultimately represents the integration of information, utterance and understanding.

Luhmann's concept of *double contingency* describes the gap that arises between two interacting systems. Luhmann's concept of *contingency* describes an option that is selected from a variety of possible options: "it describes objects within the horizon of possible variations" (Luhmann, 1995a, p. 106). As Luhmann explains, "a fact is contingent when seen as selection from other possibilities which remain in some sense possibilities despite selection" (Luhmann, 1976, p. 509). Thus, contingency is an option that is chosen from a field of options that could still be chosen. As such, double contingency is what occurs when two psychic systems choose options out of a group of options (that could still be chosen) in relation to one another. Both individuals are completely opaque and unpredictable to one another; neither individual can know anything about the other individual or the other individual's understanding. However, each individual knows that whatever option is chosen will be contingent on how the other individual receives it.

To illustrate this problem of double contingency, imagine a woman wishes to pay for a soda at her local shop. If the act of taking the debit card out of her wallet and putting it on the counter is not understood by the shopkeeper as the intention of paying, there is no understanding possible. In such a case, the communication cannot continue, and the issue of double contingency cannot be addressed: i.e. the payment cannot be made. However, assuming the shopkeeper does understand that the gesture of removing the debit card does imply an interest in making a payment, the shopkeeper may communicate by making a reciprocal gesture (e.g. picking up the card) that the shopkeeper expects will also be understood by the customer. In other words, "communication goes on [...] when the problem of double contingency on both sides of the 'understanding' of that communication is addressed. Communication that is not mutually understood will not continue" (Moeller, 2006, p. 22). Resolving the problem of double contingency that occurs when "two black boxes, by whatever accident, come to have dealings with one another" (Luhmann, 1995a, p. 109) requires communication, and "this communication inevitably constitutes a social system as a network of meaningful reciprocal selections" (Vanderstraeten, 2002, p. 88). Thus, communication arises to resolve the problem of double contingency and, in turn, creates social systems. Communication can thus be defined as "a network of meaningful reciprocal selections" (Vanderstraeten, 2002, p. 88). Accordingly, the ability to observe and understand society relies on social systems making sense of information and utterances and extracting meaning through communication. As Luhmann states: "as soon as any communication whatsoever takes place [...], social systems emerge" (Luhmann, 1982a, b, p. 70). Thus, social systems are simply systems of communication; the challenge is to understand how social systems perceive communication as *meaningful* and how double contingency is resolved in a manner that is structured and reliable in order to maintain social order. The obliged entity sending a suspicious activity report to a financial intelligence unit is an example of meaningful communication. This is explored in the following section.

Function Systems and Binary Codes

In order to understand how social systems end up perceiving communication as *meaningful*, it is fundamental to first examine what Luhmann's social systems are. As documented in Fig. 2.1, Luhmann argues that there are three types of social systems, interactions, organisations and societies, also referred to as function systems.

Interaction systems refer to face-to-face interactions and require "co-presence and reflexive perception" (Borsch, 2011, p. 68). Indeed, inspired by Goffman (1963, 1974), Luhmann argues that having two psychic systems in the presence of one another is not sufficient for an interaction system to emerge. Such a system occurs when psychic systems perceive the perception of another (and vice versa) and alter their behaviour accordingly. This happens, for instance, when taking a taxi or queuing up at the supermarket—communication can be both verbal and nonverbal.

The second category of social systems is that of organisations. This is of great interest to Luhmann who dedicated a whole book to the subject (Luhmann, 2011; Luhmann 2018). Organisation systems are more important to Luhmann than interaction systems, since (unlike interactions) organisations can process complexity in a way that interactions cannot. Indeed, organisations are neither spatially nor temporally limited: they reach across geographical location and exist over a wider time horizon than do interactions; they continue to exist even if members die or leave the organisation. In addition, organisations can communicate (in Luhmann's sense) a wider number of topics than interactions can because they have the ability to bridge a number of different function systems. For example, an obliged entity such as a bank that provides banking services and ML prevention and sponsors the Premier Championship bridges the economic system, the legal system and the sports system.

According to Luhmann's system theory, society has evolved into a number of function systems that perform and fulfil a specific purpose, or *function*. Indeed, according to Luhmann, modern society is differentiated into the political system, the scientific system, the educational system, the economic system, the religious system, the legal system, the art system and the mass media (Borsch, 2011); this list is likely not exhaustive. Roth and Schütz (2015), for example, have also recognised the sport system among others. Function systems appear after inventions become fundamental and necessary to society. The invention of money has thus led to the differentiation of the economic system. Similarly, certain conventions of power concentration have resulted in the differentiation of the political system (Moeller, 2006).

Since function systems are social systems, their key operation is communication. Thus, "buying a meal is communication functioning economically; the casting and counting of a vote is communication functioning politically; presenting an argument in court is communication functioning legally" (Moeller, 2006, p. 24). Each of these systems has its own environment (Luhmann, 1982a, b) which is constituted by other function systems as well as by interactions and organisations. To Luhmann, society consists of everything that is understood as communication by interaction, organisation and function systems. More specifically, "society is the encompassing social system which includes all communication, reproduces all communication and constitutes meaningful horizons for future communication" (Luhmann, 1982a, b, p. 131).

Hence, when psychic systems exchange information on bad weather, the state of conflict in Syria, the recent Beirut explosion, the increasing rate of teenage pregnancy or the Paradise Papers, this may be the product of interactions; however, such exchanges are *not* communication as defined by Luhmann. Indeed, they become communication only when they are perceived as having significance for one or more of society's function systems—for example, bad weather as a by-product of climate change (scientific function system), the conflict in Syria as a by-product of Russia's attempt to assert greater power in the region, the Beirut explosion as related to Iran's control of the Lebanese government (political function system) or increasing teenage pregnancy rates as related to a decrease of faith and family values (religious function system). Fundamentally, nothing is part of society until it has been communicated and has meaning to society (in terms of at least one function systems). Accordingly, "society represents the boundaries and the limits of all that is recognized as societal communications" (King & Thornhill, 2003, p. 8) with respective function systems converting information into meaning and having their very own function in relation to how meaning is organised. As such:

> the function system of *religion* manages the inevitability of contingency, science provides a way of distinguishing between what is true and what is not, the economy responds to and regulates scarcity for society via payments. Together they represent a collection of autonomous but inter-dependent processes, and as such constitute society. (King & Thornhill, 2003, p. 11)

Luhmann identifies three types of social differentiation as predecessors of functional differentiation (Luhmann, 1977, 1995a): segmentary differentiation, centre/periphery differentiation and stratified differentiation. Segmentary differentiation describes tribal societies, centre/periphery differentiation describes major societies (e.g. the Roman Empire), and stratified differentiation describes societies that are based on hierarchical social order—for example, societies based on social classes and castes. Stratified societies are the immediate predecessor of functionally differentiated societies that emerged between the sixteenth and the eighteenth century (Moeller, 2006). Function systems are not ranked and do not have a gravitational core: "Whereas in the case of stratified differentiation every subsytem defines itself through the difference in rank in relation to the others and only thereby achieves an identity, in the case of functional differentiation every function system determines its own identity" (Luhmann, 1997, p. 745).

Function systems evolved based on what Luhmann calls *symbolically generalised media of communication*, which improve the chances for successful communication, address double contingency and thus enable social order. According to Luhmann, "even if communication is understood there can be no assurance of it being accepted. By 'success' I mean that the recipient of the communication accepts the selective content of the communication (the information) as a premise of his own behaviour" (Luhmann, 1981, p. 124). Accordingly, Luhmann first identifies language as a tool to increase successful communication and describes the development of the media of dissemination (e.g. writing, printing, radio, television, etc. and of course although Luhmann did not live long enough to see its evolution, the Internet), which tackles spatiotemporal limitations to successful communication. Finally, to address the challenge of ensuring that the communication is not only understood but accepted (thus enabling social order), Luhmann identifies symbolically generalised media of communication (which are highly specialised communication tools) as the solution to the problem of double contingency:

> We would like to call 'symbolically generalized' the media that use generalisations to symbolise the nexus between selection and motivation. That is, represent it as a unity. Important examples are: truth, love, property/money, power/law; and also, in rudimentary form, religious belief, art, and today standardised 'basic values.' In all these cases this—in a very different way and for very different interactive constellations—is a matter of conditioning the selection of communication so that it also works as a means of motivation, that is, so that it can adequately secure acceptance of the proposed selection. The most successful and most relevant communication in contemporary society is played out through these media of communication, and accordingly, the chances of forming social systems are directed towards the corresponding functions. (Luhmann, 1995a, p. 161)

Media of communication provide a code framework (called the binary code, discussed below) within which the function systems can evolve and emerge (Luhmann, 1976): "each of the media gave way to a binary code and this constituted the backdrop to the development of independent, autopoietic and operationally closed function systems" (Borsch, 2011, p. 80). As their names suggest, such systems have their own specific functions. For instance, the purpose of the political system is "characterised as supplying the capacity to enforce collectively binding decisions" (Luhmann, 1990a, p. 73), while the legal system aims to "stabilise normative expectations" (Luhmann, 2004, p. 148), and the scientific one looks at producing scientific knowledge and "making it available to other function systems" (Moeller, 2006, p. 25). Function systems reconstruct what they observe through system-specific distinctions; this not only enables them to attribute meaning to their environment but also reinforces their own identity, existence and function in relation to—and yet independent of—their environment.

Thus, each function system processes information and meaning and communicates through its very own and specific medium which foments its own language, called the binary code. This binary distinction enables the function system to identify operations pertaining to itself along the following model: positive/negative distinction. It is, as the name suggests, purely binary and has only two values excluding all others. "The system introduces its own distinctions and grasps the states and events that appear to it as information" (Luhmann, 1989, p. 18). Essentially, this means that events exist within a system's environment or within the system itself. The events are then registered and processed by the observing system that converts it to information on the basis of its code. The implications of this are that systems are limited by their binary code, as what does not fit around the code cannot easily be understood as communication to that system. On the other hand, the advantage is that "the binary code frees the function system of the burden of having to take into account what other systems consider important" (Borsch, 2011, p. 71). Furthermore, binary codes are amoral (Luhmann, 1994): the positive side of the binary distinction does not have a higher (or better) value or standing than the negative side of the binary distinction (and vice versa) implying a fundamentally amoral (*not* immoral) modern society. Finally, in order to regulate the application of the code, function systems have

2.1 Luhmann's System Theory (LST) and Social Systems

Table 2.1 Function systems, function, binary codes and medium (Moeller, 2006; Roth & Schütz, 2015)

Function system	Function or purpose	Programmes	Binary code	Medium
Law	Standardising norms	Laws, constitutions	Legal/illegal	Jurisdiction
Politics	Enabling collective binding decisions	Ideology	Government/opposition	Power
Science	Producing knowledge	Theories, methods	True/false	Truth
Religion	Eliminating contingency	Dogmas, Holy scriptures, Confession	Immanence/transcendence	Faith
Economy	Reducing shortages	Budget, Price	Payment/non-payment	Money
Media	Information	Topic	Information/non-information	Medium

developed what Luhmann calls programmes. Programmes define "given conditions for the suitability of the selection of operations" (Luhmann, 1995a, p. 317) meaning that they identify and develop the criteria that enable the binary distinction to be made. For instance, the scientific system has developed protocols and methods to ensure adequate application of the true/untrue code, while the legal system has laws and constitutions in order to ensure adequate application of the legal/illegal code.

Table 2.1 provides an overview of function systems, function, programmes, binary codes and symbolically generalised media of communication.

This list is not exhaustive; Luhmann has also identified the function systems of art, education, family and health (Luhmann, 1990b, d, 1998, 2000b). Luhmann never intended for the list of function systems to be immutable and static and was, for instance, working on defining social movements as function systems (Borsch, 2011; Moeller, 2006). Hence, the existence of a comprehensive list of function systems is a source of debate among scholars, and Roth and Schütz (2015) argue that Luhmann himself is responsible for this. They point out that while listing function systems, Luhmann had added "and so on" (Luhmann, 1995a, p. 48), thus signalling that society can be further functionally differentiated. As Roth and Schütz clarify, "we find that the mention of 'the legal system, the economic system, the system of education, the system of art,' is regularly preceded by a *'for example'* (Seidl, 2004, p. 407; emphasis added)" (Roth & Schütz, 2015, p. 13). A number of additional function systems have been proposed by other scholars, including morality (Reese-Schäfer, 1999, 2007), culture (Henkel, 2010), family (Burkart, 2005), social work (Baecker, 1994), sports (Roth and Schütz), civil society (Reichel, 2012), sexuality (Lewandowski, 2004), technology and AML (Demetis, 2010).

Each function system has its own binary code (or distinction), which creates order and provides assurance that decisions that are made may be relied upon by other function systems. However, the validity of decisions made on one function system's positive/negative code may not necessarily transfer to other function systems. Some function systems will reject the operations and communications of other systems as invalid. For instance, as seen in the response to scientific evidence regarding climate change, the current US president, Donald Trump, regards the scientific determination of climate change as truth to be invalid, due to its impact on the political binary code he relies upon. In another example regarding the so-called "paradise papers" leak of 2017, while tax avoidance schemes may be legal according to the legal function systems, they may nevertheless be considered unacceptable by other function systems. Finally, the current discourse around "fake news" coinciding with the Trump presidency represents a particularly interesting case in which a politician seeks to entirely undermine the information/non-information code of the media system in order to reduce the potential impact of the media system on his political subsystem, by, in the words of Republican senator Jeff Flake, "wag[ing] war on objective reality for nearly two solid years, calling real things fake and fake things real" (ABC News, 2018).

Thus, while function systems encapsulate decisions made by applying their own binary logic, they face an environment that may not validate these decisions. This is the result of a decentred society in which no single function system has primacy over another. Nevertheless, some function systems may have an evolutionary advantage over others. For instance, the economic system "has a highly effective symbolic media and (is) able to further refine these (money into stocks, and so on)" (Moeller, 2006, p. 27). Furthermore, function systems may not align with other function systems because each system observes phenomena in different ways through application of their own codes: "Society remains the same but appears different depending upon the functional system (politics, economy, science, mass media, education, religion, art and so on) that describes it. The same is different" (Luhmann, 1995a, p. 48). Accordingly, a concern pertaining to the economic function system may be perceived differently from the perspective of a religious or legal function system, for instance. As such, it is unclear whether function systems are truly equipped to deal with social issues that affect a number of different function systems.

Organisations and Decisions

Organisations (Luhmann's third type of social system) can be thought as a bridge of a number of different function systems because, through their very structure, organisations encompass different communicative logics and codes pertaining to diverse function systems. Unlike function systems, organisation systems are not bound by a single code and can observe the same issue through the lens of multiple codes. Organisations are located within function systems (for instance, courts of law or universities) but are not necessarily constrained by a single function system. For instance, a university may bridge all scientific, education and economic function systems. Accordingly, organisations should have the ability to "cross the divides between function systems and therefore a way for society to observe how its

Fig. 2.5 The form of decision and its paradox (Åkerstrøm Anderson, 2001)

functional differentiation produces limits to societal problem management" (Borsch, 2011, p. 106). For instance, financial institutions are organisations that bridge legal and the economic function systems as well as subsystems of AML and even ML itself. Indeed the Danske Bank case identified that there were ten ML accomplices within the institution who supported and enabled ML activities. Accordingly, organisations can enable function systems and their competing codes (and hence rationales) to be seen by second-order observers who may be capable of unpacking complex social issues that run through a number of function systems. Hence, since a wide array of organisations perform AML (e.g. international bodies, regulators, obliged entities, financial intelligence units, etc.), the keys to locating failures within the AML framework may lie with one of these organisations, or it may necessitate cooperation between several or all of them. This is explored in the findings and discussion chapters (Chaps. 4 and 5), but first it is necessary to review organisational decision-making in the context of Luhmann's system theory as this will enable the reader to better understand the cross-case analysis performed and documented in Chap. 4.

Organisations are "social systems which are able to stabilise forms of action and behaviour by deciding about more or less strong conditions of membership and about their practices and procedures" (Nassehi, 2005, p. 185). Whereas communication for interactions and societies take the form of language and binary code, respectively, the communication units of organisations are decisions. Accordingly, Luhmann calls organisations systems of decisions (Moeller, 2006; Seidl & Mormann, 2015). For Luhmann, decisions are organisations' communication units and indicate a selection: alternatives could have also been selected. Hence, each decision marks the distinction between fixed contingency (what has been decided) and open contingency (what has not been decided). In sum, communication with psychic and function systems communicates content, whereas the power of a decision is qualitatively different in that a decision communicates that "there were alternatives to the selected content that could have been—but were not—selected" (Seidl & Mormann, 2015, p. 23). Essentially, the decision determines that "before" the decision was made, an array of options was available. "After" the decision was made, a conclusion was reached but other options could have been chosen.

Figure 2.5 illustrates this point through the nesting of two distinctions. The first marked side (in blue) indicates the decision made by a decision-maker and distinguishes the marked side (i.e. all the alternatives—chosen and excluded) from the unmarked side.

Within the marked side of the blue distinction, a second distinction is made (in green) and distinguishes the chosen alternative, or fixed contingency (marked side), from the excluded alternatives or open contingency (unmarked side). "The paradox is that no decision can reach a final state because it always simultaneously potentializes different decisions. A decision (fixed contingency) as opposed to a non-decision (open contingency) is paradoxical because it always contains the non-decidable" (Åkerstrøm Anderson, 2001, p. 12). For instance, when financial institutions perform large-scale high-risk customer remediation exercises (to avoid regulatory sanction, for instance), often "high*er-r*isk" customers will be identified among high-risk customers in order to apply a risk-based approach and mobilise remediation efforts. While the unmarked side of the blue distinction represents low-risk customers, within the marked state of the blue distinction (high-risk customers), a second distinction is made, that of high*er*-risk customers, represented in the figure above as the chosen alternative, on the left-hand side of the green distinction.

The decision is therefore the communication of the chosen alternative as well as the implicit communication of the contingency of the decision: alternatives that have been excluded but that could have been chosen. Indeed, the following statement "I have *decided* to take job A" communicates that the other jobs or alternatives were considered. The more that decision appears to be obvious, the less the discarded options appear as credible contenders. Put differently, if the decision describes options as nonoptions, the chosen option will not appear as a decision per se: there was not much to *decide* in the first place, the option was obvious! This is the rationale behind Luhmann's following statement: "Only questions which are fundamentally undecidable can be resolved" (Luhmann, 1993, p. 12). Hence decisions are fragile communication units because they communicate their own contingency (as understood by Luhmann) and are therefore paradoxical in nature.

Luhmann argues that the purpose of decisions is to manage high levels of complexity and *absorb uncertainty*. To an observer, perceived uncertainty is suppressed the moment a decision is made. Through selectivity, organisations restrict their possibilities and thus mould their reality into a less complex environment. Any subsequent decision uses the first decision as its reference point and does not have to deal with the uncertainty related to previous alternatives; these were discarded the moment the previous decision was made. As such, every decision produces a stable reference for the next decision: a decision becomes a decision as soon as the ensuing decision is made, not before. "In other words, not until a decision is recognised as a decision premise is it decided" (Åkerstrøm Anderson, 2001, p. 10). Thus, by not having to question the previous decision, perceived uncertainty and complexity relating to the past are reduced. "Every single decision (unless just ignored, in which case it would not be a 'real' decision) serves as a decision premise for later decisions" (Seidl & Becker, 2006, p. 27). Similarly, the questioning and

Fig. 2.6 Deparadoxisation (adapted from Knudsen, 2007)

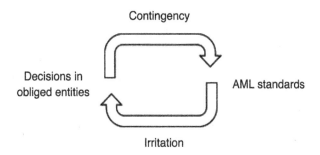

rejection of a decision have to be communicated as decision too, which, itself, becomes a decision premise for subsequent decisions.

A decision is thus fundamental to handling complexity, but it also is a highly fragile communication event, since by communicating its own contingency, it communicates its alternatives and thus communicates how it could be deconstructed. Thus, if decision units, or organisations' communication events, are to be successful as per Fig. 2.6, specific communicative tools are required to camouflage the intrinsic paradox of the decision. Such specific tools are what Luhmann calls deparadoxisation tools, i.e. tools that organisations have had to develop in order to address this issue of paradox. Those tools enable organisations to make the contingency of their decisions less visible or to displace them to a less disturbing place (Knudsen, 2007, p. 117). Luhmann identifies several deparadoxisation tools, namely, operative closure, attribution of the decision to a decision-maker and finally, the most important tool, decision premises.

Seidl and Mormann explain that operative closure refers to the fact that the organisation gives the *decision* the status of the only legitimate communication unit, "even the deconstruction (i.e. the rejection) of a decision in an organization has to be communicated as a decision" (Seidl & Mormann, 2015, p. 25). The second deparadoxisation tool is the attribution of a decision to a decision-maker as opposed to the organisation. Luhmann argues that the "decision-maker" responsible for making decisions is an organisational fiction (Luhmann, 1995a, 2018). Motives are attributed to a decision-maker and, as such, decisions are justified through the assumed rationality of the decision-maker. However, rationality, according to Luhmann, is "a retrospective scheme of observation, dealing with the contingency and the paradox of decision-making processes" (Nassehi, 2005, p. 186). Hence, an observer would question the rationale that made the decision-maker decide upon that particular alternative. "Therefore, whether or not a decision is accepted as a decision premise by later decisions depends on whether it is assumed that the (fictional) decision-maker had good ('rational') motives" (Seidl & Becker, 2006, p. 29). This essentially shifts the attention away from the decision and its intrinsic paradox towards the fictional decision-maker and his or her motives, be they "rational" or not.

The final and most relevant deparadoxisation tool for this research is that of decision premises. For Luhmann, decision premises create the framework that enables decision-making but also restricts it. Indeed, "decision premises regulate which decisions have to be accepted under what conditions, including who can make what kind of decisions that are binding for certain other decisions" (Seidl & Mormann, 2015, p. 26). Luhmann recognises four types of decision premises (Luhmann, 2018): decision programmes, communication channels, personnel and the undecidable decision premises. Decision programmes define the preconditions required to ensure adequate decision-making. Communication channels aim to formalise and regulate communication, for instance, who can communicate with whom, through which forums and at what hierarchical level. Personnel relates to the recruitment, transfer or dismissal of organisation members, and, finally, undecidable decision premises relate to an organisation's culture and will be discussed below. At this point, the author focuses on the decision premise with relevance to this research, namely, "programmes" (Luhmann, 2003, 2018).

> Decision programmes define conditions for correct decision-making: goal programmes define certain goals that are to be reached (i.e. the respective decisions are expected to contribute to achieving the goal), while conditional programmes describe what decisions to take in what situations. (Luhmann, 2003, p. 45)

Thus, programmes identify key criteria that enable adequate decision-making. Conditional programmes have the "if/then" format: for example, if a customer is a politically exposed person (PEP), *then* he or she should be classified as high risk for ML. Goal programmes have a decision-making process defined by goals. For instance, if the *goal* is to reduce the likelihood of regulatory fines for the period 2018–2020, one must reduce the amount of non-resident customers by $x\%$ by date y.

Figure 2.6 illustrates deparadoxisation. The organisation displaces the contingency of its decision to the AML standards and regulations set out by the FATF and relevant national governments. "When the question 'why this decision' is answered with 'because the standard says so' then the contingency is moved from decision to standard" (Knudsen, 2007, p. 119).

Figure 2.6 also shows that the standard irritates (i.e. influences) the decision. "But the term irritation also indicates that it is not a causal relation: it is the organisation itself which determines how it can be irritated, influenced and how it should react to the irritation" (Knudsen, 2007, p. 120).

To summarise, decisions are fragile communication units because they are paradoxical. Accordingly, decisions need deparadoxisation tools to enable the original paradox emerging from the decision to be ignored "by shifting attention to the decision premises which cannot be questioned" (Seidl & Becker, 2006, p. 29). In addition, decisions are produced by a network of decisions that are encased in the decision premise: "the focal decision, while ultimately undecidable, is *presented* (to a large extent) as merely the programmable application of fixed decision premises" (Seidl & Becker, 2006, p. 29). This enables uncertainty absorption because uncertainties associated with previous decisions have become irrelevant. As stated by Luhmann, "uncertainty absorption takes place when decisions are accepted as decision premises and taken as the basis for subsequent decisions" (Luhmann, 2005, p. 96).

To illustrate the empirical application of Luhmann's systemic theory of organisations and decisions, the author refers to the 2015 Barclays Bank case resulting in a GBP 72 million fine. In 2011 and 2012, Barclays Bank Plc. executed a series of transactions amounting to GBP 1.88 billion on behalf of ultrahigh-net-worth clients that were PEPs (Financial Conduct Authority [FCA], 2015). In order to take on the clients as quickly as possible and to generate GBP 52.3 million in revenue, Barclays decided not to apply standard procedures, consisting in performing enhanced customer due diligence as required by the RBA. The identity of the clients was so sensitive that the bank agreed to pay them GBP 37.7 million should their names ever be revealed. In November 2015, the FCA (the UK regulator) fined Barclays GBP 72 million. At the time, the FCA made the following statement: "While we make no finding that the transaction involved financial crime, the circumstances of the transaction gave rise to a number of features which indicated a higher level of risk. This required Barclays to adhere to a higher level of due skill, care and diligence but Barclays did not follow its standard procedures" (FCA, 2015a, b). In addition, the FCA made the following statement:

> Barclays failed to follow its own standard procedures, failed to implement any adequate alternative procedures, and failed to have sufficient regard to the JMLSG Guidance and other relevant guidance in issue during the relevant period. Barclays focused on its objective of entering into the business relationship and executing the transaction quickly and on the exceptional confidentiality restrictions in place, rather than on the importance of completing the EDD required and making a careful and considered assessment of the potential financial crime risks. (FCA, 2015a, b, p. 22)

When observed through Luhmann's decision processing system, this case illustrates the following points: the decision to not apply enhanced customer due diligence on a sensitive PEP was determined by the network of previous decisions (decision premises) made within Barclays as opposed to one decision-maker. The responsibility of the decision was distributed across a number of individuals, and, again, such responsibility could not be assigned to any single decision-maker. Indeed, the FCA report documenting the case states the following:

> While several members of Barclays' senior management were aware of and endorsed the transaction, there was no consistent understanding among the senior managers who were working on the transaction as to who would be approving Barclays' entry into the Business Relationship and the nature of the approvals that they would each be giving. For example, during interviews with the Authority, five different individuals were identified as giving part of the approval. (FCA, 2015a, b, p. 15)

This case highlights the following: identifying a sole decision-maker would have forced Barclays to admit that the decision-maker made the rational decision to breach AML regulation and that such decision would then become decision premise to future decisions. The decision to distribute the decision-making role across five separate individuals may have been made in order to protect Barclays Bank. Essentially, since the decision to breach AML regulation cannot be attributed to a single decision-maker and his or her rational motive, this decision cannot be seen by the regulator as a decision premise for future decisions.

It is important to note that the decision by Barclays Bank to take on the sensitive PEPs and apply "a lower standard for reviewing the financial crime risks associated with the Business Relationship than it typically did for its other business relationships with PEPs" (FCA, 2015a, b, p. 17) is not documented or described by the FCA's 2015 report as a decision. The report focuses on Barclays' failures to apply adequate measures and includes 51 references to Barclays' failure to act adequately, versus seven references to Barclays' decisions relating to accepting the sensitive and high-net-worth PEPs. The remaining eight references made to decisions and decision-making relate to the regulator, who is explicitly identified as the decision-maker (FCA, 2015a, b, p. 28). Indeed, since decisions are justified through the assumed rationality of the decision-maker (Luhmann, 2003, 2018), recognising that Barclays decided to accept customers with inadequate AML checks could question, if not undermine, Barclays' decision premises. This point invokes the fourth decision premise, the undecidable decision premise. Luhmann defines organisational culture as the undecided prerequisite for decision-making: a structure that emerges through the practice of the organisation itself (Luhmann, 2003, 2018).

The Barclays' case has implications in relation to organisational culture, especially in light of the backlash that financial institutions faced over the years regarding the number of financial sanctions they have incurred (see Chap. 1 for details on fines). Repetitive scandals involving Barclays, HSBC, Deutsche Bank and Danske Bank, to name a few, have led the general public to question the banking culture and label it as greedy, shoddy and deceitful (Randal, 2012). Indeed, Cohen, Fehr and Maréchal have conducted a study that strongly suggests that the business culture within the banking industry "weakens and undermines the honesty norm" (Cohn et al., 2014, p. 86). Thus, referring back to Barclays' 2015 case, the FCA was unwilling to label the decision to apply a lower level of customer due diligence on those high-net-worth PEPs as a decision. In addition, the regulator was unable to identify a decision-maker. As such, it seems that the decision may have been the by-product of the undecidable decision premise in conjunction with the goal programmes of the front office seeking to reach a certain level of sales by a certain date.

Nevertheless, this trend of heavy fines triggered by the banking industry's culture has generated a strong interest in culture auditing as evidenced by the UK's Financial Services Code issued by the Institute of Internal Auditors (2013), by the increasing number of consultancy firms offering such services and by private institutions (e.g. Credit Suisse) setting up "people risk and culture" departments. The challenge is understanding the implications and the paradox of setting standards and expectations in relation to an undecidable decision premise.

Table 2.2 summarises Luhmann's theoretical concepts pertinent to the Barclays Bank case discussed above.

Now that LST and its key concepts have been introduced and discussed, the following section focuses on Luhmann's sociology of risk

2.1 Luhmann's System Theory (LST) and Social Systems

Table 2.2 Barclays Bank 2015 regulatory fine through LST

Luhmann's theoretical concepts	Barclays Bank's case	Description as per the FCA report (2015) and *author's comments*
Binary code	Barclays made a payment of GBP 1.88 billion on behalf of high-net-worth customers	"Barclays established the business relationship with the clients in respect of the transaction in 2011. The transaction involved a structured finance transaction comprised of investments in notes backed by underlying warrants and third party Bonds. A number of companies were used to make the investments and the Proceeds of the investments were held in a trust of which the clients were beneficiaries" (p. 2). *Barclays Bank uses the payment/ non-payment code. What the FCA report highlights, however, is the fact that Barclays marked the transactions as non-suspicious when in fact the FCA would have expected Barclays to mark them as suspicious instead*
Organisation bridges many function systems	Barclays as a financial institution is in charge of maximising profits for shareholders as well as meeting its regulatory requirements for the prevention of ML	"The transaction was the largest of its kind that Barclays had executed for natural persons. Deals over GBP 20 million were commonly referred to within Barclays as elephant deals because of their size and the transaction, which was for an amount of GBP 1.88 billion, was also referred to as an elephant deal" (p. 2). "In order to prevent the UK financial system being exposed to financial crime risks, regulated firms are required to comply with certain obligations when entering into New business relationships. These obligations are set out in the Authority's handbook and the 2007 regulations and are supported by the JMLSG guidance, together with statements from the authority and other bodies" (p. 8). *Barclays Bank bridges the economic and the legal function systems*
Deparadoxisation tool	Barclays established a confidentiality agreement	"The terms of the confidentiality agreement were onerous and were considered by Barclays to be an

(continued)

Table 2.2 (continued)

Luhmann's theoretical concepts	Barclays Bank's case	Description as per the FCA report (2015) and *author's comments*
		unprecedented concession for clients who wished to preserve their confidentiality" (p. 9). "In view of these confidentiality requirements, Barclays determined that details of the clients and the transaction should not be kept on its computer systems. A select team, including representatives from senior management, was brought together from across Barclays' divisions and offices around the world to carry out the checks required to establish the business relationship and to arrange and execute the transaction" (p. 9–10). *Through the confidentiality agreement, Barclays has given its decision to bank-sensitive and high-net-worth PEPs the status of the only legitimate communication unit. In addition, Barclays has made the contingency of its decisions less visible*
Undecidable decision premise	Barclays has unveiled its organisational culture	"Barclays focused on its objective of entering into the business relationship and executing the transaction quickly and on the exceptional confidentiality Restrictions in place, rather than on the importance of completing the EDD required and making a careful and considered assessment of the potential financial crime risks" (p. 22). *Barclays Bank's front office and drive for profits and commission was the main motivation for the decision to bank high-net-worth Qatari clients without adequate application of regulatory requirements*
Fiction of the decision-maker	5 senior managers were designated as decision-makers on IT systems, but they denied having such responsibility	"Those who were identified on Barclays' systems as having given the approval referred to in paragraph 4.23(a) above did not know that they were named on Barclays' computer system as having given

(continued)

Table 2.2 (continued)

Luhmann's theoretical concepts	Barclays Bank's case	Description as per the FCA report (2015) and *author's comments*
		this approval. They did not accept that they had this responsibility in interviews with the authority" (p. 15). *This case illustrates an extreme version of Luhmann's fiction of the decision-maker: The rationale of the decision made by a decision-maker, unaware that he was made decision-maker, cannot be questioned*

2.2 Luhmann's Sociological Theory on Risk

Luhmann's premise is that risk is not ontologically real; it is a social construction:

> The already familiar discussions on risk calculations, risk perceptions, risk assessment and risk acceptance are now joined by the issue of selecting the risks to be selected or ignored. And once again, discipline specific research can reveal that this is not a matter of chance but that demonstrable social factors control the selection process. (Luhmann, 1993, p. 4)

Based on Spencer-Brown, Luhmann considers risk to be a two-sided form. If risk is the marked state, what is the unmarked state? Luhmann argues that risk is often determined by its counterconcept, security (Luhmann, 1993, p. 19) or safety (Gephart Jr., 1993), which can be expressed as follows:

$$\overline{\text{risk}}\,|\,\text{security}$$

As already seen in the previous section, Luhmann's premise is that words are distinctions and that their meanings can be further understood by looking at their unmarked side: distinctions enable an observer to further define a concept. For instance, a shift from risk/security or safety to risk/certainty and then from risk/certainty to risk/danger will generate three different interpretations, understandings and hence meanings of *risk* as a concept.

Thus, Luhmann proposes defining risk by proceeding "from reflection of risk to reflection on risk" (Luhmann, 1993, p. 225). He distances himself from the belief that risk is linked to individuals acting a certain way, focusing instead on *decision* which, as seen in the previous section, is one of the building blocks of Luhmann's framework. Hence, reiterating the example from Chap. 1 of the maritime merchant who decides to ship his goods without knowing whether they will reach their destination or not, the connection between the decision to ship the goods and the uncertain consequences of that decision helps define risk as a "consequence of a decision that will occur in the future but that is unknown" (Japp & Kusche, 2008, p. 80). In summary, all decision-making is based on the selection of one decision from an array of multiple decisions which, had they been selected, could have led to other consequences. Ultimately, "the uncertainties of non-knowledge are dealt with by decision-making" (Japp, 2000, p. 225). This is *contingency*, and, since the selection from alternatives is always contingent, decision-making is always risky.

Hence, Luhmann argues that modern societies are characterised by contingency; every alternative to a decision made is risky and nothing is safe or certain. As such, the observer must assume uncertainty on both sides of the distinction since uncertain consequences are inevitable whether the outcomes are positive or negative. Accordingly, "certainty in reference to the non-incidence of future losses doesn't exist, therefore the opposite term of risk is not security or certainty but danger" (Voss, 2005, p. 5). The distinction between risk and danger does not hinge on certainty or safety but on attribution: risk is attributed to the system's decisions, while danger is attributed to the environment. Risk is "the possibility of future damage, exceeding all reasonable costs, that is attributed to a decision" (Luhmann, 1990c, p. 225), while "danger is a possible loss considered to have been caused externally" (Luhmann, 1993, p. 22). However, from the perspective of an individual who did not make the decision or accept the associated risks, the possibility of a loss is perceived as a danger that is caused by an external force. Thus, even though a decision may be made as part of a democratic process, the possibility of loss or damage is not voluntarily accepted by all potentially affected parties through the decision-making process:

> Decisions are always the decisions of somebody, not the decisions of everybody. Therefore the real dangers in modern society are the decisions of others. Almost all other dangers, including natural disasters, can be avoided, for instance by moving out of a region threatened by storms or earthquakes and settling elsewhere. But the danger that results from the decisions of others cannot be avoided because others are everywhere. (Luhmann, 1990c, p. 226)

Accordingly, risk takers within systems internalise external threats, thereby transforming them into risks. What emerges is the coexistence of risks and dangers not just within systems, but also across them: a system is aware of its own risks but is also aware of the risks within other systems. This "not only impedes communication between systems but draws into relief the conflict over what are considered rational rules" (Rosa et al., 2014, p. 104), thus creating further tension between risk takers and those who were not involved in the risk taking, i.e. the victims (Holmström, 2007) or affected parties. The 2008 financial crisis illustrates this point. Senior management and shareholders of the big financial institutions that were deemed "too big to fail" (Sorkin, 2009) perceived the possibility of a financial crisis as a risk, while taxpayers perceived it as a danger. Victims perceive a society full of danger, while risk takers need to justify their decisions and perhaps "as a means for exculpation, use formal tools of risk analysis to justify and legitimize the acceptance of risks" (Rosa et al., 2014, p. 105).

Figure 2.7 illustrates Luhmann's risk model.

There are two systems, A and B. The environment is outside of both systems, and System A is part of system B's environment, while System B is part of system A's environment. Danger originates from the environment and irritates system A, which,

2.2 Luhmann's Sociological Theory on Risk

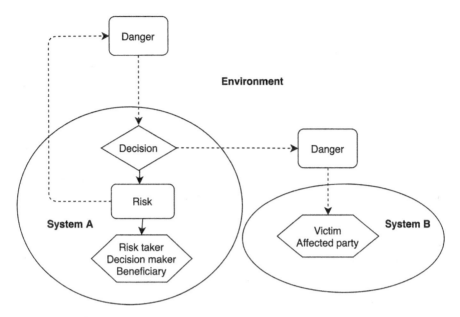

Fig. 2.7 Luhmann's risk model (Luhmann, 1993)

for the sake of illustration, is a financial institution. The financial institution makes a decision in order to internalise the danger. Once internalised, the danger becomes a risk: a self-referential risk because it originates from within the system. However, actions selected by the risk takers also produce second-order dangers that are external to the system and may affect System B who is the victim, the affected party in this scenario. The risk/danger distinction changes depending on who the observer is. In the above framework, the observers are, on the one hand, the risk takers who internalise the danger and transform it into risk and, on the other hand, the victims who were not involved in the decision-making process but who nevertheless face the dangers resulting from the decisions made by the risk takers.

As such, the same event is perceived differently depending on who the affected party or the risk taker is. In addition, it is also perceived differently across different function systems which, as previously discussed, apply different communication logic to the same events. For instance, from the perspective of the economic system, the financial crisis may be perceived as presenting a danger to liquidity and as threatening the ability to make payments. In contrast, the scientific model may perceive it as representing a danger to the knowledge and truth behind market and credit risk models. No common ground can be met across different function systems, and it has been argued that the only way that a function system can deal with risk is to transfer it to another function system (Japp & Kusch, 2008; Rosa et al., 2014).

Luhmann's understanding of risk as a social construction is, for example, supported by Borsch, who argues that the increase of risk awareness in modern society is the result of "the emergence of a new semantics, a new vocabulary with which society describes itself" (Borsch, 2011, p. 102). Similarly, Zinn's (2010) study investigating the increase in the risk discourse in "leading newspapers in the US and the UK such as the New York Times, The Washington Post and the London Times" indicates that "risk seems not to be a phenomenon which mainly rests on the objective state of current societies but is an expression of how we think about uncertain futures and possible harms" (Zinn, 2010, p. 106–7). Although Beck argues that improved science and technological advancements produce more actual risks to society (Beck, 1986, 1992), Rosa et al. (2014) argue that "real" threats have not necessarily increased; they argue that when systems internalise dangers into risks, this creates the illusion that risks are increasing. Luhmann states that the increase of risk perception is due to a convergence of function differentiation and increased and widespread decision-making processes within society; as such, it can be argued that the emergence of risk semantics is engrained in the structure of modern society and is a "distinctly modern phenomenon, inherently linked to functional differentiation" (Japp & Kusche, 2008, p. 77).

The perceived increase of risks is driven by risks in one function system that are perceived as dangers by different function systems and thus operate as irritations to those systems. As Rosa et al. (2014) clarify:

> In advanced modernity the diversity and plurality of systems have reached a point where the coexistence of competing rationales (generated by each system) within a society cannot be ignored. Systems have become more and more aware of not only the risks within their systems, but also the risks (dangers) outside their systems. (p. 104)

Indeed, functionally differentiated systems each have their own risks perceived as dangers to other function systems through the form of irritations, for instance. Such dangers can only be internalised by other function systems in accordance to each function system's specific communicative logic, thus potentially creating further irritations and thus dangers to other function systems (i.e. their environment) which in turn will need to internalise the newly created dangers.

To provide an empirical illustration of Luhmann's risk/danger model, the author moves to a discussion of the "de-risking" trend that emerged between 2015 and 2017 and which, as argued in Sect. 1.9, has been facilitated by the application of the RBA. A number of institutions, including the BIS, FATF, Moneyval and the UK regulator (FCA), have identified a trend in financial institutions seeking to de-risk their businesses (FATF, 2015; FCA, 2015a, b; Moyano & Ross, 2017). Indeed, "according to data by the Financial Stability Board of July 2017, the number of correspondent relationships by global banks with eastern European banks has decreased between 2011-2016 by 20% (almost twice as much as in other regions of the world, such as the Caribbean or Africa)" (Moneyval, 2018, p. 30).

De-risking has been defined by the president of Moneyval as "financial institutions deciding to avoid—rather than to manage—possible money laundering or terrorist financing [TF] risks, by terminating business relationships with entire regions or classes of customers" (Moneyval, 2018, p. 8). The association for AML specialists (ACAMS) extends the list of dangers that financial institutions aim to avoid through de-risking, stating: "The aim is to reduce ML and TF risks exposure

2.2 Luhmann's Sociological Theory on Risk

and limit potential financial sanctions or expensive remediation programs, should regulators identify AML and/or CFT framework failings" (Bukola, 2014). Of course, it should be noted that while ML and TF are identified as risks in these quotes, these would properly be called "dangers" in Luhmann's risk/danger framework. The de-risking phenomenon affects two separate observing systems: the financial institution and the regulator. Furthermore, de-risking signals that financial institutions are refusing to internalise the (Luhmannian) dangers as "risks" within their own systems or are externalising previous risks back to dangers. For financial institutions, such dangers cannot be consistently internalised as risks because they are unsure of their ability "to produce, govern, manage, reduce, or manipulate [them], regardless—more or less—of their probability of occurrence or severity or outcome" (Rosa et al., 2014, p. 106).

To regulators, de-risking clearly represents a danger, as it "may drive financial transactions underground which creates financial exclusion and reduces transparency, thereby increasing money laundering and terrorist financing risks" (FATF, 2015). This concern is also expressed by the FCA which states: "we require banks to put in place and maintain policies and procedures to identify, assess and manage money-laundering risk. This requires banks to use an effective risk-based approach" (FCA, 2015a, b). Thus, when a financial institution transforms a danger "that was formerly seen as external into processable [. . .] and manageable activities" (Renn, 2004, p. 103), its decision generates danger for entities that neither took part in the decision-making process nor benefited from the decision. In this case then, the entities are the regulators (and customers) that were the *victims* of the de-risking process. Thus, alongside the risk/danger distinction, another distinction emerges—that of decision-maker/victim or risk taker/victim (Holmström, 2007).

To protect themselves, financial institutions may simply have aimed to move risks into dangers by moving them out of their own systems into the environment. Thus, by de-risking their own systems financial institutions create irritations for regulators, thus triggering developments (also called resonance in LST) in the regulator subsystems. However, while financial institutions can produce irritations for regulators, they cannot steer regulators' responses to these irritations, which can only be determined within the regulator subsystems themselves. In the UK, for example, regulators threatened to fine financial institutions that could not provide robust rationale for de-risking activities, thus creating dangers and irritations for financial institutions, who then had to decide whether to internalise such newly generated dangers as risk or not. As such, there is a self-perpetuating logic associated with the risk/danger distinction. Danger re-enters the environment because a system makes the decision not to internalise dangers (e.g. ML, TF and regulatory risks) as risks. Thus, another system (e.g. a regulator) may decide to internalise this new danger in the environment as a risk within its own system and may then respond to this risk. In our scenario, the regulator may then respond to the risk of ML, TF, etc. by threatening to fine any financial institution performing unjustified de-risking. This decision then generates new dangers that are perceived as irritations by financial institutions that now need to decide whether to internalise the danger of new regulatory fines or not. Thus, since the financial institution (System A) is located

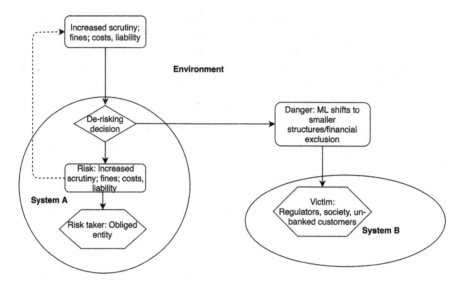

Fig. 2.8 De-risking through Luhmann's risk/danger model (Bukola, 2014; Durner & Shetret, 2015; FCA, 2016)

in the environment of the regulator (System B) and vice versa, decisions in System A generate dangers that may be internalised as risks in System B. System B then responds to the risk by creating new dangers for System A, which may, in turn, decide to internalise these dangers as risks and may then respond by making new decisions perceived as dangers by System B so on and so forth. Thus, the risk/danger distinction is self-referential and reproduces itself at every step of the decision-making chain. As Demetis (2010) explains, "risk cannot therefore be specified or pointed out simply because it is categorised, even when the perception of risk is communicated; its re-genesis will transcend any system that attempts to manipulate it" (p. 113).

Figure 2.8 illustrates de-risking through Luhmann's risk/danger model.

In Fig. 2.8, the top box represents danger external to the system, which, in this context, is a financial institution. Because of increased regulatory scrutiny and dangers associated with certain customers judged as higher ML risks, the financial institution makes the decision to de-risk and thus terminates these relationships. This allows the financial institution to transform a risk into a danger; it generates danger for entities that were not involved in the decision-making process: i.e. the regulator, customers, thus potentially impacting the wider financial system's stability. De-risking may be perceived by regulators as a danger that may affect consumers or create wider competition problems. De-risking may push ML into smaller institutions that lack the resources and expertise needed to manage high-risk customers. Furthermore, it could also push ML and TF into financial mechanisms, such as alternative remittance systems, that exist outside of regulatory scrutiny. Furthermore, de-risking can exclude legitimate businesses and consumers from the financial system, which can have negative effects on a country's economic and social development. Finally, such dangers can threaten the credibility of regulators should they fail to address them. Thus, if regulators find an institution's de-risking to be unjustified, they may create the danger of fines against a financial institution, which, if levied, would then represent a risk that the financial institution would have to internalise because it made the decision to de-risk.

Hardy and Maguire (2019) explore this self-referential phenomenon in the context of how the chemical bisphenol A (BPA) and its effect on the environment and human health have been managed across different stakeholders. The authors explore how organisations have interpreted and perceived risks associated with BPA differently (i.e. toxicologists versus regulators versus endocrinologists) and the way risk management decisions impact other institutions' risks. This, they argue, results into an ecology of risks where institutions' risk management heighten other's risks and connect different stakeholders in a strengthening chain displaying, in the author's opinion, characteristics of structural coupling. Indeed, in the context of AML, the regulator's activities and decisions are structurally coupled to that of financial institutions, while the latter's risk management decisions are structurally coupled to that of regulators. Hence while Perrow argues that risk is an indigenous source of consequences embedded in work (Perrow, 1984), the author believes that risk is indigenous to risk and risk management.

Based on Hardy and Maguire (2019), the following figure aims to illustrate the regenesis of risk described by Demetis (2010) and illustrated by the de-risking phenomenon explored above (Fig .2.9):

Each stakeholder represented in the above diagram has deconstructed ML risk or, as per Hardy and Maguire (2019), translated ML risk into a set of risks that are familiar to them and thus easier to manage. However, as represented by the black arrows, each stakeholder's risk management decisions impact others' risks. The red arrows illustrate how the different stakeholders have become increasingly structurally coupled.

In summary, risks cannot be observed independently of one another ignoring their interconnectedness. As stated by Ackermann, Eden, Williams and Howick, "risks can be seen as a network of interrelated possible events, which may be referred to as risk systemicity" (2007, p. 40).

Risk Governance and Communication According to Luhmann

In Luhmann's risk/danger framework, risk governance concerns either transferring risks to other systems, as per the case above, or "translating the respective codes of each system, leading to a social agreement or collective perception, among systems, that the remaining risks are controllable, manageable, or worth taking" (Rosa et al., 2014, p. 108). For example, the economic sanctions imposed on Russia or North Korea illustrate successful translation of the political system's binary code of power/no power or government/opposition (Luhmann, 1995a; Roth & Schütz, 2015) into

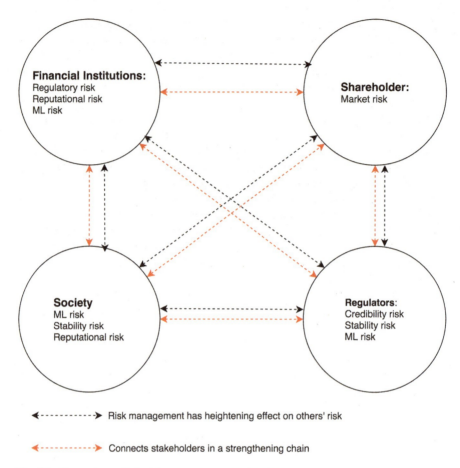

Fig. 2.9 The ecology of ML risk (adapted from Hardy & Maguire, 2019)

payment/no payment. It is important to note, however, that extant literature does not explore how systems translate their respective binary codes and what conditions or circumstances are required for successful translation across systems. This is explored in Chap. 5.

This section aims to further discuss the implications of risk governance in Luhmann's systems theory and, specifically, in his risk/danger model. According to Luhmann, "risk is the hopefully avoidable causal link between decision and damage. In fact the modern obsession with risk management has the practical function of teaching one how to avoid the regret of regrettable decisions" (Luhmann, 1990c, p. 225). Nevertheless, in reviewing the literature that accounts for how institutions handle or avoid the regret of regrettable AML decisions, it would seem that post-decisional regret is never actually avoided. Furthermore, it should be noted that the literature presents ML-related damages and/or losses exclusively as danger related rather than associated with risks that financial institutions have internalised

2.2 Luhmann's Sociological Theory on Risk

by means of decisions. For the purpose of this work, the author defines risk governance as "the identification, assessment and prioritisation of risks followed by coordinated and application of resources to minimise monitor and control the probability and/or impact of unfortunate events" (Njogo, 2012, p. 100). In short, risk governance is "being smart about taking chances" (Hubbard, 2009, p. 10).

In the context of AML, risk governance can be described as follows: the financial institutions' RBA to risk management programmes starts with the identification of the elements or components of the overall risk faced by the firm. Financial institutions then deconstruct risk into identifiable parameters in order to understand the risk they face. The financial institutions observe and deconstruct risk in order to then reconstruct it using predefined distinctions that are system specific. The FATF provides guidance for financial institutions regarding the identification of ML subcategories and terrorism financing risks—"products, services, delivery channels, location of the business and activities, clients and business relationships" (FATF, 2014a, b, p. 7–10). This reiterates that a system "can observe and realise only from within the specific meaning boundaries of the system" (Holmström, 2007, p. 260). Indeed, the obliged entity, as observer, reconstructs risk through parameters "programmed by descriptions enslaved by linguistic frames" (Luhmann, 1990c, p. 223). Thus, the issue is "that category is not truth, but merely cognitive fiction, an act of choice" (Demetis & Angell, 2007, p. 415). Once risk is deconstructed, the observer aims to measure the overall risk through the lens of each of its supposed components and measures the "riskiness" of those components. Each subcategory is evaluated in order to determine whether it represents a low, medium or a high risk of ML. Accordingly, risk profiles emerge across risk departments summarising the constructed risk discourse pertaining to each financial institution and feeding into risk governance programmes. This governance framework is a decision programme. It defines the preconditions required to ensure adequate decision-making in relation to performing the risk/danger distinction.

Thus, communication is an essential aspect of risk governance, and like any system, the AML system (Demetis, 2010) communicates through its binary code:

> Codes are abstract and universally applicable distinctions. Although formulated in terms of a distinction between a positive and a negative value, they contain no indication of which attribution is correct, the positive value or the negative one. It is only under the condition of openness towards both the positive and the negative condition that a social system can identify with a code. If this occurs, it means that the system recognizes as its own all operations that are guided by its own code—and rejects all others. The system and the code are then coupled. The code is the form with which the system distinguishes itself from the environment and organizes its own operative closure. (Luhmann, 1993, p. 78)

For example, alerts relating to a customer or transactions use the suspicious/non-suspicious code (Demetis, 2010). Hence, in order to communicate and to subsequently quantify ML risk and danger, financial institutions are required to apply this suspicious/non-suspicious code to their transactions or customers. Once an alert is generated, it triggers the following decisions: the event communicated through the alert can be acknowledged and internalised by the system as a risk or the financial institution can trigger a SAR instead and communicate it to its environment (i.e. the FIU), as danger.

However, this code seems ambiguous; ML involves multiple types of dangers making it uncertain whether the code can be successfully communicated or not. As documented in the 2015 FCA report on de-risking, as well as the FATF's guidance on the RBA, financial institutions perceive regulatory fines as a major danger intertwined with that of ML. This contrasts with governments', FIUs' and regulatory bodies' understanding of ML danger: having the financial system enable or facilitate either knowingly or unknowingly ML activities. Interestingly, when the UK regulator (called at the time the FSA) adopted the RBA, dangers were defined as "risks to FSA's achievement of its statutory objectives" (Black, 2004, p. 23). They referred to the external environment, consumer and industry-wide developments and regulated industries, all of which represent Luhmannian dangers in terms of the regulator's statutory objectives.

This reflects the differences in how financial institutions and regulatory bodies perceive and communicate ML danger and thus risk (as per Luhmann's information, utterance and understanding). The Barclays Bank case illustrates this gap. As previously discussed, in November 2015, the FCA fined Barclays GBP 72 million. In order to secure a GBP 50 million profit, Barclays arranged and executed a GBP 1.88 billion transaction for clients who were ultra-high-net-worth PEPs. The FCA stated:

> While the FCA makes no finding that the transaction, in fact, involved financial crime, the circumstances of the transaction gave rise to a number of features which, together with the PEP status of the individuals, indicated a higher level of risk [...]. This required Barclays to adhere to a higher level of due skill, care and diligence but Barclays [...] did not follow its standard procedures, preferring instead to take on the clients as quickly as possible and thereby generated GBP 52.3 million in revenue. (FCA, 2015a, b)

This highlights a pertinent point: Barclays Bank was not fined for enabling financial crime but for not following its own internal procedures informed of course by the third AML directive at the time, echoing the financial sector's belief that "the greatest threat to the Banking Industry lies in the regulatory and political backlash that has taken place against banks" (Lascelles & Patel, 2014, p. 4).

This raises the additional issue of competing rationales, and hence systemic codes, within the very same system. For the sake of this example, Barclays will be simplified as a system, and focus will be on just two of Barclays' subsystems: the compliance department and the front office. The compliance team communicated the GBP 1.88 billion transaction in terms of the suspicious/non-suspicious code, while the sales team communicated the GBP 1.88 billion transaction in terms of the payment/non-payment code (refer to Table 2.2). Both subsystems have competing rationales thus rendering the coexistence of both subsystems difficult. Unable to either communicate through code translation or to transfer the danger to the environment, Barclays as a system became the victim (as per the decision-maker/victim distinction made earlier) and faced the GBP 72 million fine (i.e. the danger). Yet, it could also be argued that such a fine is the risk that the front office internalised (along with that of potentially laundering dirty money) in exchange for the GBP 52.3

2.2 Luhmann's Sociological Theory on Risk

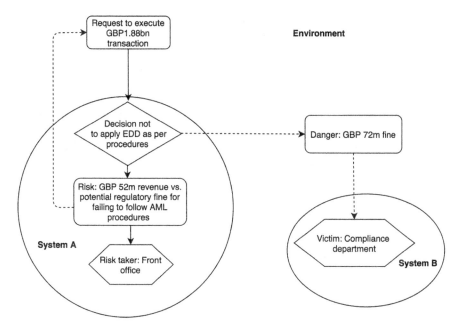

Fig. 2.10 Barclays Bank 2015 fine through Luhmann's risk/danger model (FCA, 2015a, b)

million in revenue. The fact that the fine exceeded the revenue resulted in post-decisional regret, but such a fine remains a risk to the decision-maker.

Indeed, based on Luhmann's systems theory, organisations should have the ability to bridge function systems and hence to bridge communicative logic despite their competing codes. Regardless of contradictory agendas across subsystems, the system as a whole should work towards its goal and avoid internal conflicts. Ultimately, Barclays is a financial institution driven by revenue, profits and shareholder approval; as such, the compliance subsystem could be interpreted as having had to "surrender" to the greater will of the system. The following extract from the FCA report documenting the circumstances leading to the fine certainly points in that direction:

> On the basis of the EDD information available to it at that time (which, as outlined in paragraphs 4.32 to 4.47 below, was inadequate) Legal and Compliance did confirm that the appropriate level of EDD had been conducted, including that the PEPs had been properly identified, and that the Clients' sources of wealth were legitimate. This was not compliant with Barclays' usual procedures that required the front office to give this confirmation. In addition, Legal and Compliance did not have the benefit of the knowledge held by front office senior management about the Business Relationship and a number of relevant issues that had emerged during negotiations between the Clients and senior management. (FCA, 2015a, b, p. 16)

Figure 2.10 illustrates Barclays' case. The front office here is represented as System A, while the compliance department is system B. Both are subsystems of Barclays, which, if represented in Fig. 2.10, would be a circle englobing both A and

B. System A's decision not to apply enhanced due diligence in order to fast track the GBP 1.88 billion transaction and secure GBP 52 million in revenue may result in a potential fine which is the risk that the front office has decided to internalise. The compliance department is the victim who, not having been part of the decision-making process, sees the GBP 72 million fine not as risk but danger.

At this point, the key building blocks of Luhmann's systems theory should be clear; the relevance of Luhmann's work on risk and the risk/danger distinction has been illustrated through two indicative cases, Barclays Bank's 2015 regulatory fine and the de-risking phenomenon, thus demonstrating the versatility of Luhmann's theoretical framework for exploring and understanding the AML domain.

References

Ackermann, F., Eden, C., Williams, T., & Howick, S. (2007). Systemic risk assessment: A case study. *The Journal of the Operational Research Society, 58*(1), 39–51.

ABC News. (2018). *Flake calls Trump-Putin summit an 'Orwellian moment'* [Video]. Accessed Aug 8, 2018, from https://www.facebook.com/ABCNews/videos/10157477658978812/?video_source=permalink

Åkerstrøm Anderson, N. (2001). *The Undecidability of decision* (Copenhagen Business School Working Paper No. 12/2001). Accessed Feb 24, 2016, from https://research-api.cbs.dk/ws/portalfiles/portal/58900668/wp122001.pdf

Ashby, R. (1956). *An introduction to cybernetics*. Chapman & Hall.

Baecker, D. (1994). Soziale Hilfe als Funktionssystem der Gesellschaft. *Zeitschrift für Soziologie, 23*(2), 93–110.

Baecker, D. (2001). Why systems? *Theory, Culture & Society., 18*(1), 59–74.

Beck, U. (1986). *Risk Society*. Sage Publication Ltd.

Beck, U. (1992). *Risk society: Towards a new modernity*. Sage Publications.

Black, J. (2004). *The development of risk-based regulation in Financial Services: Canada, the UK and Australia*, ESRC Centre for the Analysis of Risk and Regulation, London School of Economics. Accessed Oct 15, 2018, from https://www.researchgate.net/profile/Julia_Black/publication/268395436_The_Development_of_Risk_Based_Regulation_in_Financial_Services_Canada_the_UK_and_Australia_A_Research_Report/links/54d5c60b0cf24647580 83251/The-Development-of-Risk-Based-Regulation-in-Financial-Services-Canada-the-UK-and-Australia-A-Research-Report.pdf

Borsch, C. (2011). *Niklas Luhmann*. Routledge.

Bukola, A. (2014) *AML de-risking: An effective method of plugging AML control failures*? ACAMS. Accessed Feb 12, 2016. Available online: http://www.acams.org/wp-content/uploads/2015/08/AML-De-Risking-Aneffective-method-of-plugging-AML-control-failures-B-Adisa.pdf

Burkart, G. (2005). Die Familie in der Systemtheorie. In G. Runkel & G. Burkart (Eds.), *Funktionssysteme der Gesellschaft. Beiträge zur Systemtheorie von Niklas Luhmann* (pp. 101–128). VS Verlag.

Cohn, A., Fehr, E., & Marechal, M. A. (2014). Business culture and dishonesty in the banking industry. *Nature, 516*, 86–89.

Demetis, D., & Angell, I. (2007). The risk-based approach to AML: Representation, paradox and the 3rd directive. *Journal of Money Laundering control, 10*(4), 412–428.

Demetis, D. (2010). *Technology and anti-money laundering: A systems theory and risk-based approach*. Edward Elgar.

References

Douglas, M., & Wildavsky, A. (1982). *Risk and culture. An essay on the selection of technological and environmental dangers*. University of California Press.

Durner, T., & Shetret, L. (2015). *Understanding Bank De-risking and its effects on financial inclusion*. Oxfam. Accessed Feb 3, 2016, from https://www.globalcenter.org/wp-content/uploads/2015/11/rr-bank-de-risking-181115-en.pdf

Egmont Group. (2019). *About*. Accessed Mar 27, 2018, from https://egmontgroup.org/en/content/about

FATF. (2010). *Money laundering using new payment methods*. FATF. Accessed Sep 8, 2018, from http://www.fatf-gafi.org/media/fatf/documents/reports/ML%20using%20New%20Payment%20Methods.pdf

FATF. (2014a). *Guidance for a risk based approach: The banking sector*. Accessed Jun 2, 2015, from http://www.fatf-gafi.org/media/fatf/documents/reports/Risk-Based-Approach-Banking-Sector.pdf. : FATF.

FATF. (2014b, October 23). "*FATF clarifies risk-based approach: Case-by-case, not wholesale de-risking*", conclusion from FATF Plenary on 22 October, Paris. Accessed Sep 2, 2020, from https://www.fatfgafi.org/documents/documents/rba-and-de-risking.html

FATF. (2015). *FATF takes action to tackle de-risking*. FATF. Accessed Feb 12, 2016, from http://www.fatf-gafi.org/publications/fatfrecommendations/documents/fatf-action-to-tackle-de-risking.html

Financial Conduct Authority. (2015a). *Final notice 2015: Barclays Bank PLC–November 2015*. Accessed Dec 5, 2015, from https://www.fca.org.uk/publication/final-notices/barclays-bank-nov-2015.pdf

Financial Conduct Authority. (2015b). *FCA fines Barclays £72 million for poor handling of financial crime risks*. (Press release 26 November) Accessed Dec 5, 2015, from http://www.fca.org.uk/news/fca-fines-barclays-72-million-for-poor-handling-of-financial-crime-risks

Financial Conduct Authority. (2016, February 24). *Derisking banks' management of money-laundering risk–FCA expectations*. [Company announcement] Accessed Feb 12, 2016, from https://www.fca.org.uk/about/what/enforcing/money-laundering/derisking

Francot-Timmermans, L.M.A. (2008). *Normativity's re-entry. Niklas Luhmann's social systems theory*. PhD thesis. Utrecht University. Accessed Jun 10, 2019, from https://www.researchgate.net/publication/27709640_Normativity's_Re-entry_Niklas_Luhmann's_Social_Systems_Theory_Society_and_Law

Foucault, M. (1991). Governmentality. In G. Burchell, C. Gordon, & P. Miller (Eds.), *The foucault effect, studies in governmentality* (pp. 87–104). Harvester/Wheatsheaf.

Gephart, R. P., Jr. (1993). The textual approach; risk and blame in disaster sensemaking. *Academy of Management, 36*(6), 1465–1514.

Goffman, E. (1963). *Stigma: Notes on the management of spoiled identity*. Prentice-Hall.

Goffman, E. (1974). *Frame analysis: An essay on the organization of experience*. Harper & Row.

Hardy, C., & Maguire, S. (2019). Organizations, risk translations and the ecology of risks: The discursive construction of a novel risk. Academy of management. Accessed Mar 4, 2020, from https://www.researchgate.net/publication/332824257_Organizations_Risk_Translations_and_the_Ecology_of_Risks_The_Discursive_Construction_of_a_Novel_Risk

Henkel, A. (2010). Systemtheoretische Methodologie: Beobachtung mit Systemreferenz Gesellschaft. In R. John, A. Henkel, & J. Rückert-John (Eds.), *Die Methodologien des Systems* (pp. 181–200). VSVerlag für Sozialwissenschaften.

Hubbard, D. W. (2009). *The failure of risk management: Why It's broken and how to fix it*. John Wiley & Sons, Inc.

Holmström, S. (2007). Niklas Luhmann: Contingency, risk, trust and reflection. *Public Relations Review, 33*(3), 255–262.

Interpol. (2013). *Guide to carbon trading crime*, INTERPOL. Accessed May 3, 2015, from http://www.interpol.int/en/News-and-media/News/2013/PR090/

Japp, K. P. (2000). Distinguishing non-knowledge. *The Canadian Journal of Sociology/Cahiers canadiens de sociologie, 25*(2), 225–238.

Japp, K. P., & Kusche, I. (2008). Systems theories and risk. In J. O. Zinn (Ed.), *Social theories of risk and uncertainty* (pp. 76–102). Blackwell Publishing.
King, M., & Thornhill, C. (2003). *Niklas Luhmann's theory of politics and law.* Palgrave Macmillan.
Kneer, G., & Nassehi, A. (1993). *Niklas Luhmanns Theorie sozialer Systeme.* Wilhem Fink Verlag.
Knudsen, M. (2007). Structural couplings between organizations and functions systems. *Cybernetics and human knowing, 14*(2–3), 111–131.
Lascelles, D., & Patel, K. (2014). *Banking banana skins.* Centre for the Study of Financial Innovation (CSFI). Accessed July 29, 2015, from https://www.pwc.com/gx/en/banking-capital-markets/banana-skins/assets/pwc-banking-banana-skins-2014-v2-april.pdf
Lee, D. (2000). The Society of Society: The grand finale of Niklas Luhmann. *Sociological Theory, 18*(2), 320–330.
Lewandowski, S. (2004). *Sexualität in den Zeiten funktionaler Differenzierung. Eine systemtheoretische Analyse.* Transcript.
Luhmann, N. (1962). Function und kausalität. *Kölner Zeitschrift für Soziologie und Sozialpsychlogie, 19,* 615–644.
Luhmann, N. (1976). Generalized media and the problem of contingency. In J. J. Loubser, R. C. Baum, A. Effrat, & V. M. Lidz (Eds.), *Explorations in general theory in social science: Essays in honor of Talcott Parsons* (pp. 507–532). Free Press.
Luhmann, N. (1977). Differentiation of society. *Canadian Journal of Sociology, 2*(1), 29–54.
Luhmann, N. (1981). The improbability of communication. *International Social Science Journal, 33*(1), 122–131.
Luhmann, N. (1982a). The world society as a social system. *International Journal of General Systems, 8*(3), 131–138.
Luhmann, N. (1982b). *The differentiation of society. Translated from German by Holmes, S., and Larmore, C.* Columbia University Press.
Luhmann, N. (1983). Insistence on systems theory: Perspectives from Germany–an essay. *Social Forces, 61*(4), 987–998.
Luhmann, N. (1989). *Ecological communication.* Translated by John Bednarz Jr. University of Chicago Press. Original edition, 1986.
Luhmann, N. (1990a). *Political theory in the welfare state.* De Gruyter.
Luhmann, N. (1990b). Der medizinische code. *Soziologische Aufklärung, 5,* 183–195.
Luhmann, N. (1990c). Technology, environment and social risk: A systems perspective. *Industrial Crisis Quarterly, 4,* 223–231.
Luhmann, N. (1993). *Risk: A sociological theory.* Transaction Publishers.
Luhmann, N. (1994). Politicians, honesty and the higher amorality of politics. *Theory, Culture and Society, 11*(2), 25–36.
Luhmann, N. (1995a). *Social systems.* Stanford University Press.
Luhmann, N. (1995b). The paradox of observing systems. *Cultural Critique, 31,* 37–55.
Luhmann, N. (1997). Limits of steering. *Theory, Culture & Society, 14*(1), 41–57.
Luhmann, N. (1998). *Love as passion: The codification of intimacy.* Stanford University Press.
Luhmann, N. (2000a). *The reality of the mass media.* Stanford University Press.
Luhmann, N. (2000b). *Art as a social system.* Stanford University Press.
Luhmann, N. (2000c). *Die Religion der Gesellschaft.* Suhrkamp.
Luhmann, N. (2002). Deconstruction as second-order observation. In W. Rasch (Ed.), *Theories of distinction. Redescribing the descriptions of modernity* (pp. 94–110). Stanford University Press.
Luhmann, N. (2003). Organization. In T. Bakken & T. Hernes (Eds.), *Autopoietic organization theory: Drawing on Niklas Luhmann's social systems perspective* (Oslo: Abstrakt) (pp. 125–157). Liber.
Luhmann, N. (2004). *Law as a social system.* Oxford University Press.
Luhmann, N. (2005). The paradox of decision making. In Seidl, D and Becker, H.K. (eds.), Niklas Luhmann and organization studies. : Abstrakt, Liber, Copenhagen Business School Press.
Luhmann, N. (2011). *Organisation und Entscheidung.* Springer.

References

Luhmann, N. (2018). *Organization and decision*. Edited by Baecker, D. Translated by Barrett, R. Cambridge University Press.
Maturana, H., & Varela, F. (1980). *Autopoiesis and cognition: The realization of the living*. Reidel.
Maturana, H. R. (1981). Autopoiesis. In M. Zeleny (Ed.), *Autopoiesis: A theory of living organization* (pp. 18–33). Elsevier-North Holland.
Maurer, K. (2010). Communication and language, *Pandaemonium germanicum* 16, 1–21. Accessed Feb 16, 2018, from http://www.scielo.br/pdf/pg/n16/a02n16.pdf
Mazoue, A. (2016, May 3). *Multi-billion Euro carbon-trading fraud trial opens in Paris*. France24. [Online]. Accessed Feb 15, 2017, from https://www.france24.com/en/20160503-france-trial-multi-billion-carbon-emissions-trading-fraud-opens-paris
Messner, C. (2014). Introduction to special issue SI: Luhmann. *International Journal for the Semiotics of Law, 27*(2), 313–324.
Midgley, G., & Pinzón, L. A. (2011). Boundary critique and its implications for conflict prevention. *Journal of the Operational Research Society, 62*, 1543–1554.
Moeller, H.-G. (2006). *Luhmann explained*. Open Court.
Mingers, J. (2002). Can social systems be autopoietic? Assessing Luhmann's social theory. *The Sociological Review, 50*(2), 278–299.
Moneyval. (2018). *Annual Report 2017*. Strasbourg: Council of Europe. Accessed Sep 17, 2018, from https://rm.coe.int/moneyval-annual-report-2017-eng/16808af3c2
Moyano, J. P., & Ross, O. (2017). KYC optimization using distributed ledger technology. *Business Information Systems Engineering, 59*(6), 411–423.
Murphy, J. W. (1982). Talcott Parsons and Niklas Luhmann: Two versions of the social 'system'. *International Review of Modern Sociology, 12*(2), 291–301.
Nassehi, A. (2005). Organizations as decision machines: Niklas Luhmann's theory of organized social systems. *The Sociological Review, 53*, 178–191.
Njogo, B. O. (2012). Risk management in the Nigerian banking industry. *Kuwait Chapter of Arabian Journal of Business and Management Review, 1*(10), 100–109.
Parsons, T. (1951). *The social system*. Routledge and Kegan Paul.
Pask, G. (1969). The meaning of cybernetics in the behavioural sciences. In J. Rose (Ed.), *Second-order cybernetics: Progress of cybernetics* (Vol. 1, pp. 15–45). Gordon and Breach.
Pateau, M. (2013). Niklas Luhmann and cybernetics. *Journal of Sociocybernetics, 11*(1), 75–103.
Perrow, C. (1984). *Normal accidents: Living with risk systems*. Basic.
Quick, T. (2003) *Autopoiesis*. Accessed Oct 15, 2018. Available online: http://www.cs.ucl.ac.uk/staff/t.quick/autopoiesis.html
Randal, D. (2012, July 1). Banking scandal: Greedy, shoddy, deceitful. A modern cesspit, *The independent*, [Online]. Accessed Mar 14, 2018, from https://www.independent.co.uk/news/business/news/banking-scandal-greedy-shoddy-deceitful-a-modern-cesspit-7901949.html
Reese-Schäfer, W. (1999). *Luhmann zur Einführung*. Junius.
Reese-Schäfer, W. (2007). *Politisches Denken heute: Zivilgesellschaft, Globalisierung und Menschenrechte*. Oldenbourg.
Reichel, A. (2012). Civil society as a system. In O. Renn, A. Reichel, & J. Bauer (Eds.), *Civil society for sustainability* (pp. 56–72). Europäischer Hochschulverlag.
Renn, O. (2004). Perceptions of risk. *The Geneva Papers on Risk and Insurance, 29*(1), 102–114.
Rosa, E., McRight, A., & Renn, O. (2014). *The risk society revisited: Social theory and risk governance*. Temple University Press.
Roth, S., & Schütz, A. (2015). Ten systems: Towards a canon of function systems. *Cybernetics, 22*(4), 11–31.
Seidl, D. (2004). *Luhmann's theory of autopoietic social systems*, Munich Business Research. Accessed Feb 11, 2016, from http://www.zfog.bwl.uni-muenchen.de/files/mitarbeiter/paper2004_2.pdf.
Seidl, D., & Becker, K. H. (2006). Organizations as distinction generating systems. *Organization, 13*(1), 9–35.

Seidl, D., & Mormann, R. (2015). Niklas Luhmann as organization theorist. In P. Adler, P. du Gay, & M. Reed (Eds.), *Oxford handbook of sociology, social theory and organization studies: Contemporary currents*. Oxford University Press.

Spencer Brown, G. (1969). *The laws of form*. The Julian Press, INC.

Sorkin, A. R. (2009). *Too big to fail: The inside story of how wall street and Washington fought to save the financial system from crisis--and themselves*. Viking.

Vanderstraeten, R. (2002). Parsons, Luhmann and the theorem of double contingency. *Journal of Classical Sociology, 2*(1), 77–92.

Varela, F. J., Maturana, H. R., & Uribe, R. (1974). Autopoiesis: The Organization of Living Systems, its characterization and a model. *Biosystems, 5*, 187–196.

Voss, M. (2005, January 29–29). Towards a reopening of risk societies: A contribution to the debate on risk and danger. *Learning about Risk, Launch Conference ESRC, Social contexts and Responses to Risk*. Canterbury. Accessed Nov 11, 2015, from http://www.kent.ac.uk/scarr/events/finalpapers/martin%20voss.pdf

Von Bertalanffy, L. (1968). *General system theory: Foundations, development*. George Braziller.

Von Foerster, H. (1981). *Observing systems*. Intersystems Publications.

von Foerster, H. et al. (1974). *Cybernetics of cybernetics, BCL Report 73.38, Biological* Computer Laboratory, Dept. of Electrical Engineering, University of Illinois.

Von Glasersfeld, E. (Ed.). (1991). *Radical constructivism in mathematics education*. Kluwer.

Von Heiseler, T.N. (2008, Feburary 4). *Interview mit Humberto Maturana*. Accessed Feb 11, 2018, from https://www.scribd.com/document/339122660/Interview-Humberto-Maturana

Zinn, J. O. (2010). Risk as discourse: Interdisciplinary perspectives. *Critical Approaches to Discourse Analysis across Disciplines, 4*(2), 106–124.

Chapter 3
Case Studies and Empirical Findings

This chapter documents the main findings from the comparative cross-case analysis that was carried out over a 4-month period in two financial intelligence units (FIUs) that are based in the EU. Section 3.1 provides a brief overview of the research methodology; Sect. 3.2 summarises the suspicious activity reports (SARs) receipt and analysis process. Sections 3.3–3.6 document the findings pertaining to the SARs regime, the RBA, financial institutions' risk appetites and the de-risking/re-risking phenomenon. Finally, Table 3.2 summarises all 28 findings, which will subsequently be analysed and discussed in the discussion chapter that follows.

3.1 Fieldwork and Research

The author secured access to two financial intelligence units for her research. Once access was granted, interviews with the FATF, regulators, finance practitioners, the economic crime bureau, the US Secret Services and ML defence lawyers were also conducted. The variety of interview subjects provided an enormous scope for investigative depth. While the majority of the research for this book was conducted within financial intelligence units, the ability to complement the research with interviews from experts in the field of ML prevention across a wide array of organisations was illuminating and enriched the integrity of the research.

Table 3.1 provides a list of interviewees both within and external to the FIUs, identifying their position, interview type (semistructured or unstructured), organisation type and number of interviews conducted.

Access to the first research site (hereafter referred to as FIU1) was granted from November 2015 to early February 2016. Access to the second site (hereafter referred to as FIU2) was granted between November 2017 and December 2017. Since the interviews were held between 2015 and 2017, the AML community was generally focused on the Fourth AML Directive (effective June 2017); however, the directive was not yet legally binding at the time of the interviews. During this time, the Fifth

Table 3.1 List of interviewees

Interviewee no.	Position/semistructured or unstructured interview	Firm type	No. of interviews
01	Senior manager—semistructured	FIU1	2
02	MLRO—semistructured	Corporate bank	1
03	CFO—unstructured	Lending institution	3
04	Director—semistructured	Regulator	3
05	Strategic analyst—semistructured	FIU1	1
06	FIU director—semistructured	FIU1	3
07	Consultant—semistructured	FIU1	2
08	Senior manager—semistructured	FIU1	1
09	Analyst—semistructured	FIU1	1
10	AML risk practitioner—semistructured	Retail bank	2
11	Detective—unstructured	Police, Economic Crime Bureau	1
12	MLRO—semistructured	Retail bank	2
13	Detective—unstructured	Police, Cybercrime Bureau	1
14	Special agent—unstructured	US Secret Service	1
15	Non-executive director (NED)	Management funds company	1
16	Partner—unstructured	Law firm	1
17	Analyst—semistructured	FIU2	1
18	Secretariat—semistructured	FIU2	1
19	Secretariat—semistructured	FIU2	1
20	Analyst—semistructured	FIU2	1
21	Analyst—semistructured	FIU2	1
22	Analyst—semistructured	FIU2	1
23	Policy analyst—semistructured	FATF	1
24	Representative of the Wolfsberg Group—semistructured	Wolfsberg Group	1
25	Senior partner—unstructured	Big 4	1
26	Analyst—semistructured	FIU2	1
27	FIU director—semistructured	FIU2	3
28	MLRO—semistructured	Management fund company	1
29	Partner—unstructured	Consultancy, Big 4	1
30	Global markets CFO—semistructured	Investment bank under sanctions regime	1

AML Directive had also been announced, thus generating further uncertainty across the AML community.

A nondisclosure agreement (NDA) with FIU1 and a confidentiality agreement with FIU2 were signed. Therefore, to comply with both of these agreements, all data have been anonymised, and secondary checks have been conducted to eliminate the possibility of de-anonymisation (e.g. through inferences regarding location/identity). The author selected FIU1 and 2 because of their respective differences in terms of geographical location, organisational culture, culture, FIU type, neighbouring jurisdictions and types of ML threats faced. A comparative cross-case analysis (George, 1979; George & McKeown, 1985) was performed to identify and analyse common and divergent themes, which facilitated the comparison of commonalities and differences regarding events, actions and processes faced in the two different organisations.

3.2 The SAR Analysis and Escalation Process: Summary

Summary of FIU1's SAR Process

FIU1 calls its SARs *suspicious transaction reports* (STRs); however for consistency with FIU2 and to avoid confusion, the author refers to FIU1's STRs as "SARs" as well. FIU1 receives its SARs via email or via XML files submitted by obliged entities. They are all eventually manually entered into their system which is a very time-consuming process. FIU1 receives, on average, more than 10,000 SARs per year, but the majority are threshold based (i.e. they are currency transaction reports), not actual suspicious activity reports.

The preliminary analyst of the FIU1's secretariat inputs the SAR data into an Excel spreadsheet and decides either to archive the SAR or to open a case file, based on the following criteria: (a) connections with previous SARs, (b) any pre-identified trends relating to the SAR (e.g. small denominations exchanged for larger notes), (c) whether the SAR contains the name of an individual who has already been flagged and (d) any relation to objective indicators of a predicate crime (e.g. narcotics). SARs that have been flagged by reporting entities as urgent are prioritised for analysis, as are any SARs relating to asset confiscation and sanctions.

SARs that are archived are not analysed further because they are considered to be either immaterial are currency transaction reports (the Fourth AML Directive requires obliged entities to report transactions above EUR 10,000) that do not represent an ML threat or the workload necessitates archiving them. However, they are treated as intelligence and can be transferred to the case file list if a relevant trend emerges or if associated monetary amounts warrant that. According to the FIU1 director, SARs are retained for 10 years after receipt.

SARs that have a case file status are escalated to the head of analytics who then evaluates whether the case file status should be maintained or whether the SAR should be archived. The analyst and the head of analytics explained that a case file is opened based on objective indicators of ML, although identifying a predicate offence is not required. The list of FIU1 "objective indicators" is publicly available on the FIU's website and is designed to facilitate the reporting process. However, the problem with this approach is that launderers can access this list and identify how to avoid detection. Such indicators vary widely, ranging, for example, from an individual's behaviour to an individual's legal address being listed as post-box. If a decision is made to maintain the case file status, then the head of analytics distributes the SAR to the analysts.

Analysts can have up to 15 cases running at the same time, and the FIU disseminates case files to other countries or to law enforcement agencies (LEAs) for relevant intelligence-sharing purposes. If a case leads to prosecution, the case file is sent to the prosecution office. Once a year, the FIU reviews its database to evaluate the stage of its case files, monitor general progress and track those that have been passed on to LEAs for intelligence-sharing purposes. It should be noted, however, that all case files have the same status in the system.

Summary of FIU2's SAR Process

The FIU2 process is different from that of FIU1 because it relies completely on a software into which obliged entities manually input all relevant information relating to their SARs, thus saving the FIU the effort. This is particularly important for FIU2 because they receive an average of 30,000 SARs per year. This volume is driven by electronic commerce platforms operating in FIU2's jurisdiction, which, at the time of the fieldwork, are responsible for approximately 80% of the SARs logged into the software.

Driven by the categorisation options available in the software, FIU2 manages different types of SARs depending on whether they relate to terrorism financing, have associated transactions, are behavioural (e.g. based on refusal to provide certain documents when opening an account) or are logged by commerce platforms operating within their jurisdiction. Again, for consistency with FIU1, the author refers to all FIU2's suspicious reports as SARs.

FIU2 uses a rota system. Every week, a different analyst is given the task of reviewing *all* incoming SARs, requiring the analyst to assess the integrity of the data submitted and assess whether there are any links to existing SARs. Then, each SAR is risk scored and a decision is made to (self-)assign the SAR to the analyst on duty or forward it to an analyst whose expertise is better aligned with the SAR (e.g. trade-based ML, terrorism financing or cyberbased ML).

FIU2 uses a risk scoring matrix that helps the analyst on duty to risk score new SARs that come in and assign them to the appropriate analysts. The risk scoring matrix (documented in more detail in Chap. 4, "The FIU: externalizing danger and de-risking") works by mapping the probability of the ML event from happening against the impact of the event. The impact is defined as the consequences of the event and is broken down into a set of criteria, such as life endangerment, country or regional political stability (e.g. terrorist attacks, human trafficking, kidnap for ransom schemes, corruption), physical and mental safety (e.g. extorsion), economic stability (e.g. insider trading, tax evasion) and financial losses ranging from severe to small. Analysts explain that the impact is generally evaluated based on the amount of money associated with the SAR, although SARs associated with terrorism financing

3.3 The SARs Regime 93

are not evaluated on monetary associations because terrorism financing amounts are typically low. This approach is not devised to maximise potential asset confiscation; rather, it aids analysts' risk scoring. The primary fields on the software that the analyst fills in are *reporting entity, predicate offence, associated prosecutor* and *risk score*.

Risk scores determine whether a SAR will be archived, analysed (case created) or passed on to the LEA. Thus, in cases of SARs relating, for instance, to abuse of vulnerability (a recognised criminal offence in the FIU2 jurisdiction), pedophilia or terrorism, the SAR is disseminated to the relevant LEA and/or the intelligence services. A *minimum* score of 5 (on a scale of 1 to 10) is assigned to such SARs. Cases of false wire transfers are passed on to the secretariat. SARs with medium scores (3 or 4) are taken seriously and are assigned a "case-created" status. The analysis of certain SARs can take many months, as analysts rely on information from the reporting entity, other obliged entities that may have information on the SAR, other FIUs or governing bodies. When the analysis is complete, the case is sent to the LEA office via a software and is reviewed. If nothing happens within 3 or 4 weeks, the report is closed, which requires the LEA office to issue a closing letter, meaning that the case has ended and no further actions will be required or that there is enough information to move forward with prosecution.

If the SAR is given a risk score of 1 or 2, the report is considered "not opened", and the LEA office is not involved. Such cases generally relate to banks refusing to onboard customers, false transfers or names that have appeared in the media (for instance, in the context of the Paradise and Panama papers). To summarise, both FIUs have different setups, processes and technology access. This determines the FIUs' respective approaches to SARs receipt, analysis and dissemination functions, which are explored in the following sections.

3.3 The SARs Regime

As seen in the previous section, FIU1 does not apply a formalised RBA to the receipt and analysis of the SARs it receives nor does it risk rate the obliged entities who submit those SARs. Similarly, FIU2 does not risk rate the obliged entities from which it receives SARs but does use a formal RBA methodology for risk rating the SARs it receives. Hence, as described in the summary above, when a SAR is submitted to FIU2, it is subjected to a risk scoring process in which an analyst assigns a risk score of between 1 and 10. The risk is assessed based on the client or transaction(s) to which the SAR relates, but the risk profile of the obliged entity (as per the FIU's observation) does not influence the SAR's assigned risk score. This is surprising since interviews held with analysts from both FIUs indicate that obliged entities develop reputations regarding their risk profiles and appetites. For instance, one FIU1 analyst explained that "there are serious tax evasion schemes from Scandinavian banks" (Interviewee no. 09). Similarly, the FIU2 director stated: "the vulnerability or weakness of obliged entities generally manifests itself through obliged entities who submit few SARs" (Interviewee no. 27).

Yet, despite the awareness of obliged entities' weaknesses, vulnerabilities or propensity to facilitate ML or tax evasion, neither FIU collects intelligence relating to the risk profiles of obliged entities even though such intelligence would support FIUs in their analysis of SARs and would possibly impact the SAR prioritisation processes. Thus, despite FIUs' knowledge and awareness of the risk profiles of obliged entities, the lack of formalised data relating to the risk profiles of obliged entities is malaligned with the current AML framework, which is based on obliged entities' customer risk profiles, SAR submissions and the naming, shaming and sanctioning that occurs when such entities are identified as facilitating or failing to prevent ML. Indeed, as stated by one interviewee, an economic crime defence lawyer, "the law and the penal code make no distinction between the actual money launderer and the professional obliged entity" (Interviewee no. 16) since, ultimately, "the professionals are the ones who get heavily sanctioned when wrongdoing is identified" (Interviewee no. 16). Indeed, the Fourth AML Directive states: "The importance of combating money laundering and terrorist financing should result in Member States laying down effective, proportionate and dissuasive administrative sanctions and measures in national law for failure to respect the national provisions transposing this Directive" (Council Directive 2015/849 of 20 May 2015, Paragraph 59).

Accordingly, it is astonishing that FIU intelligence related to obliged entities' vulnerability to ML or tax evasion, for instance, is not taken into account when assessing SAR submissions. Indeed, an FIU2 analyst stated that "some banks have a known risk profile within the FIU and, in such cases, a training is delivered to the relevant institution along with an informal monitoring and communication made with the regulator" (Interviewee no. 26). However, despite the intelligence relating to an institution's risk profile, the FIU2 director explained: "ML risk must be assessed in relation to the client and not the institution that submits the SAR" (Interviewee no. 27). This contradicts statements from FIU analysts who clearly acknowledge institutional risk profiles and appetites and is clearly illustrated by the multiple tax evasion scandals involving, for example, UBS and Deutsche Bank.

Finding 1: FIUs do not use their knowledge of financial institutions' risk profiles as intelligence in the analysis of SARs. Thus, intelligence is excluded at early stages of SAR prioritisation and analysis.

In addition, FIUs do not and are not expected to systematically apply a formalised and standardised RBA when analysing their SARs—this despite the FATF's drive for an enhanced RBA, reflected in paragraph 22 of the Fourth AML Directive, which emphasises a holistic RBA; paragraphs 29 and 30, which underscore the need for enhanced due diligence; and paragraphs 21 and 24, which both call for the application of national risk assessments. According to the FIU2 director "The RBA is a

3.3 The SARs Regime

concept of vigilance. There is no RBA on suspicion" (Interviewee no. 27). However, as indicated in the summary of the SAR analysis process above, FIU2 does apply its own RBA to assign resources and prioritise certain SARs due to the sheer volume of SARs they receive. Indeed, in direct contradiction to his previous statement, the FIU2 director stated: "once the SAR hits the FIU, at that point the FIU applies its own RBA" (Interviewee no. 27). Hence, it is possible to apply an RBA based on suspicion of potential wrongdoing, despite the Interviewee no. 27's earlier claim.

The FIU2 director's statement highlights the variability in applying the RBA. What is striking, however, is that while obliged entities must each employ the RBA as per the FATF's requirements, FIUs do not need to have a robustly formalised or documented RBA applied at all, as observed in FIU2 where associated monetary amounts and existing workload drives the prioritisation of SAR analysis. While obliged entities are expected to apply and justify their RBA and their overarching AML framework, FIUs are held to different standards.

Finding 2: Unlike FIs, FIUs are not required to use an RBA when analysing the SARs they receive. This means that FIUs use different methods to prioritise and manage their SARs.

The underlying logic of this is, of course, driven by the fact that obliged entities are perceived as potentially performing or at least facilitating money laundering activities, while FIUs serve a governmental and regulatory purpose and are not viewed as ML gateways into the financial sector. According to the FIU2 director, "the drive to increase revenue is clearly an element of the failures that are observed [in banks] and clearly beyond a certain threshold, negligence becomes guilty" (Interviewee no. 27). Corroborating the view of FIU2's director, an analyst asserted that "banks want to make money and, right now, very little is made with mortgages; banks therefore focus on private banking and want to share very little information and intelligence with FIUs" (Interviewee no. 20). A banking risk practitioner interviewed in the FIU1 jurisdiction stated that "the key issue is that banks want to do less SARs-related work while FIUs feel that banks do not do enough work in relation to the SARs they submit" (Interviewee no. 10). Thus, in terms of the end-to-end SAR process, issues of accountability and clarity of ownership emerge. Although FIUs own the SAR process, they heavily depend on obliged entities, which appear to be essential to SAR creation and thus the SAR process. Yet, other than being required by law to log SARs, obliged entities have few performance incentives and SAR reporting motivations, which is explored in more detail below.

FIUs constitute a fundamental element of a country's AML framework, but there is no business as usual type governance in place to oversee their performance and no tools available to monitor and assess whether the current SAR process actually works despite its ambiguous end-to-end accountability and ownership issues. The FATF's interpretative note to Recommendation 29 goes as far as to state that "the FIU should be operationally independent and autonomous, meaning that the FIU should have the authority and capacity to carry out its functions freely, including the autonomous decision to analyse, request and/or disseminate specific information" (FATF, 2021, p. 103).

The case of the German FIU illustrates how bad things have to become for an external authority to intervene. In 2020, the German prosecution office launched an investigation into the German FIU's failure to analyse and disseminate 46,000 SARs. In addition, the FIU had failed to forward 8 SARs relating to transactions to Africa, worth EUR 1.7 million (Vedrenne & Couvée, 2020, n. p.). While some German investigators "labelled the FIU a significant danger to domestic security" (ibid., n.p.), Switzerland's ex-FIU head stated that it is any FIU's raison d'être to filter SARs which ultimately do not evidence criminal behaviour per se.

In essence, "due to a lack of prescriptive international standards, FIUs maintain significant differences as regards their functions, competences and powers" (Council Directive 2018/843 of 30 May 2018, Paragraph 16). This was clearly observed during the research undertaken at both FIU1 and FIU2: there is no monitoring as to whether the *right* SARs (i.e. SARs that relate to an activity that is not only suspicious but truly related to ML) make it to the FIU in the first place and, if reported to the FIU, whether the right SARs make it past the analysis stage and are forwarded to LEA offices. As stated by the FIU1 director, "right now we have no way of determining which SAR is good for resolution and which one is not" (Interviewee no. 06). This ultimately comes down to the fact that while "there are objective indicators of ML, there are no indicators of an actual predicate offence" (Interviewee no. 06).

The difficulties associated with identifying a predicate offence based on SARs alone are consistently raised by interviewees from the banking industry, the police force, legal practices, the regulatory industry and FIUs alike. According to a midsized bank risk practitioner operating in FIU1's jurisdiction: "[for SARs related to Russia], FIUs have no information about predicate offences and without that, there is not much FIUs can do" (Interviewee no. 10). Similarly, a police investigator stated: "the problem is that it is not easy to find out specifics of predicate offences based on suspicions. The predicate offence is not obvious so there is no criminal offence as such to prosecute" (Interviewee no. 11). Furthermore, although money laundering is an offence in and of itself; it is not easy to prove that money is indeed being laundered and is thus difficult to prosecute. For instance, even when looking at activities on the dark web where predicate offences are clearly documented and advertised, prosecution is not straightforward. As a cybercrime police investigator explains "the dark net offers a wide market for (online) child sexual exploitation, weapons, drug selling, malware purchasing. You find traditional crime and not just cyberrelated crime. But, again, identifying the predicate offence is tricky, as crime occurs all over the world" (Interviewee no. 13). A lawyer specialising in AML explained that "a SAR has no geographical nor temporal limits. The bank denounces the transaction. The law is geared against the laundering of money and not against the individual initiating the laundering, i.e. the launderer" (Interviewee no. 16). For instance, at the time of the investigation, a high-profile case of money laundering was uncovered and heavily discussed in the media. However, when interviewed on the matter, the FIU1 director stated: "those transactions just passed through our jurisdiction, the SARs do not show us anything" (Interviewee no. 6). Similarly, the FIU1 head of analytics asserted that such transactions were "transit money only and they did not know it came from suspicious sources. The obliged entity should have asked for more information, what kind of business it was and why an offshore company has the account in a specific country, but they did not" (Interviewee no. 01). Another analyst stated that "because of the absence of a clear link to a predicate offence, there are not a lot of SARs that make it to LEAs" (Interviewee no. 26).

Finding 3: The current AML framework focuses on identifying and punishing obliged entities executing ML, as opposed to individuals initiating ML. However, the SAR regime focuses on individuals initiating ML.

Finding 4: SARs do not establish evidence of predicate offences nor money laundering. SARs rarely result in ML investigations and prosecutions, leading AML practitioners to question the efficiency of the SAR regime.

Such feedback on SARs certainly explains the absence of data relating to the conversion rate of SARs into actual prosecutions. Analysts and LEAs are unable to consistently access sources to identify a predicate offence. For instance, in 2016, FIU2 transferred more than 500 cases to LEAs. When the author asked for data relating to SARs that had been escalated to a LEA and led to actual prosecution, analysts from FIU1 responded that they did not have robust data on the matter. Interviewee no. 9, a SARs analyst, stated that "only 10% of SARs end up as criminal reports that make it to the prosecution office". However, the head of analytics reported that "70% of SARs are sent to law enforcement" (Interviewee no. 1). Similarly, while the FIU1's 2016 annual report states that 50% of computer fraud-related court decisions were initiated by SAR submissions, when interviewing analysts and other FIU practitioners, there was no clarity regarding the origin of such figures nor who had performed the data mining. When the author approached the Economic Crime Bureau to get further information regarding the source of these figures, the police officer interviewed stated that "10 to 20% of the cases investigated by the economic crime bureau come from the FIU" (Interviewee no. 11); however, he was not able to tell the author anything about the source of these figures. Similarly, the FIU employee in charge of performing strategic and data analyses stated that "there was no analysis nor overview of SARs passed onto LEAs or [information regarding] decisions taken by courts or how many court decisions were triggered by the FIU work" (Interviewee no. 5).

The author found this astonishing, as she expected that both FIU1 and FIU2 collected data relating to court proceedings, court decisions and funds confiscated and seized based on SARs passed on to LEAs. However, this was not the case, and neither FIU seems to have a system in place to identify and manage such data, even though such data would certainly contribute to the organisation's performance indicators and enable the monitoring and assessment of FIU performance. When challenged on this point, the FIU2's director responded that "evaluating the SAR system based on conviction rates is inadequate as what matters is the quality of legal proceedings. In addition, the SAR regime is designed as a prevention tool and not a repression tool. If it were the latter, such a system would have repercussions for the financial stability of a country" (Interviewee no. 27). Interestingly, the FIU2 Annual Report states that "a report given to the prosecution office is not the provision of proof but aims to open an investigation". However, if only a small number of investigations are opened in response to the large volume of SARs reports generated, the utility of such reports seems questionable.

Furthermore, many of the ML scandals that have been reported and documented in the media over the past 5 years were not identified by FIUs (e.g. 1MBD, Danske, ABLV, Versobank, Pilatus, BNP Paribas, Credit Agricole, SocGen, BPCE, Deutsche Bank, Santander, ING, Credit Suisse, Rothschild, HSBC). Rather, the majority of prominent ML scandals were brought to light via US-led investigations, sanctions violations, whistleblowing and/or media investigations. Discussions with FIU1 and FIU2 confirm that neither of these organisations identified the prominent ML scandals that impacted their jurisdictions. However, both organisations supported investigations pertaining to the cases above insofar as they were relevant to their respective jurisdictions. Such support, however, was retroactive and not deployed preventatively. It might be assumed that under such circumstances, the relevant FIU would have been asked to justify its performance and/or existence as an investigative body or that it would have faced some sort of backlash for failing to act pre-emptively. This, however, does not seem to have been the case, at least not publicly.

This point was raised with an analyst, who responded by saying that "no matter what, the FIU has to exist and, as such, there is no illusion to be had in relation to the overall system and its level of sophistication" (Interviewee no. 17). Indeed, FATF Recommendation 29 states that "countries should establish a FIU that serves as a national centre for the receipt and analysis of: (a) suspicious transaction reports and (b) other information relevant to money laundering" (FATF, 2016, p. 22), and the IMF stresses the importance of FIUs as "steps in combating financial crime" (World Bank, 2004, p. 5). Similarly, the Fourth AML Directive states the following:

> All Member States have, or should, set up operationally independent and autonomous FIUs to collect and analyse the information which they receive with the aim of establishing links between suspicious transactions and underlying criminal activity in order to prevent and combat money laundering and terrorist financing. An operationally independent and autonomous FIU should mean that the FIU has the authority and capacity to carry out its functions freely, including the autonomous decision to analyse, request and disseminate specific information. Suspicious transactions and other information relevant to money laundering, associated predicate offences and terrorist financing should be reported to the FIU, which should serve as a central national unit for receiving, analysing and disseminating to the competent authorities the results of its analyses. All suspicious transactions, including attempted transactions, should be reported, regardless of the amount of the transaction. Reported information could also include threshold-based information. (Council Directive 2015/849 of 20 May 2015, Paragraph 37)

3.3 The SARs Regime

Hence, the point made by Interviewee no. 17 indicates that despite these statements by the IMF, World Bank and the European Union, analysts are aware of the inability of SARs to effectively generate LEA-led investigations. The SARs regime thus seems incapable of acting as a preventive tool (as it cannot effectively and consistently trace sources back to a predicate offence). In addition, based on the vertiginous list of ML violations, it also does not appear to act as a repressive tool. Ultimately, FIUs are simply not required to justify their own performance. Although mutual evaluation reports review each country's compliance to FATF recommendations including FIUs' processes, remediation and associated progress reports are performed over a number of years depending on the mutual evaluation assessment and whether the jurisdiction falls under the "enhanced follow-up process" or "regular follow-up process". Similarly, national risk assessments do not look at FIUs' individual performances in relation to SARs initiating ML prosecutions or asset confiscation. Instead such reports document SARs and break them down in terms of typology, reporting entities or number of analyses started.

Hence, FIUs do not compete with any other type of organisation in terms of the receipt, analysis and resolution of SARs. They are not incentivised to justify their legitimacy. This absence of competition may be a driving factor motivating the issues raised by Interviewees 5, 11, 12 and 17. Hence, if SARs rarely result in ML investigations and prosecutions as per Finding 4, and are useful neither as repressive tools (as they employ ineffective incentives resulting in underreporting) nor preventative tools, it would seem that national governments should consider re-evaluating the current SAR process.

Finding 5: SARs represent neither repressive nor preventive tools.

Finding 6: FIUs do not analyse nor review their performance since FIUs do not need to compete with other bodies in terms of SAR analysis.

Hence, what emerges from the interviews mentioned above is the fact that FIUs essentially act as a conduit for information transferred between obliged entities and law enforcement agencies. Indeed, as an organisation, FIUs rely heavily on two separate types of organisations—namely, law enforcement agencies and obliged entities—for preventing ML and initiating prosecution. As one analyst pertinently stated: "SAR cases are worked within the framework that the financial institution has given the analyst and *that* says it all" (Interviewee no. 09). This is compounded by the fact that "obliged entities do not provide sufficient information when submitting their SARs" (Interviewee no. 18). Another analyst confirmed that "obliged entities do not submit much information in their SARs because they believe that their job is done once a SAR is submitted to the FIU and, given that an FIU analyst does this day in day out, the obliged entities assume that the analyst will be able to fill in the gaps. Obliged entities do not realise that an analyst cannot and does not have a global view of the SAR" (Interviewee no. 26). Similarly, the head of analytics within FIU1 wondered "how FIUs are meant to give typology reports when, ultimately, financial institutions are on the frontline and really see what the typologies are, such as cryptocurrency abuse, for instance" (Interviewee no. 01). According to a money laundering reporting officer who also worked in the police force and FIU1, "obliged entities do not provide much information in SARs because there are not many ML cases and it is more about suspicion or softer elements relating to an analyst's gut feeling. As such, there is no point in sending account details because they will not be analysed by the FIU and they will be archived" (Interviewee no. 12). Similarly, Interviewee no. 18 confirms that "the quality of SARs submitted by banks is low. In light of the fact that fiscal infractions are now a predicate offence, SARs flagged as related to fiscal infractions have, of course, gone up in volume, but the quality of information is so low that FIU analysts often have to change the infraction category in the system to *undetermined*". Hence, regarding low SAR quality, one FIU1 analyst explained that some SARs are simply archived and "waiting for their time" (Interviewee no. 9).

Another issue concerns accessing and understanding the data that obliged entities submit. Once a SAR is submitted to the FIU, the latter requests information in order to create and analyse a case. This information request relates to raw transaction data pertaining to one account, one customer, related accounts and related customers. This may involve transaction data dating to the beginning of the relationship, the past 5 years, the past 10 years, etc. Such requests entail great bureaucratic efforts for obliged entities, and FIUs take this into account by building into their process flows timelines of, for example, 2 weeks, 4 weeks, 2 months and sometimes even 6 months for the information to be returned by the obliged entities. It is important to note that these time frames generated by the FIU's internal process itself substantially complicate the money trail, sometimes beyond recognition, thus undermining potential asset confiscation efforts. Thus, as Interviewee no. 3 explains, in institutions there is:

> extremely poor data quality, as information is often maintained in multiple systems, which are legacies of previous institutions that have been merged with the current one and sit on top of one another. The data is therefore fragmented. Also, there is the problem of data definition even within the same organisation. One department will define a customer one way while another department will define it differently. For example, how do you define a customer? Are three accounts held by one legal person classified as the "same customer" or as three separate customers? It is therefore important to define each data point and to realise that data contextualisation is important to understanding it. (Interviewee no. 3)

Finding 7: The SAR analysis performed by FIUs is limited by the poor quality of SAR information submitted to FIUs.

Finding 8: The SAR process depends on FIUs who rely on obliged entities completely and obliged entities who, constrained by regulation, cooperate reluctantly. This creates inefficiencies.

Because of the limitation of SARs in terms of not only the scant information that obliged entities submit through them, analysis and dissemination to LEAs are limited, due to the difficulty in identifying a predicate offence associated with an actual SAR and the challenges associated with information requests. SARs often therefore have no other utility than becoming part of a database. Thus, ultimately, the purpose of SARs being sent on to FIUs has increasingly become less about identifying a predicate offence and more about creating a network of ML intelligence. This ML intelligence may or may not lead to the identification of predicate crimes and thus prosecution if the right connection is made to the right archived SAR. As asserted by the FIU2 director when challenged on the effectiveness of SARs: "what matters is having a database that enables analysts to establish links *between* SARs" (Interviewee no. 27, emphasis added). This statement leads the author to question the role of FIUs in the current framework and how it is positioned in relation to regulators and obliged entities. The FIU2 2017 Annual Report clearly states that the purpose of the FIU is to kickstart an investigation and does not aim to provide irrefutable proof of an infraction. As such, the FIU's role is to act as an intermediary, assessing obliged entities' SARs, adding ML intelligence to them and selecting which SARs should be passed on to LEAs. The persisting issue, however, is that there is a low proportion of SARs that result in investigations and a high number of SARs that are archived, thus leading the author to question the overall process and the efficacy of the current function of SARs, as well as FIUs. In sum, while SARs aim to flag ML risk, the existing system fails to isolate and address this risk. This topic is explored and discussed in the following chapter.

Before moving on to the following section, it is worth mentioning the 2018 Bruun & Hjejle "Report on the Non-Resident Portfolio at Danske Bank's Estonian Branch", as it provides a rare insight into how SAR reporting and investigations may fail to convert into prosecution. The report documents that from 2007 to 2015, the Estonian branch of Danske Bank filed 653 SARs based on 10,000 high-risk non-resident portfolio customers to which it provided services. Based on those 653 SARs, 1007 customers were investigated by the FIU. However, while SARs filed in relation to the non-resident portfolio accounted for 13% of SARs filed by the Estonia branch of Danske Bank between 2007 and 2015, the non-resident portfolio accounted for 30% of the FIU inquiries received by the Estonian branch during this time period (Bruun & Hjejle, 2018, p. 30).

Yet, despite a greater percentage of FIU inquiries based on the non-resident portfolio, and as confirmed by Howard Wilkinson, Danske Bank's whistleblower, the Estonian FIU was unable to initiate court proceedings. This was despite the fact that some of those SARs were linked to activities that are now known to have been illegal, again confirmed by Howard Wilkinson at the November 2018 European parliamentary hearing. This strongly highlights the weakness of the current test of suspicion. While, "the boundary between unease and suspicion is unrealistic and difficult to identify" (Law Commission, 2018, p. 106), the boundary between suspicion and prosecution appears almost impossible to cross.

FIUs Develop Competitive Advantages Over Others

The FIU's environment is determined by the government of its jurisdiction, its political and economic environment, reporting entities, the FIU's geographical location and, finally, the other FIUs it interacts with in the context of SAR analysis and investigations. The interviews conducted for this study indicate that an FIU's environment indirectly determines an FIU's advantages or disadvantages in comparison with other FIUs. This section documents FIU environments and explains how they drive certain FIU operations.

Technology

Technology funding and access is one field in which some FIUs develop a competitive edge. The high volume of SARs that FIUs receive is a topic that has been heavily discussed and addressed in the AML industry and academic literature (Financial Intelligence Group, 2017; Chaikin, 2009; Levi, 2002; Goldby, 2013). The current study aligns with this research in that it has identified the high volume of SARs as an issue worthy of investigation. The previous FIU1 director explained: "We do receive a lot of SARs, roughly 11,000 a year. Those are threshold-based reports (i.e. currency transaction reports). We also receive roughly 2,000 more traditional SARs per year" (Interviewee no. 12). Similarly, the FIU1 head of analytics stated that "each analyst will have 10 to 15 cases going at the same time" and that "the manual workload is too high right now and that is a real issue: SARs coming in from the obliged entities come in different formats so, in essence, a lot of manual conversion and input is being performed by analysts" (Interviewee no. 01). Additionally, problems with SAR quality (discussed in Sect. 3.3) compound the volume issue, as underscored by Interviewee no. 01: "I wonder what needs to be done to ensure that financial institutions give better information when submitting their SARs. Systematically we need to go back to them and ask for additional information and data that they do not think of adding in, even though they could".

FIU2 interviews and documents reflect similar issues associated with handling a high volume of SARs. The 2016 FIU2 Annual Report mentions a vertiginous increase in SAR submissions over 2015, and 2015 SAR submissions had already increased by more than 50% over 2014. The FIU2 director indicated that this increase in SARs was the result of "the implementation of two electronic-commerce companies within [the jurisdiction] who report suspicious activities relating to all 28 Member States of the European Union. This decision was of course driven by politics and the role of the FIU2 secretariat changed drastically when [Company 1 and 2] arrived in [FIU2's jurisdiction]. We had to perform a lot of data input manually" (Interviewee no. 20).

Another issue mentioned by one of the interviewees is the fact that "the laundering of fiscal fraud has just been recognised as a predicate crime in [the jurisdiction] and, as such, there is a tsunami of defensive reporting" (Interviewee no. 16).

3.3 The SARs Regime

Obviously, this impacted the volume of SARs and is acknowledged in the jurisdiction's 2017 FIU report, which attributes the increase of over 7000 SARs (over 2016) to not only a greater presence of electronic commerce companies and accrued awareness of and sensitivity to terrorism financing but also to tax crimes. A number of the interviewees labelled the issue of tax fraud being categorised as a predicate offence as a political decision that has a number of consequences. Indeed, one FIU2 analyst stated that "this decision will ultimately mean more SARs and more work for us" (Interviewee no. 21). This was confirmed by the FIU2 director who said: "each directive is a political decision. In our jurisdiction, taxes are taken from the source but there has been a big increase of tax-related SARs internationally and this is it" (Interviewee no. 27). Similarly, the AML legal specialist stated that "for [FIU2 jurisdiction], the choice to categorise fiscal fraud on the list of predicate offences is the result of political pressure and not that of legal constraints" (Interviewee no. 16). In an email exchange, he further explained:

> A close reading of the Fourth Directive shows that the FATF's choice of states to define tax evasion as sufficiently serious to be considered a primary money-laundering offense was indeed maintained by the Fourth Directive in its article 3 §4 subparagraph f: all offenses, including criminal tax offenses relating to direct and indirect taxes and as defined by the national law of the Member States, which are punishable by deprivation of liberty or a measure of maximum duration of more than one year or, in those Member States whose legal system provides for a minimum threshold for offenses, all offenses which are punishable by deprivation of liberty or a security measure of a minimum duration of more than six months; [FIU2 jurisdiction] defines primary offenses by the minimum threshold criterion. Tax scam is punishable by a minimum of one month's imprisonment, and until January 1, 2017 was not a "designated offense" (that is, listed in Article [anonymised] of our Penal Code) nor was it included in the last indent of Article [anonymised] (...) and any other offense punishable by a minimum of six months' imprisonment). So, to strictly read the text of the Fourth directive, the [FIU2 jurisdiction] legislator was not obliged to classify tax fraud as one of the primary offenses. Under international pressure, [FIU2 jurisdiction] has ceded and registered aggravated tax fraud (newly created) and tax fraud in the list of designated offenses of Article [anonymised] of the Penal Code. The Fourth Directive is not yet transposed, [which] therefore leaves the choice to the Member States to choose whether or not tax fraud is a primary offense. (Interviewee no. 16)

The above interviews highlight the level of political pressure that is imposed on FIUs when governments consider launching national initiatives. For instance, in FIU1's jurisdiction, an initiative was announced in 2016 that aimed to attract more investment into the country. However, when the banking sector realised that the government had changed neither the law nor AML regulation to enable the banking sector to support the initiative while adhering to national AML regulation, the project was postponed and finally relaunched in 2018 on a more modest scale. When interviewed about this, the money laundering reporting officer of a small-to-midsized retail bank (who was the previous FIU1 director and had also supported the regulator in performing the national risk assessment) stated the following: "I do not like that project at all. Suddenly the project became bigger and the government decided to open it to a great number of individuals. It has implications from a tax revenue perspective and generates problems from an ML perspective. There is a need to invest in knowledge and infrastructure first" (Interviewee no. 12). Similarly, when interviewed on the matter, the regulator stated that "this project may lead to such a big risk. The industry is aware of the risks and is looking at building greater technology" (Interviewee no. 4). Hence, what emerges from such interviews is the importance of the right support, namely, investment in infrastructure, training and technology. If such requirements are not enabled by the government or regulating bodies, important national initiatives may collapse before they even have a chance to launch or, if launched, endanger the wider AML framework and expose jurisdictions to further ML or TF risks.

While conducting interviews, a certain frustration on the part of the bankers emerged: they felt that banks were under pressure to deliver the government's vision without having adequate assurances from the government or regulators that should any ML risks arise, they would be supported and protected. Indeed, as stated by the money laundering reporting officer of a small corporate bank: "There are requirements in place for onboarding. But, only last week did the ministry of [anonymised] sign a paper so that banks can [perform onboarding a certain way] and not [another way]. The idea is moving towards the use of [electronic channels for onboarding] but this will take some time" (Interviewee no. 2). When discussing matters of nationwide initiatives aimed at improving a jurisdiction's economy, the FIU2 director, in contrast to the FIU1 director, expressed that they had adequate support. He stated that "the main risk in relation to accepting the implementation of such big electronic commerce companies in [the jurisdiction] would have been for the FIU2 to not have the right tools to process and disseminate the SARs they submit" (Interviewee no. 27).

Indeed, the fieldwork performed within both FIU1 and FIU2 highlighted the contrast in resources and technology to which different FIUs have access. More specifically, the above summary of FIU2 identified the use of two applications: goAML, available to all UN member states and self-funded, and the Financial Intelligence Unit Network (FIU.NET), the EU information exchange platform available to all EU member states and EU funded. According to the UN's website, 49 FIUs are currently using goAML. And, while all European Union FIUs have access to FIU.NET, it is not possible to ascertain how many of the 28 FIUs within the EU actively use it. In fact, during the 3 months spent within FIU1 conducting research, the interviewees never mentioned using FIU.NET. Interestingly, a 2019 EC report on the cooperation between FIUs states "this tool has not been used by the FIUs to its full potential and the issue of a better engagement by the FIUs has been a recurring item on the EU FIUs' Platform agenda" (European Commission, 2019, p. 8).

Nevertheless, the purpose and use of both applications should be briefly explained: goAML is a platform that enables the collection, management (through queries and matching), analysis, tracking and reporting of SARs. For example, within the FIU2, "once a week, the analyst in charge of sorting out new SARs receives them all through goAML" (Interviewee no. 17). In this case, goAML also acts as the interface that is downloaded and used by obliged entities. The advantage of the tool is that "all the procedures are documented and stored in goAML presented as workflows that have been specifically configured to match the needs of the FIU"

(Interviewee no. 18). Another advantage is that "goAML tracks all the SAR case files, average resolution time and number of closed case files" (Interviewee no. 26).

FIU2 told the author that goTrace would soon be implemented: "This is a product that has also been developed by UNDOC and enables FIUs to compare and match different FIUs databases" (Interviewee no. 18). The advantage of such a tool is that it foments FIU cooperation while preserving data privacy, as goTrace encrypts the records. Thus, goTrace offers FIUs the ability to see whether the SARs they are working on are related to a greater network of SARs, thus facilitating intelligence exchange and, eventually, potentially increasing prosecution rates.

FIU.NET is the result of Council Decision 2000/642/JHA and was also adopted to promote the cooperation and exchange of intelligence between EU's FIUs in the EU. It is designed to enable multilateral exchanges of SAR-related information. For FIU2, the main advantage of FIU.NET is that it is a SAR exchange platform that enables obliged entities to directly communicate with other FIUs without using FIU2 as an intermediary. FIU.NET is a decentralised system; hence all connected FIUs have their FIU.NET tool and manage their own information. Thus, in the case of the FIU2 jurisdiction, which, as previously mentioned, is home to two electronic commerce companies, FIU.NET is an excellent tool. For all SARs relating to transactions across the entire EU, instead of reporting to SARs to FIU2, the electronic commerce companies use FIU.NET to report "such SARs straight to the concerned country. The FIU2 does not even have to deal with those" (Interviewee no. 17). Indeed, when interviewing the FIU2's secretariat, the author was advised that, ultimately, "the secretariat's role changed when [Electronic Commerce Company 1 and 2] arrived in [the jurisdiction]. Our role was about manual input. It became too much with [Electronic Commerce Company 1 and 2]. And then we transferred this job back to [Electronic Commerce Company 1 and 2]" (Interviewee no. 18). It is interesting to note that "[Electronic Commerce Company 1 and 2] invested a lot of money in their own systems in order to improve their reporting" (Interviewee no. 26).

This cross-border reporting has also greatly impacted other FIUs. Indeed, the FIU2 director reported that "certain FIUs, state that such SARs are none of their concern given that the declaring party (i.e. the electronic commerce company) is not based in their jurisdiction" (Interview no. 27). This is part of a wider issue; he notes that "there is access to a lot of data via FIU.NET sitting across 28 member states and, as such, this increases the number of SARs FIUs have to deal with. In essence, FIUs need to adapt because we are ultimately talking about millions of entries. (...) There is clearly an increase in the amount of information received and more and more exchanges between FIUs. There will be countries who will happily work with other FIUs and others who will aim to deliver the strict minimum" (Interview no. 27).

Indeed, as an analyst explained, in addition to data exchange, FIU.NET also enables the use of another tool: Ma^{3}tch (autonomous, anonymous, analysis), which is a matching tool within FIU.NET that enables FIUs to match names in order to identify relevant data located at other FIUs. Since the data is anonymised, there is no breach of the General Data Protection Regulation (GDPR): "FIU2 uses this feature once a month and downloads a list of potential matches it has with other FIUs and assesses whether the risk score that was assigned to a SAR should be re-evaluated" (Interviewee no. 21). An important issue raised by both the secretariat and the FIU2 director is the fact that "FIU.NET has issues with processing such [a large] volume of data and there may be a risk that it may not be able to disseminate SARs to relevant jurisdictions" (Interviewee no. 27). This issue was also raised in the FIU2 2016 Annual Report, the 2017 Europol meeting on the FIU platform and the 2020 European Commission on FIUs cooperation. All three sources indicate that "FIU. NET is a victim of its own success" (FIU2 2016 Annual Report, p. [not reported]).

In summary, while FIU2 uses tools such as goAML that enable obliged entities to submit SARs in a standardised format, FIU1 works with three different types of SAR submission formats and manually inputs the information into an Excel spreadsheet. Similarly, through the use of FIU.NET, FIU2 has the ability to transfer a very high volume of SAR information processing back to its obliged entities. As mentioned by the FIU2 director "there is almost a competitive disadvantage for certain FIUs that are simply not able to process the data they receive" (Interviewee no. 27). In addition, goAML enables FIU2 to tweak SAR acceptance rules and make them stricter. The FIU2 director states that "to manage the high influx of SARs, rejection rules are stricter, especially in relation to mandatory fields that are not completed by obliged entities. (...) [An example of] such a field is the typology indicator that obliged entities do not populate when submitting a SAR" (Interviewee no. 27). The FIU2 director confirms that although the FIU cannot develop stricter rejection rules (as it cannot risk being accused of complicating the SAR reporting process), FIU2 has the ability to control the flow and the quality of SARs being logged. In contrast, FIU1 does not have this capacity.

Compared to FIU2, FIU1's manual workload is excessive. Analysis of the end-to-end process confirms that SARs come in different formats and, as such, a great deal of manual conversion and input is required. In addition, FIU1 cannot easily establish links between SARs and previous disseminations of information because the database used by analysts has limitations. As explained by the FIU1 director, some SARs are archived because there is either a high workload or the SAR contains intelligence that has very little relevance as a stand-alone SAR. In addition, because FIU1 (in contrast to FIU2) uses nonstandardised reports, some key information will be missed by obliged entities. However, discussion with FIU2 clarified that the standardised SAR form doesn't necessarily prevent obliged entities from "missing" information. As Interviewee no. 12 explains:

> there are not many ML cases and it is more about suspicions than anything else, it is about softer elements relating to the analyst's gut feeling. As such, there is no point in sending account details because the underlying SAR will not be analysed and will end up archived. Actually, Professor Levi has written an article that claims that the SAR system has not impacted ML whatsoever. (Interviewee no. 12)

Finding 9: *Although some FIUs have the ability to manage SARs quality and/or flow, they are nonetheless expected by law not to reject SARs and to analyse them, as FIUs cannot be seen as impeding the SAR reporting process.*

Finding 10: Some FIUs benefit from the willingness of governments and obliged entities to invest in specific software and technology, enabling FIUs to pass certain processes to other organisations, thus facilitating day-to-day operation.

Geographical Location

Interviews held with both FIUs emphasised the importance of geographical location and its influence on the operations of different FIUs. Depending on the jurisdiction and its neighbouring countries, the FIU faces different kinds of ML typologies, handles transactions coming from certain jurisdictions of ill repute and engages with other FIUs using varying levels of goodwill and cooperation. At the time of research, an ML event emerged in FIU1's jurisdiction. When pressed by the author on the topic and what the FIU could have done differently to prevent ML, the FIU1 director's response was "this money was transit money, and the Russian FIU is difficult, it will not co-operate, they simply do not help." Hence, to cooperate effectively, FIUs must take into account the particular characteristics of other FIUs, which may be influenced by the political climate of the geographic region in which they are located. The FIU2 director described the great levels of cooperation the organisation enjoyed with its counterparts in western Europe. However, in contrast to the FIU2 director, Interviewee no. 1 from FIU1 complained about slow responses from the French FIU, on par with Russia or Italy, but claimed that Baltic FIUs tend to deliver quick responses.

In sum, the *danger* (as per Luhmann's framework, see Chap. 2) that FIUs must contend with is represented not only by the threat of underperforming counterparts but also by their geographical proximity to ML hubs. The proximity of FIUs to ML hubs is an issue that came up throughout the empirical research. A number of practitioners discussed how the globalisation of the financial world has led to the globalisation of the ML business; for example, Russian and Azeri money made its way to the UK in the 2017 case involving Russian and Azerbaijani laundromats (OCCRP, 2017). Interviewee no. 7 stated that "clean up here in [FIU1 jurisdiction] is focused on Russia. But the problem is that Russian customers cannot be removed. They have a high presence here with contacts in Ukraine and Russia" (Interviewee no. 7). Likewise, Interviewee no. 10 explained that "Russia and Ukraine transit through [anonymised jurisdiction] and the cash makes its way to our jurisdiction" (Interviewee no. 10). Interviewee no. 12 asserted that "[FIU1 jurisdiction] is a transfer platform for Russia and Ukraine. This is its main risk. In addition, with us being part of the ex-USSR, there is a big stigma attached to that and a reputational risk". Finally, the regulator in FIU1's jurisdiction suggested that the proximity to [anonymised jurisdiction] is a danger in itself: "They are very open to Russian money and aspire to become the Switzerland of eastern Europe. They attract Russian money: Non-resident deposits represent 55% in [anonymised jurisdiction] of which 95% is from Russia. To give you a sense of what that means, here in the FIU1 jurisdiction, only 15% of non-resident money is Russia related" (Interviewee no. 4).

Finding 11: An FIU's jurisdiction and/or proximity to certain problematic jurisdictions are indicators of potential support or cooperation as well as potential dangers or vulnerabilities that need to be internalised by the relevant FIUs.

Law and Constitution

Another advantage that some jurisdictions have over others involves their own laws and constitutions. Indeed, while certain jurisdictions allow for the reversal of the burden of proof, others are required to strictly abide by the principle of the presumption of innocence. The FATF president's report "Experience, Challenges and Best Practices" on AML and CFT for judges and prosecutors (FATF, 2018) documents that "countries that permit a shifting or dynamic burden of proof have expressed that this has proven to be very useful" (FATF, 2018, p. 28). This ultimately means that the predicate offence would not need to be proven in order to prosecute an ML offence, which was discussed in the FATF president's report and the FIU1's 2016 and 2017 Annual Report. Thus, the laws and constitution of a jurisdiction may moderate an FIU's minimum standards and requirements regarding the depth and the extent to which SAR analyses and investigations are required to demonstrate a predicate offence. Thus, FIUs that are not required to prove a predicate offence in order to initiate prosecution associated with a SAR would have a competitive advantage in this regard.

Finding 12: An FIU's geographical location, law, or constitution may either facilitate FIU operations or represent a danger that FIUs need to internalise and convert into risk.

3.4 The Risk-Based Approach

Financial Institutions and Their Relationships with AML and ML

Discussions with the regulator and FIU analysts in both jurisdictions investigated highlight the certainty across the industry that financial institutions are ultimately profit driven and not incentivised to enforce the AML framework to the best of their abilities. As seen above, despite the threat of financial and regulatory sanctions, a number of analysts expressed their scepticism about the integrity of financial institutions. One interviewee working at the FATF stated that "the biggest financial institutions understand very well the RBA, but they simply do not wish to see risks. Or they refuse to implement the right measures based on identified risks" (Interviewee no. 23). The long list of financial institutions that have been fined for ML provides ample evidence of this. At the time of writing, Danske Bank, Deutsche Bank, Swedbank and Nordea had all been fined for ML, indicating failure to meet their AML obligations (Jensen and Virki, 2018; Harding, 2019). This demonstrates that the trend of ML violations is certainly not decreasing. Yet, despite the avalanche of shortcomings, the FATF, the European Commission and national governments continue to entrust financial institutions with key AML responsibilities. They hold financial institutions accountable for failures to enforce and apply AML and expect them to continue managing ML risks by using the RBA.

Furthermore, the FIU2 director lamented the fact that "the RBA has become more complicated under the Fourth AML Directive. Just have a look at Annex III and see for yourself!" (Interviewee no. 27). Indeed, Annex III of the Fourth AML Directive sets out a list of *potential* higher-risk situations that obliged entities must consider when performing their risk-based assessments. Essentially, the more compliance that is required by firms, the more that transactions need to be monitored, and the more in-depth customer due diligence that needs to be performed and documented. Similarly, the FIU1 head of the supervision division explained that not only will some obliged entities struggle with such new requirements, but such requirements will also lead to unforeseen complications:

> With the Fourth AML Directive, all OEs will need to discuss their risks and mitigate them. OEs such as pawnshops will need to do that, but the question is how will such institutions do it? It could be decided to actually exempt them from such a requirement. The other issue is accounting service providers. They are likely to describe their risks in the least risky kind of way to circumvent Fourth AML Directive requirements. This new process will force me to review the rationalization that is being performed by OEs and the risk associated with that is the launching of court cases, should they not agree with my opinion in relation to the risk rating that has been performed. I will therefore need to advise sectors as to what risks they really are facing. (Interviewee no. 08)

Interviewee no. 08 obviously has clear concerns regarding obliged entities' integrity and ability when it comes to complying with their RBA responsibilities and believes that he will be required to monitor and enforce adherence. Interestingly, in terms of ML prevention, risk practitioners working in obliged entities also raised the potential lack of integrity among their peers as an issue. The compliance director and money laundering reporting officer of an independent management company for over 50 investment funds stated that there is "a certain element of intentionality" (Interviewee no. 28) when discussing the case of a well-known private bank that had recently been sanctioned. Similarly, the ML risk practitioner of a large retail bank highlighted the fact that "[anonymised bank] used to knowingly do high-risk business (the interviewee is referring here to taking big deposits of non-resident Russians) and did not take informal warnings of the regulator (into consideration)"

(Interviewee no. 10). Likewise, the money laundering reporting officer of a medium-sized commercial bank stated that "[anonymised bank] has had two fines in a row from the regulator. Back in 2015 this fine related to insufficient controls in relation to a beneficial owner. There is a poor compliance culture there" (Interviewee no. 02).

Such concerns are also reflected in the secondary data reviewed as part of the research. For instance, the report on ING's criminal investigation produced by the Netherland's Public Prosecution Office indicates that for ING NL, "compliance was often considered less important than the business" (Openbaar Ministerie, 2018, p. 17). Also, regarding the biggest ML scandal of 2018, the report on the non-resident portfolio at Danske Bank's Estonian branch (Bruun & Hjejle, 2018) documents the investigation performed by the Bruun and Hjejle law firm and suggests that Danske Bank's Estonian branch may have been actively involved in ML activities rather than simply a passive entity whose infrastructure was exploited for ML purposes. The investigation addressed "possible cooperation between customers and employees with the Estonian branch (internal collusion)" (Bruun & Hjejle, 2018, p. 4) and analysed the 2013 whistleblowing report sent to a member of Danske Bank's executive board, entitled "Whistleblowing Disclosure—Knowingly Dealing with Criminals in Estonia Branch" (Bruun & Hjejle, 2018, p. 51). *The Financial Times* confirms the report's content, stating that in December 2018, ten former employees of Danske Bank Estonia had been detained by the Estonian prosecutor on suspicion of "knowingly enabling money laundering" (Milne, 2018b).

Thus, interviews with risk practitioners along with review of secondary data indicate that both ML and AML activities are performed alongside one another within financial institutions. FIU1, for instance, stated in its 2017 Annual Report that there are market participants that are willing to break rules and enable ML to a certain extent. The regulator of FIU1's jurisdiction stated:

> In the financial sector, on top of general risk mitigation measures, real-life events such as the Panama Papers scandal, the Russian Laundromat case, the Moldova case, the exit of Deutsche Bank from the correspondent bank's market, heavy financial sanctions for AML regulations breaches in Nordic and Baltic countries have had more influence than regulatory advice or policy recommendations. As a result, a self-regulating and cleansing process has been triggered and there is, at the moment, greater sensitivity to ML risks. Right now, everyone in the banking industry is changing their risk scoring models. (Interviewee no.4)

This point was confirmed by a risk practitioner working in retail bank in northern Europe, who noted that "in light of the regulatory environment and pressure, we upgraded our risk segmentation program at the bank" (Interviewee no. 10). The regulator's statement above also implies that such crises are almost welcomed because, like government-sponsored policies, they act as regulating forces and ultimately help to refine the operations of the financial sector.

Finding 13: ML scandals support the regulator's AML agenda by triggering the wider financial sector to assess and adjust its ML risk models.

3.4 The Risk-Based Approach

However, the current RBA and resulting risk scoring models do not acknowledge, explore nor capture the juxtaposition of ML and AML frameworks within the same financial institution or examine what this implies. This task generally falls to fraud teams, but there is no acknowledgement of collusion risk in the RBA. Indeed, as seen in the Third and Fourth AML Directive, customer, product, services, delivery channels and geographical risk factors are flagged as the key categories to consider when assessing risk. However, no mention is made of collusion risk based on an institution's culture, risk profile or appetite. Furthermore, although all risk practitioners interviewed were able to identify the lax compliance culture in other institutions, a blind spot was revealed when it came to discussing their own institutions: "having a Russian offshore business has an impact and needs to be managed, there are always reputational issues, but the [regulators from two concerned countries] seem happy" (Interviewee no. 10). At the time of writing, the institution that Interviewee no. 10 worked for had been implicated in yet another ML scandal. Thus, this blind spot may be caused by the recurring rhetoric of risk practitioners: "Banks are not the police" (Interviewee no. 10) or the uncomfortable truth that this invokes within obliged entities. As rightfully stated by one interviewee, a risk practitioner and Wolfsberg Group member: "business as usual is exposure [to ML risk] and when one has four billion transactions at any point in time, some of it will be illicit" (Interviewee no. 24). Accordingly, with such volumes and a commercial role that trumps the prevention, financial institutions may have neither the ability nor the incentive to identify and observe what could be called a conflict of interest within their systems.

Finding 14: Financial institutions, despite being caught laundering money with criminal intent, as a result of incompetence or due to the sheer volume of transactions they face, are maintained by regulators at the forefront of ML prevention.

Finding 15: The RBA methodology fails to capture collusion as a factor of ML risk.

Regulators themselves are unable to grasp such conflicts of interest. The National Risk Assessment (NRA) exercise performed in FIU1's jurisdiction in 2016 indicates a failing on the regulator's part. In late 2016, the author discussed the NRA process and outcomes with the FIU1 regulator, who stated: "the National Risk Assessment is not publicly available I'm afraid. But we used the methodology as per World Bank's recommendations and there were *no surprises with the results*" (Interviewee no. 04). However, based on a series of publicised ML scandals involving the FIU1 jurisdiction, the author contacted the regulator in May 2017 to ask about his thoughts and comments in relation to the NRA and to ascertain whether the NRA had, in fact, accounted for all relevant ML-related events. Essentially the author wanted to know whether such scandals were in line with the "no surprises" position of the NRA, given that there was no opportunity for public review of this assessment. His response confirmed that the ML scandals that impacted his jurisdiction had indeed come as a surprise: "actually the AML/CFT governmental committee agreed to launch the new NRA program next year. The methodology depends on the lifecycle of the Supra-NRA project run by the European Commission. We hope that in light of what happened it would make more sense to discuss the risk scoring and assessment process at the national level as opposed to EU level" (Interviewee no. 04). Incidentally, the "Supra-NRA" referred to Article 6 of the Fourth AML Directive, which required the commission to complete a report identifying, analysing and evaluating the ML and TF risks at the European Union level by June 26, 2017.

In order to get a better understanding of the FIU1 jurisdiction's NRA process and identify why it failed to capture actual ML dangers and risks, the author interviewed another practitioner who was involved in the NRA process. He stated:

> the NRA debacle was linked to the tool provided by the World Bank. Too much effort was required to understand the tool. I worked with [the regulator] on it and we had to define a lot of items such as what a Private Banking customer is. We ended up having to focus more on the tool as such than on risks per se. In addition, the fact that financial institutions had limited input and no visibility of the process was in hindsight an issue, yes. The Ministry of [*anonymised*] has an overview of the results relating to the NRA but it was an overview only and high level. The overview was also given to the [*anonymised*] Banking Association. (Interviewee no. 12)

This quote clearly suggests that the failure to capture risks faced by the FIU1's jurisdiction was the result of an inadequate World Bank risk scoring tool, whereby the very act of technology use and becoming familiar with the software interfered with the task of identifying and documenting risks. This was not an isolated case, and practitioners have faced similar issues in dealing with transaction risk scoring tools. When discussing risk scoring within his institution, Interviewee no. 12 stated that "the scientisation of risk scores through software confuses the process and we end up with misspent resources. The transaction per se may be high risk but the customer may not. For example, I could have a customer who sends money to Syria, which my tool will pick up as being high risk, but there will really be no risk at all there". The above scenarios suggest that, in spite of its burdensome complexity, the tool may nevertheless flag cases too broadly to be useful.

Finding 16: The application of a transaction monitoring software based on the scientisation of risk generates false positives. This hinders AML efforts, creating further dangers that require internalisation.

Finally, another reason for the NRA's failure is that obliged entities are not sufficiently involved in the risk assessment process, which echoes Interviewee no. 12's comments on the lack of visibility of the NRA process. Indeed, before the ML scandals that emerged in FIU1's jurisdiction, one interviewee stated that despite having had some input in preliminary NRA data gathering, "the NRA was not shared with banks" (Interviewee no. 10). Similarly, interviews held with FIU1 indicated that the NRA had also not been shared with the FIU either, which in turn prevented its use in wider strategic work. The NRA was an exercise performed in isolation of key AML stakeholders within the FIU1 jurisdiction.

Finding 17: The ML intelligence available across financial institutions was not adequately leveraged by the regulator and the committee in charge of completing the NRA in FIU1's jurisdiction. Thus, potentially relevant information relating to ML risks and dangers was ignored.

The Role of the Regulator

The NRA debacle highlights that there is a double standard of expectations in relation to performance between regulators and practitioners when it comes to ML prevention. As stated by one of the interviewees, "look at the public sector's role in prevention! It's not doing very well compared to the private sector which is expected to perform 99% of the time" (Interviewee no. 24). When discussing the anti-corruption initiative, a similar discourse emerged. Although discussions with financial institutions indicate that the latter is aligned with policy efforts to tackle corruption and tax evasion, they do condemn the limited amount of support provided by the public sector as well as the dichotomy of what is expected from financial institutions versus what is expected from the private sector. Interviewee no. 12 explained that domestic corruption is often related to small amounts of cash:

> The average corruption is observed locally, not so much at parliament level. I have seen corruption occur at school director level for example[1]. So that means that moving forward, all small amounts of money being exchanged will need to be monitored. And people such as school directors are not even covered by the local PEPs/anti-corruption initiative. The state needs to do its job when it comes to battling corruption and provide the names and the positions that they believe represent a higher risk. The Central Criminal Police Anti-Corruption Bureau has this information, that is for sure, but they refuse to give it to us. Furthermore, the directive excludes local government, and this is an issue as real corruption is at that local level. A lot of the PEPs covered by the Directive such as MPs or members of government are required to fill economic declaration anyways, stating what their revenue is, what stocks they own. This is a yearly exercise. So, what is the added value of the Fourth AMLD? This information is necessary to the state not the banks and this can be done by mapping the individuals that should be identified along with their associated parties. Then this information should be passed on to banks. This new regime will end up being yet another tick boxing exercise, requiring a lot of resources and real corruption will not be targeted and addressed adequately. (Interviewee no. 12)

Thus, financial institutions feel that they do not receive sufficient governmental and regulatory support for their AML activities despite being held to a higher standard of accountability compared to the regulator. The counterargument,

---

[1] The 2019 US university admissions bribery case is an illustration of this.

however, is that financial institutions are expected to perform at a higher standard because they are on the front lines: it is their systems that enable ML, not those of regulators. Hence, expectations regarding their performance in terms of ML prevention need to be set at a higher level because they are the gatekeepers responsible for keeping dirty money out of the financial/economic system and detecting it if it is there. However, given that prevalent banks are failing to deliver their AML duties, one questions why regulators are not stepping up and offering the support and guidance needed by financial institutions.

Regulators, however, do not seem to have a framework enabling them to identify when obliged entities' failures to identify or prevent ML are suspicious. Such a system would, of course, assist governments, regulators and society as a whole, in understanding whether ML scandals are the result of incompetence or criminal behaviour. The case of Barclays reviewed in Chap. 2 indicates that, despite the lack of ML evidence, the British regulator decided to nevertheless fine the institution. Yet, interviews with risk practitioners indicate that a number of institutions manage to avoid regulatory fines or, when fined, incur sanctions that are disproportionately small compared to the damages that have been caused. For instance, *The New York Times* ran an article in 2018 lamenting the fact that although HSBC had been fined for laundering drug traffickers' money, none of its staff had been "prosecuted, despite claims from federal prosecutors that the conduct involved stunning failures of oversight—and worse" (The New York Times, 2018). Interestingly, Interviewee no. 10 confided that his own institution had "'escaped' a fine in [anonymised foreign jurisdiction]." Again, when the matter was raised with the FIU1 regulator, the latter was unwilling to share information pertaining to obliged entities that had escaped regulatory sanctions. Since such information is not easily accessible in public records or in the media, there are no records documenting whether punishment faced by banks is disproportionately small compared to the damage that is caused by ML and AML decisions.

The most recent source providing insight into regulatory failings is the 2018 Bruun and Hjejle report on Danske Bank, which provides a chronology of how regulators failed to ascertain their authority to supervise and regulate a bank appropriately within an adequate time frame. Indeed, the report explains that:

> In 2007, the Estonian FSA came out with a critical inspection report, and at the same time Danske Bank at Group level received specific information from the Russian Central Bank, through the Danish FSA. This information pointed to possible "tax and custom payments evasion" and "criminal activity in its pure form, including money laundering", estimated at "billions of roubles monthly". (Bruun & Hjejle, 2018, p. 8)

More precisely, the inspection performed by the Estonian Financial Services Authority concerned Sampo Pank's non-resident customers that were transferred to Danske Bank after acquisition. This inspection report was sent to the Danish Financial Services Authority. The information provided by the Russian Central Bank also related to Sampo Pank's non-resident customers and stated that "clients of Sampo Pank permanently participate in financial transactions of doubtful origin" (Bruun & Hjejle, 2018, p. 41). There is no explanation as to why neither the Danish

3.4 The Risk-Based Approach

nor the Estonian financial services authorities pursued this matter further. The report indicates that the executive board of Danske Bank was able to provide assurance to the Danish regulator, stating that:

> the Estonian FSA's conclusion of the inspection was that the bank complies with the existing laws and regulations, and that the Estonian FSA had had no material observations. The reply also stated that the AML concept of Danske Bank Group had been implemented in the Estonian subsidiary, and that reporting lines had been set up. The Danish FSA convened a meeting with the bank on 3 September 2007, at which Group Legal provided equally comforting information. (Bruun & Hjejle, 2018, p. 41)

The report then explains that the Estonian regulator issued a 2009 inspection report based on a follow-up assessment of the Estonian branch of Danske Bank. The report was less critical than the 2007 report and was shared with the Danish regulator and stated that "the attitude of branch employees concerning the objectives of and compliance with statutory requirements had improved considerably" (Bruun & Hjejle, 2018, p. 42). In 2010, there were news reports linking Danske Bank's Estonian branch to sanctions breaches and ML; however, it appears that neither the Estonian nor the Danish regulator intervened. Subsequently, in 2012, the Danish regulator sought comments from Danske Bank on matters of AML and CFT and risk patterns identified at the Estonian branch (this action was triggered by a letter issued by the Estonian FSA). Group Legal and Group Compliance and AML responded that the controls and systems in place were commensurate with the actual risk faced by the branch.

In the context of Danske Bank's application to set up a branch in the USA, the financial institution submitted an AML action plan to the US Federal Reserve. The action plan was reviewed and updated and "on 30 October 2012, the Danish FSA issued a statement of support to the US Federal Reserve" (Bruun & Hjejle, 2018, p. 46) on the adequacy of ML and TF prevention. In 2013, there was further communication between the Danish and Estonian FSAs and Danske Bank. Based on email exchanges, it would appear that the Danish regulator was worried, given the assurance it had given to the US authorities, while the Estonian FSA was concerned about the Estonian branch risk appetite which "looks above the average comparing with Estonian banking sector in general" (Bruun & Hjejle, 2018, p. 47). In 2014, based on the whistleblowing findings report, there was an informal call with the Estonian regulator. In addition, the Estonian FSA performed an inspection of the bank and issued a report stating that the institution was monitoring neither clients nor transactions effectively and that "economic interests prevailed over the obligation to apply enhanced due diligence measures" (Bruun & Hjejle, 2018, p. 60). In 2015 and 2016, Danske Bank was finally fined by both the Estonian and Danish regulators for 12.5 million Danish crowns in Denmark. The amount of the Estonian fine is not available in public records. The report then explains that in 2016 and 2017, there were a series of actual ML cases confirmed in the media implicating Danske Bank's Estonian branch. In 2017 "the Danish FSA initiated an investigation into Danske Bank's management and governance in relation to the AML case at the Estonian branch" (Bruun & Hjejle, 2018, p. 20).

The above timeline indicates that there were three regulators and supervisory authorities focusing on Danske Bank, and while failures were identified in relation to controls and processes, Danske Bank's high-risk business continued until 2015. Furthermore, it took 10 years for Danske Bank to be named and shamed, not by the regulators, however, but by the media. This timeline indicates that the media and public perception of a lax regulator is valid. However, Danske Bank is considered to be a "systemic bank", meaning a bank that is key to a country's financial system and hence to the wider economy and society. As such, it could be argued that the regulators' refusal to aggressively enforce the AML framework on that occasion may have been necessary to preserve Denmark's and Estonia's wider economic systems and reputations.

Finding 18: The regulator needs to maintain its own credibility and reputation to preserve itself as an organisation. At times, this may conflict with its role in preserving the stability and the reputation of the economic and political systems.

Another striking point in the Danske Bank timeline is the fact that the Russian Central Bank is the institution that kickstarted the inquiry, identifying tangible issues pointing to ML activities and tax evasions in 2007. Hence, the Russian regulator (of what is considered to be one of the most corrupt countries of the world—Russia ranks 138th on the Transparency International Index list [TI Index, 2019]) intervened and aired its suspicions to the regulators of Denmark (ranked 1st on the TI Index) and Estonia (ranked 18th on the TI index).

This point highlights the complex interaction between the different elements feeding into ML risk as a whole and the implications this has for the AML system. Throughout this research, a large number of interviewees confirmed the extent of Russia's corruption and involvement in ML. For instance, Interviewee no. 01 explained that "the Russian FIU is extremely slow" when it comes to cooperating on ML cases. Likewise, Interviewee no. 10 explained that "corruption issues are intrinsic to Russia". Interviewees no. 02, 04, 05, 07, 08, 10 and 12 all confirmed that Russia represents an extremely high ML risk. What also emerged from conversations with the above interviewees is that Russia is very keen to prevent individuals from protecting their assets by "cashing out of Russia given that there is corruption at all levels" (Interviewee no. 10). Interviewee no. 10 explained that Russian authorities have set up strong restrictions on money flows and seek to curb tax fraud. However, under the current political circumstances, wealthy Russians obviously want their assets to be shielded from their corrupt government, even if that means evading taxes. Interviewee no. 10 describes how wealthy Russians set up dollar-denominated inheritance schemes for their children in order to avoid disputes in Russian courts. Wealthy Russians also attempt to hide that they are the ultimate beneficial owners of companies or accounts because "in Russia one day the individual is good and the next he is branded as bad by the government. Just look at the opposition leader Navalny and what happened to him" (Interviewee no. 12). This

3.4 The Risk-Based Approach 117

comment was made prior to Alexei Navalny's 2020 poisoning and refers to the court judgement finding him guilty of embezzlement in 2017 and 2018, which barred him from running against President Putin. Similarly, Mikhail Khodorkovsky (owner of Yukos gas and oil), Russia's wealthiest man at the time of his 2003 arrest, was prosecuted and incarcerated for tax fraud, embezzlement and money laundering. His wealth was frozen and seized by Russian authorities. Western media such as *The New York Times* (2018) have claimed that Khodorkovsky's arrest and imprisonment were politically motivated.

Thus, as explained by Interviewees 1, 10 and 12, Russian authorities use the current AML framework and its provisions for tax evasion to assist them in dispossessing individuals and confiscating their funds. Generalising from that, it could be argued that, on occasion, the AML framework becomes a tool used by corrupt governments to maintain and preserve their status quos. Likewise, the AML system is used by democracies to maintain and preserve their legitimacy and transparency. In addition, as discussed above, governments and regulators may also decide to enforce the AML framework more or less strictly in order to preserve the reputation and stability of economic and financial systems. The absence of documented cases of obliged entities that have avoided fines makes it hard to evaluate the robustness of this claim, but the chronology of what happened over a 10-year period with Danske Bank would certainly support it.

Finding 19: The AML framework is a tool that can be (mis)used to support and preserve a political, economic or financial system, regardless of the system's integrity and ethics.

The Illusion of Risk Deconstruction

The research identified that the RBA is based on the certainty that deconstructing ML risk into subrisks makes risk easier to understand, grasp and thus control. The approach consisting in identifying the supposed components of ML risk and listing them as subrisks aims to support obliged entities' attempts at identifying ML risk and is endorsed by the Fourth AML Directive:

> Member States shall ensure that obliged entities take appropriate steps to identify and assess the risks of money laundering and terrorist financing, taking into account risk factors including those relating to their customers, countries or geographic areas, products, services, transactions or delivery channels. Those steps shall be proportionate to the nature and size of the obliged entities. (Article 8)

However, the RBA misses that such subrisks are subject to feedback from one another. They permit or deny each other; they recoil from one another. Quite simply, they interact in ways that practitioners and regulators cannot account for. Hence, the current ML risk framework needs to acknowledge the existence of such interactions and feedback, despite the fact that they cannot be fully accounted for or predicted. This is fundamental to AML efforts.

At present, no matter who the observing system is, whether an FIU, obliged entity or regulator, accounting for each subrisk and the way they irritate one another is impossible. Ultimately, none of the observing systems within the AML community can observe (i.e. differentiate) ML risk in its totality and account for its complexity. For instance, while the Fourth AML Directive recommends splitting ML risk into customers, countries, geographic areas, products, etc., Deutsche Bank's internal report on the impact of the Russian laundromat identifies the ML risk it faces as being observable through regulatory risk, reputational risk, market risk, correspondent banking risk and other customers' risk (Harding, 2019). Likewise, the analysis of what led to the Danske Bank ML scandal identifies ML risk factors as customers, poorly integrated IT systems, failed internal AML procedures, staff complacency and internal collusion with ML criminals. In addition, in light of an article published in *The Financial Times* claiming that the bank had launched an investigation in the whistleblower's personal life to discredit and blackmail him (Binham, 2019), it could be argued that one of the subrisks that Danske failed to account for is whistleblowing itself.

Hence, none of the above observing systems have been able to assess where ML risk starts and where it ends. At what point, for instance, does ML risk venture into other types of risks listed in corporate risk governance manuals. Even if one assumes that AML stakeholders have a clear understanding of where ML risk ends and where other risk begins, there is evidence that different risk types irritate one another, generate further complexity and thus result in further risks. Hence, not only is the task of splitting ML risk into subrisks futile; attempts at splitting the environment within which ML risk evolves are similarly pointless. Although there exists within the current AML framework the strong conviction that a reductionist method will "simplify the question being asked through the elimination of as many variables as possible, such that the environment of the object of observation can be controlled" (Webb, 2013, p. 18), this approach can lead to a misevaluation of risks and the way they ultimately interact with one another. Indeed, the communication between different risks and different observers of risks leads to the emergence and the formation of more risk. Risk thus displays an autopoietic behaviour similar to that of a system.

When discussing ML risk with interviewees, they clearly believed that once an ML risk scandal is known to the general public and acknowledged by relevant regulators and institutions, ML risk reduces in size. Indeed, in the context of the Russian and Azerbaijani laundromat scandals, Interviewee no. 10 stated: "The ML risk is stable here. There have been no new trends. Risk is now smaller. Bearing in mind that Russia and Ukraine transit their dirty money through [other jurisdiction in ex-Soviet area] and the cash finds its way back to [FIU1 jurisdiction]" (Interviewee no. 10).

At the time, regulator and risk practitioners were not anticipating the impact that news relating to the Danske case would have on public opinion and on the wider

3.4 The Risk-Based Approach

region's reputation. Ominously, the previous FIU director stated in 2015: "we don't want to become the next [anonymised jurisdiction] that was associated with systemic ML" (Interviewee no. 12). Furthermore, as already mentioned, at the time of writing, another branch of a northern European bank based in the FIU1 jurisdiction (for which Interviewee no. 10 worked) was implicated in an ML scandal. This indicates that even in 2015, the regulator and other obliged entities had failed to account for the "contamination" effect of the ML scandals within the FIU1 jurisdiction and beyond, across northern and eastern Europe. As Interviewee 10 himself stated, "after the series of laundromat scandals and the sanctioning of [anonymised bank], I expect ML risk to move from banks to payment service providers. Banks will now focus on vanilla products to make money" (Interviewee no. 10). What subsequently happened is that while ML risk may have moved to payment service providers, the media has further investigated the laundromat scandals and identified banks that enabled them. Thus, in 2018, Danish newspaper *Berlingske* issued a series of reports documenting Danske Bank's responsibility and involvement in the laundromat scandal, which was not anticipated by interviewees and is beyond what risk practitioners traditionally call reputational risk, especially in light of the suicide of Danske Bank Estonia's CEO.

In addition to reputational risk, another risk that interacts and feeds into ML risk is regulatory risk. This is a phenomenon that is discussed in Chap. 1 and documented in the academic literature (Power, 2004a, 2004b; Ryder, 2012; Simonova, 2011) as well as in industry (KPMG, 2014). Essentially, in contrast to the media's belief and public opinion that banks "get away with everything", there is the certainty among practitioners that "the greatest threat to the banking industry lies in the regulatory and political backlash that has taken place against banks" (Lascelles & Patel, 2014, p. 4). However, interviews held with risk practitioners indicate that while the regulator is indeed perceived as a danger, the main danger is not necessarily the regulator's sanctioning power or perceived lack of understanding of the RBA, but its inability or refusal to "take responsibility for ML risk. Part of the problem is the dichotomy between the regulation per se and regulatory expectations. All responsibility is passed on to the private sector! The challenge is thus having to manage the risk of a regulator who does not understand the RBA. The RBA as it is enforced does not accept the possibility of failure" (Interviewee no. 24). This statement is unsurprising and echoes what was discussed in Chap. 1 in relation to the dichotomy between the actual codified regulation of the RBA and the regulator's expectations of how obliged entities should implement it. However, not all ML risks can be mitigated, and, provided that obliged entities demonstrate that the RBA has been adequately implemented and applied, regulators should not penalise financial institutions when ML events emerge.

Another issue raised by interviewees is the fact that regulations are in constant mutation: as Interviewee no. 16 stated, "In [FIU2 jurisdiction] AML law and regulations have changed ten times since 2004!" Similarly, according to Interviewee no. 24:

Sometimes regulation seems like a knee-jerk reaction and not a lot of thinking goes into it. (...) The Fourth AML Directive has not even been transcribed in law and the Fifth AML Directive is already being drafted and expected to be implemented into national law by January 2020. Regulators are constantly changing requirements which creates further implementation issues and there are of course challenges relating to harmonisation. It is down to each country to implement such regulatory requirements.

There is no certainty of what laws will look like, and, as such, FIUs, in addition to all the obliged entities that were interviewed, state that such uncertainty is beyond frustrating and has implications regarding the processes and systems that need to be implemented to comply with the law. The uncertainty of current and future regulation, coupled with the belief that the regulator does not understand the RBA and how to enforce it, leads interviewees to perceive the regulator itself as a risk—or, in line with Luhmann's depiction of the risk/danger distinction, a danger that cannot easily be internalised and thus converted into risk.

Another point raised by interviewees when discussing ML risk is that of legal and privacy risks appearing to feed off AML initiatives. For instance, Interviewee no. 08 questioned who was looking at the legal implications of potentially challenging certain obliged entities on their risk assessment, as per Fourth AML Directive requirements. Similarly, Interviewee no. 10 expressed concerns about privacy risks, explaining that "updating KYC has been an issue in [FIU1 jurisdiction]. I had to go on the radio to explain the national initiative because here in our country we are not comfortable with sharing data. I felt that there would be legal risks attached to updating the KYC" (Interviewee no. 10). Similarly, according to Interviewee no. 16:

> the Fourth AML Directive's Beneficial Owner register is a big unknown. The ideology of transparency is completely disconnected from reality and the expectation that all can access such registers is dangerous. Furthermore, who will be populating and updating the data? What happens when we are looking at investment funds, trust funds or anonymous companies? In France, a US citizen has sued the French government because she had set up a trust and under the Fourth AML Directive and the Beneficial Owner register, inheritors would have been able to see who else was this trust's beneficiary. She did not want her inheritors to battle one another. Ultimately the French Conseil Constitutionnel declared that this law regarding beneficial ownership was unconstitutional. (Interviewee no. 16)

Thus, the way such risk elements interact with one another introduces a complexity that is not captured under the current framework and that cannot be broken down into a set of indicators that neatly fit a reductionist-inspired framework. The current AML framework needs to account for the interrelationship of different types of risks and the fact that ML risk is not an entity that can be kept tightly in a box, separated from legal, reputational or regulatory risks. In addition, the current AML framework needs to understand and account for the channels that such subrisks use when irritating one another and spawning new risks. This is discussed in further detail in the following chapter.

Finding 20: ML risk and the environment within which it evolves encompass an array of subrisks and systems that feed off, resonate and irritate one another. This generates additional risks and frictions. The current framework cannot capture this complexity.

3.5 Risk Appetite, Intelligence and Re-entry

Risk Appetite and Intelligence

An element that is particularly striking is the fact that while there is increased focus on intelligence and data sharing for FIUs (refer to Articles 51–57 of the Fourth AML Directive)—to the point of actually creating danger for such entities struggling with the processing and management of an increasing volume of data—risk practitioners in the finance and banking industries assert that "there are no good standards on how banks could exchange their AML intelligence with FIUs" (Interviewee no. 10).

Initiatives such as Transaction Monitoring Netherlands (TMNL) or AML Bridge in Estonia (currently in pilot phase) facilitate greater collaboration in the monitoring of transactions or financial crime data exchange across FIs. Such initiatives, however, do not necessarily tackle issues associated with the exchange of intelligence between the private sector and FIUs. When asked why banks do not submit all the information relating to a customer along with a SAR, Interviewee no. 12 explained that most SARs end up being archived; consequently, from a data privacy point of view "there is no point in sending account details". In sum, financial institution data is a goldmine of information and can be used in the fight against ML, but the absence of a workable sharing framework between FIUs and the private sector means that, currently, this intelligence is not leveraged.

Finding 21: There is currently no framework nor standards in place for FIUs to adequately leverage existing financial institutions' ML intelligence.

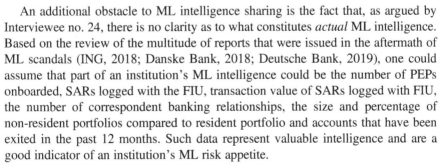

An additional obstacle to ML intelligence sharing is the fact that, as argued by Interviewee no. 24, there is no clarity as to what constitutes *actual* ML intelligence. Based on the review of the multitude of reports that were issued in the aftermath of ML scandals (ING, 2018; Danske Bank, 2018; Deutsche Bank, 2019), one could assume that part of an institution's ML intelligence could be the number of PEPs onboarded, SARs logged with the FIU, transaction value of SARs logged with FIU, the number of correspondent banking relationships, the size and percentage of non-resident portfolios compared to resident portfolio and accounts that have been exited in the past 12 months. Such data represent valuable intelligence and are a good indicator of an institution's ML risk appetite.

However, what emerges from interviews and review of secondary data is that there is no explicit ML risk appetite documentation nor official communication between financial institutions and regulators. For instance, the published FATF guidance on the RBA (FATF, 2014a, 2014b) mentions risk appetite just twice and does not provide guidance as to how an institution could or should articulate it. Furthermore, the FATF statement concerning ML risk appetite is not specific: "supervisors have to take steps to check that their staff are equipped to assess whether a bank's policies, procedures and controls are appropriate in view of the risks identified through the risk assessment, and its risk appetite" (FATF, 2014a, 2014b, p. 15). Similarly, financial institutions' remarks regarding ML risk appetite are vague. Financial institutions' "risk appetite statements often contain broad definitions of acceptable risk, such as minimal tolerance for residual Financial Crime risk" (Artingstall et al., 2016, p. 8). In addition, this FCA-sponsored research on de-risking states: "we find that ML/TF risk appetite is difficult to articulate and measure, perhaps unsurprisingly. Banks are still developing this art and in particular find it difficult to 'price' (in broad terms) ML/TF risk, as well as a reluctance to adopt an explicit compliance cost-base for pricing accounts" (Artingstall et al., 2016, p. 23).

This may be due to the fact that banks do not have much accumulated data on associated losses, as exists, for example, for losses associated with market or credit risk. It is possible that banks do not feel that such risks incur much of a loss to banks in comparison to the profits they make through exposure to ML risk. Indeed, "HSBC, made a USD 20.6bn profit in 2012 and paid its CEO a USD 3m bonus, (...) in spite of the fact that HSBC was fined a record USD 1.9bn for doing business with Mexican drug lords, terrorist financers and pariah states" (Global Witness, 2013).

As stated by Interviewee no. 23, an FATF policy-maker, "clearly despite what many say, there is not zero tolerance for ML risk, but what would a bank's risk appetite *actually* look like?" Financial institutions certainly have the same tools for communicating money laundering risk that they have for discussing their exposure to market risk (value at risk) or credit risk (exposure at default), for instance. Interestingly, when raising this point with the (non-executive) director of an independent investment funds management company, the response was that "risk management is more about liquidity, credit and market risk. ML risk sits under an operational function and is more of a compliance issue. It is not seen as 'risk' in the same way as credit or market risk" (Interviewee no. 15). While this opinion was not shared by the rest of the interviewees, it is interesting, nonetheless, to see that this perspective exists in the finance industry and may hinder the move towards a clearly articulated ML risk appetite.

However, the banking industry does leave an audit trail of its ML risk appetite through its SARs and risk assessment matrices operationalised through the RBA. Similarly, information reviewed by audit risk committees and board meetings also provide documentation of ML risk appetite. Discussion with Interviewee no. 15 indicates that he reviews, on a monthly basis, reports containing data such as "shareholders' countries, business classification, high-risk accounts, blocked accounts, PEPs". One wonders whether Interviewee no. 15 is even aware that he is reviewing an aspect of the investment funds company's ML risk appetite given that, to him, ML risk is not really a risk. Thus, this highlights how fundamental it is for

3.5 Risk Appetite, Intelligence and Re-entry

institutions to ensure that the data presented to the board relating to ML risk is provided through the *right* narrative. For instance, the volume of SAR reports could be a contentious issue. Discussion with a risk practitioner identified that the institution considered introducing a SAR threshold and might "consider exiting a customer if there were more than three SARs relating to a customer" (Interviewee no. 10). This point was made in relation to how the FIU would perceive receiving a certain number of SARs relating to the same customer and whether a cut-off threshold should be implemented. Based on other interviews with risk practitioners, it was unclear whether there was any guidance on how to interpret a high volume of SARs within an institution. Interestingly, the Bruun and Hjejle report on Danske Bank states the following:

> At a meeting in the Executive Board on 9 March 2010, there was a discussion of the number of suspicious activity reports ("SARs") filed by the Estonian branch on the basis of reporting. The discussion is reflected in minutes as follows (translation):
> *'The AML report states at page 5 that Estonia accounts for a 30% market share of the "Suspicious Activity Reports". According to [name], the reason for this high share is that the standard (of compliance) of Danske Bank is high compared to other banks in Estonia.*
> *[Name] expressed concern over the many Russian transfers. [Name] stated that the Russian Central Bank had been contacted, and it had agreed to these transfers. Nor had [name] come across anything that could give rise to concern'.* (Bruun & Hjejle, 2018, p. 43)

Accordingly, members of Danske Bank's executive board believed that the high volume of SARs they submitted reflected a high standard of vigilance and compliance. This is an interesting perspective and in direct opposition to Interviewee no. 10's comments pondering whether, beyond a certain threshold of SARs, a bank would face danger and would have to exit customers related to such SARs. In addition, the above excerpt indicates that the high number of transactions to Russia were not a concern once it was confirmed that the Russian Central Bank had approved them. This demonstrates that senior management may not have understood what the data were pointing towards. If Danske Bank's money laundering reporting officer had presented the same data to the risk committee through the narrative of the institution's ML risk appetite and exposure, it is possible that the information relating to a disproportionately high number of SARs along with the many Russian transfers would not have been dismissed as being of little concern. The absence of a system that (a) enables ML risk indicators to be identified as ML risk intelligence per se and (b) formalises ML risk appetite is, in the author's opinion, one of the many documented Danske Bank problems.

It could, however, be argued that financial institutions use their risk assessment score matrices as a form of ML risk appetite documentation. Informed by the RBA, it documents "what banks are comfortable with and what conversation needs to be had with the regulator" (Interviewee no. 24). However, it does not show how much is at risk and more importantly *what* is at risk (i.e. a financial loss, impacted reputation, branches closing down, etc.) should something go wrong. Ultimately, such a tool does not (a) document future ML-related damages and/or losses that may arise as a consequence of an institution's past ML-related decisions or (b) enable the institution to know how much will be incurred in damages and/or losses. Indeed, assessing what risk each business, client, jurisdiction or bank represents is one step of the process, but if this information does not tie back to what the institution is able to compensate for, there is little point to the exercise.

Finding 22: Financial institutions do not formally articulate their ML risk appetite. This makes monitoring their ML risk exposure extremely difficult.

Review of secondary data has identified that a financial institution's risk appetite appears to only be acknowledged, documented and circulated when damages associated with a financial institution's past ML-related decisions arise. Although not labelled as the institution's *risk appetite per se*, such reports are generally shared after an ML scandal and document an institution's action plan to minimise the expected impact of that scandal. This is generally performed by documenting the institution's ML risk acceptance regarding certain customers, products or jurisdictions. For example, the 2015 FCA report on Barclays' dealings with high net worth Qatari clients documents Barclays' risk appetite at the time regarding onboarding the clients in question. This is addressed in detail in Chap. 2. Likewise, the 2018 Bruun and Hjejle report on Danske Bank's non-resident portfolio is a clear documentation of the bank's ML risk appetite between 2007 and 2015. The report states that the main factors leading to the Danske Bank's ML scandal were the (a) maintenance of a non-resident portfolio, (b) high flow of funds transferred from external parties to non-resident portfolio customers, (c) customers from the Russian Federation and the larger Commonwealth of Independent States such as Azerbaijan and Ukraine, (d) customer due diligence and KYC written in a language not understood by the Head Office, (e) an information technology platform separate from that of the head office, (f) insufficient AML procedures, (g) ignoring warnings from regulators and whistleblowers, (h) higher share of profits in a specific jurisdiction and (i) higher share of SAR reports in the same jurisdiction. This clearly indicates that Danske Bank had a high tolerance for ML risk in the 2007–2015 time frame. As one interviewee reported, this is not surprising because "based on high-risk transactions a bank can make up to 50% of its revenues" (Interviewee no. 10).

Similarly, a Deutsche Bank internal report on the Russian laundromat's aftermath provides additional indirect documentation of the institution's ML risk appetite between 2011 and 2017. The Deutsche Bank's internal report, which appeared in *The Guardian* (Harding, 2019), lists its number of high-risk entities and number of associated SARs filed, along with the total value of the transactions that were filed as SARs. This report offers a good snapshot of the institution's accepted ML risk exposure and hence appetite based on the set of high-risk customers it decided to onboard.

The internal report documents the risk exposure that Deutsche Bank did not actively internalise, as it stems "from its involvement in the Russian Laundromat" (Deutsche Bank; reproduced by Harding in *The Guardian*, 2019). It does not explain why Deutsche Bank decided to engage in a correspondent banking relationship with Danske Bank, but the choice of wording is revealing because it refers to risks as being inherent to the consequences of Deutsche Bank's involvement in the Russian laundromat scandal. It does not refer to what the industry calls residual risks, i.e. when a bank decides to onboard a high-risk relationship (such as a correspondent banking relationship), but articulates how it mitigates the high-risk dimension of that relationship by implementing the processes and controls necessary to handle such risks. In sum, according to the RBA methodology, inherent risks (understood across the risk industry as risks that are intrinsic to an event or a set of circumstances in the absence of mitigating controls) are mitigated and thus essentially replaced by residual risks, defined as what that remains after mitigating measures have been deployed.

Therefore, review of Deutsche Bank's internal report (Harding, 2019) reveals that the bank treats the Russian laundromat case as if it were a danger external to Deutsche Bank's decisions in matters relating to its ML risk appetite and thus exposure. However, in reality, Deutsche Bank's involvement in the Russian laundromat scandal stems from its decision to bank with customers perceived by the AML community to be high-ML-risk businesses (Basel Institute on Governance, 2020). As such, the leaked internal report actually documents risks that Deutsche Bank should have accounted for when identifying the inherent risks involved in establishing a correspondent relationship, the associated processes and controls needed to mitigate these risks and the ensuing residual risks arising from such relationships once the inherent risks had been mitigated.

Nevertheless, the internal report labels the ML risk stemming from its involvement in the Russian laundromat scandal as *inherent* and not residual. Deutsche Bank essentially signals, in a tacit way, that it was not the decision-maker in terms of engaging in correspondent banking services and that its risk exposure represents a *danger* rather than a *risk* that emerged as a consequence of internalised dangers. This is a surprising narrative, given that all financial institutions providing correspondent banking services are required to perform adequate due diligence on respondent banks to ensure that the latter has the right systems and controls in place to manage ML risks (FATF, 2016; Wolfsberg Group, 2014).

Regardless, Deutsche Bank documents its risk exposure as if it involved dangers unrelated to Deutsche Bank's decision to provide correspondent banking services. It lists the dangers it faces as regulatory, market, client and reputational risks. However, according to Luhmann's model, such exposure should not be documented as a danger since Deutsche Bank was the decision-maker and not the victim in this case. Rather, what Deutsche Bank encountered is what Luhmann calls post-decisional regret, namely, high damages that arose from the decision it made to process some of Danske Bank's transactions.

Finding 23: When an ML scandal occurs and associated damages and/or losses emerge, the obliged entity responsible for the decision that led to the ML scandal treats the latter as a danger and not as a risk, thus initially rejecting accountability and responsibility for the decision.

One could speculate that Deutsche Bank simply did not account for such risks or felt that such risks were worth it. Either way, this not only reflects the findings documented in the previous section demonstrating that risks feed off of one another and that current risk scoring methodologies do not capture the interaction of such elements; it also illustrates that financial institutions may not be comfortable signalling that they did indeed accept a risk or that their internal systems and controls were not sufficiently robust to prevent their institution from being used for ML. As such, perhaps it is in the best interest of financial institutions to avoid articulating a formalised risk appetite policy and framework in order to prevent being held accountable for internalising risks and to present itself as a victim of ML criminal activity instead. Indeed, "there is no norm nor literature on risk appetite making it hard for financial institutions to state their ML risk appetite" (Interviewee no. 24). Yet, as confirmed by the FCA-sponsored report on de-risking, there are "no overt policies of not banking entire sectors for AML/CFT reasons. (...) However, it is true that some banks may not bank some particular types of businesses for commercial or 'bank culture' reasons. (...) Also a decision to not take a customer is easier to manage internally and externally than accepting the customer which will need review, monitoring and managing" (Artingstall et al., 2016, p. 22). Thus, financial institutions are clearly in a position to articulate their risk appetite when required.

The key issue is that "regulators need to come up with a methodology that will be approved by them and that will not be used as a beating stick" (Interviewee no. 3) should something go wrong. This sentiment was echoed by another interviewee who stated that "there is a difference between what is codified and what is actually expected of you and how you will be assessed" (Interviewee no. 24). The FCA-sponsored report on de-risking highlights a similar concern. It explains that interviewed institutions were adamant that their statements on risk appetite were not an indication of wholesale de-risking. In addition, the report states:

> We have also found examples where particular sectors are specifically mentioned. If this amounted to a complete prohibition it could be classified as 'wholesale de-risking', but we have found few examples relating solely to AML/CFT issues. Reputational risk, bribery and corruption concerns and strategic business reasons also factor into some banks ruling out the banking of certain sectors, for example the defence industry. (Artingstall et al., 2016, p.8)

Thus, in line with Interviewee no. 3's statement, a risk appetite methodology would identify, document and justify the rationale of what is within and outside ML risk appetites. However, a formalised risk appetite could also become an incriminating tool that enables regulators to accuse institutions of mindless de-risking or of having too great of a tolerance for ML risk, which is particularly problematic and raises the issues discussed above related to articulating (or not articulating) ML risk appetite.

Yet, while regulators may be comfortable enforcing financial sanctions on institutions that supposedly failed to adequately manage ML risks, they may be unwilling to force financial institutions out of the financial system, even if they are *undoubtedly* guilty of intent. Indeed, risk appetite statements may generate additional dangers for the overall system in that they may make it impossible for institutions to hide behind excuses of incompetence, ignorance or a few guilty employees. More precisely, if an institution operates outside its advertised, transparent and documented risk appetite, a regulator may have no choice other than to severely punish that institution in order to appease the media, taxpayers or any other institution that may expect some direct form of redress. Furthermore, if the stated risk appetite was approved and signed-off on by the regulator, the latter would then be required to justify its approval process and would become liable should that risk appetite prove to be excessive and should it expose the wider financial system to substantial ML risks and dangers. However, this scenario is unlikely because governance has increasingly been internalised by the private sector, thus relieving regulators and governments of their "command and control" duties. Hence, regulators moving away from such duties mitigate dangers by deflecting blame from regulators if something goes wrong, enabling financial institutions to claim incompetence rather than intent in such circumstances. As such, regulators likely seek to avoid overtly extreme sanctions because doing so protects the stability of financial and economic systems as well as their own reputations.

In some situations, however, regulators have no choice other than to destabilise the wider system through imposing extreme measures. For example, this was the case for Riggs Bank, which was disbanded following an ML scandal, and for Danske Bank, which was forced to exit the Estonian jurisdiction as a consequence of its widespread and systemic involvement in ML (Megaw, 2019). Such sanctions occur when the incompetence or criminality displayed by an institution makes the application of extreme measures the only viable option available to salvage the regulator's credibility and the jurisdiction's reputation. Furthermore, such sanctions are used to send signals to other institutions that the system's stability must be preserved at any cost.

In sum, regulators de-risk the responsibility of a scandal and associated consequences by transferring risks to the private sector (such as financial institutions). Hence, when discussing the issue of correspondent banking, Interviewee no. 24 stated: "all responsibility has been passed on to the private sector. Before, under a rules-based system, when setting up a correspondent banking relationship, one would have had to go to the regulator, to the public sector, and the supervisor of supervision, i.e. the G20's Financial Stability Board. Now the private sector is left guessing" (Interviewee no. 24).

Finding 24: The absence of a documented risk appetite means the absence of a decision-making audit trail. This preserves the reputation and credibility of obliged entities and regulators should losses or damages arise as a consequence of that decision-making.

The Re-entry of Risk

According to interviews, the above summaries of institutions' internal AML processes and a review of secondary data, once observers like FIUs and obliged entities distinguish what should be considered high risk versus low risk, the high-risk category is, in turn, subjected to another observation, a second-order distinction. This second-order observation again identifies what is low risk and what is high risk within the high-risk category.

This recurring use of the high-risk/low-risk distinction or, in Luhmann's terms, the *re-entry* of the high-risk/low-risk distinction has been observed within FIUs (in the context of handling SARs) and in banking institutions (in the context of clients' ML risk scoring). The two applications are discussed in turn.

Focusing on FIUs' operationalisation of high-risk/low-risk re-entry first, it is important to recall that when an obliged entity logs a SAR and sends it to an FIU, it does so because that entity believes that the underlying activity has reached a high-risk threshold of suspicion that merits flagging, internal escalation and external reporting. As such, each SAR that the FIU receives is assessed by the obliged entity using the high-risk/low-risk distinction and has already been identified as high-risk (i.e. the marked state as previously discussed).

This communication is performed through the decision to submit a SAR. In this scenario, the obliged entity is the first-order observer. However, as already discussed, FIUs are required to process a very high volume of SARs. Accordingly, FIUs need to prioritise SARs that represent higher ML or TF risk even though obliged entities have already submitted a SAR on these transactions. Hence, FIUs need to process each SAR, identifying and separating the ones in more urgent need of further investigation (marked as high-risk) from those that can "wait their time" (Interviewee no. 09). The FIU thus operates here as a second-order observer who observes the observation that has already been performed by obliged entities and communicates (or not) whether a SAR (as observed by the obliged entity) is high-risk (or not) to a LEA or prosecution office. Thus, the FIU reperforms the high-risk/low-risk distinction in the marked state of the distinction that was initially performed by the obliged entity. The re-entry of the high-risk/low-risk distinction was observed within both, FIU1 and FIU2.

In the case of the FIU1, there is no formalised and documented risk scoring methodology in place to assess the *riskiness* of SARs received triggering the reapplication of the high-risk/low-risk distinction in order to prioritise SARs internally. Interviews with relevant FIU1 staff revealed the following process: an analyst performs a preliminary assessment and identifies whether the SAR received is linked to criminal activities or not. The assessment is performed according to the following criteria: the obliged entity marks a SAR as high risk due to suspected ML, TF, a sanctions breach, a large cash transaction, an international request from another FIU, a spontaneous request from another FIU or a request from a LEA. Then, if the analyst also assesses the SAR as high risk, it is escalated to the head of the analytics team who applies yet another high-risk/low-risk distinction motivated by the same criteria and also assesses it in terms of instinct or a gut feeling. The head of analytics then decides which SARs should be given the status of *material* (i.e. a SAR that will be disseminated to analysts) and which should instead be archived. "For instance, if there is a clear case of terrorism financing or the bank has frozen the cash, then the SAR becomes material" (Interviewee no. 01). However, if the SAR is "not that acute

3.5 Risk Appetite, Intelligence and Re-entry

in risk [for example, it is a currency transaction report with no other risk indicators], it goes to the archives" (Interviewee no. 09). The FIU1 director explains that in the context of a SAR that is archived "if trends emerge or the currency transaction report involves an amount that is big enough then it may be moved to a case file category which is when there are *objective* indicators of ML but no actual predicate offences. It will then again be forwarded to the head of analytics who evaluates if the case needs to become a *material*" (Interviewee no. 06). The SARs analysis process thus involves multiple reapplications of the high-risk/low-risk distinction.

The FIU2 follows a similar pattern of high-risk/low-risk distinction re-entry in its dealings with SARs analysis. Indeed, the analyst in charge of receiving SARs risk scores each SAR using a risk-evaluation matrix to guide the scoring process. Hence, as previously seen, the analyst assesses the probability of the ML event using a suspicion indicator grid. More specifically, the suspicious transaction or activity that triggered the SAR is categorised according to a set of indicators that are split into three categories and are each given a score. The categories are (1) indicator linked to the physical client, (2) indicator linked to the operation or transaction and (3) indicator linked to the client's behaviour and profile. Each indicator is scored between 1 and 3, and the scores are cumulable. Once the probability of the ML event has been risk scored, the analyst assesses the likely consequences of the ML event should it happen. The potential consequence of an event can be assessed as extreme, major, moderate, minor or negligible. Each of these consequences is assigned a risk score, beginning with 5 for *extreme consequences* and going all the way down to 1 for *negligible consequences*. The probability score and the consequence scores are then added together, creating a final risk score that is between 2 and 10: 2 is described as very low risk; 3 and 4 as low risk; 5, 6 and 7 as medium risk; 8 and 9 as high risk; and 10 described as the highest possible risk level. The SAR analysis is then prioritised according to the final score.

On occasions "when there is abuse of vulnerability (a recognised criminal offence in the FIU2 jurisdiction), pedophilia, child pornography, terrorism, a report is sent to the prosecutor's office or the intelligence services and the analyst immediately sets the risk score at a minimum of 5" (Interviewee no. 26). An interesting point to note is that when interviewed, an analyst stated that "the risk score matrix is more problematic for confirmed money laundering cases" (Interviewee no. 21). This indicates that when there is confirmed ML, there is no uncertainty, and thus no risk can be associated with that uncertainty. Risk vanishes, and there is nothing to score. On the other hand, "if the risk is set at 2, the file is closed, *unopened*. The LEA is not even involved. Generally, such low-risk SARs relate to a refusal from the bank to enter into a relationship but also to false transfers or to a client's name being featured in the press or associated with the Paradise and/or the Panama papers" (Interviewee no. 26). The secretariat's analyst explains that such SARs are referred to as "closed low-risk SARs and amounted in November 2017 to 316 cases out of the 2926 *real* SARs" (Interviewee no. 19).

Note that the use of the term *real* SAR spontaneously employed by Interviewees no. 19 and 17 is intriguing because it implies that one suspicion may be real, while another may not. Of course, suspicion is ontologically ambiguous, and it ultimately relies on a feeling of unease. Interviewee no. 01 defines it as "when something is not believable, and inconsistent". Yet, while analysts reject the use of the term true and false positives when referring to SARs, a number of them seem comfortable using the term "*real* SARs" and appear to understand what is meant when using such a term. There is a tacit communication that real SARs refer to SARs that are submitted by banks in a way that is not defensive and thus recognised by relevant FIUs as a valid and justified suspicion. This point is particularly relevant because it ultimately shows that FIUs superimpose an additional distinction on top of the high-risk/low-risk distinction—that of true SARs/non-true SARs. Interestingly, the UK Law Commission consultation paper on the UK SARs regime discusses this issue stating that obliged entities have "the obligation to effectively distinguish between unusual and truly suspicious transactions" (Law Commission, 2018, p. 73) putting the onus of this differentiation on obliged entities as opposed to FIUs. Hence, the author observed the re-entry of the high-risk/low-risk distinction, but there is, in addition, the re-entry of the truly suspicious/suspicious distinction, adding to the complexity of the distinction process. The FIU cannot discard what the obliged entity has observed as suspicious and therefore uses the narrative of truly suspicious (as observed through a set of predefined indicators) versus unusual. Suspicion represents such a low and ultimately ambiguous threshold that it actually imposes an ambiguous burden on any given obliged entity that is expected to document a gut feeling when there are no indicators of ML or TF. This burden is also faced by FIUs who must discard many obliged entities' suspicions in the interest of processing high volumes of SARs. The issue, however, is determining what basis should be used to dismiss the suspicions of others.

The current Dutch system prevents FIUs from having to decide when to discard obliged entities' suspicions because obliged entities are expected to send *unusual* transaction reports to the Dutch FIU as opposed to suspicious ones. Hence, it is the Dutch FIU that explicitly performs the suspicious/unusual distinction. After the FIU performs its analysis, an *unusual* transaction report may then acquire the status of *suspicious* and be forwarded to the relevant LEA. Interestingly though, "only a small proportion of the reports received by the Dutch FIU are declared suspicious (on average around 15%), meaning that the reporting is rarely utilised for investigative purposes" (Europol, 2017, p. 10). Ultimately, although labelled differently, this is no different to what the author observed during her fieldwork in FIU1 and FIU2. In essence, the *truly suspicious/suspicious* distinction is another expression of the *high-risk/low-risk* distinction and thus generates further re-entry.

A similar process of the re-entry of the distinction between high risk and low risk has been observed within the private sector. Indeed, interviews with risk practitioners evidence that obliged entities try to assess how risky clients or business relationships really are once they are assessed as high risk. Such exercises are driven either internally or by the regulator. For instance, Interviewee no. 10 explains that his institution aims to follow the "FATF guidelines stating that there are high-risk local PEPs and low-risk PEPs but we need to understand the wider implications of this guidance because right now banks are treating local PEPs in the same way as a foreign bank would be treating them" meaning that obliged entities end up with misspent resources because the Fourth AML Directive "has not really thought the local PEP issue through" (Interviewees no. 10 and 12).

Such statements are particularly interesting, as they indicate that the regulation creates incentives for obliged entities to apply the high-risk/low-risk distinction in order to address the built-in deficiencies of the current regulations. More specifically, by applying a new high-risk/low-risk distinction to a category that was identified as high risk by legislation, the institution is able to observe the unmarked state, i.e. the low-risk category, to a lesser extent, thus making its job easier by not having to apply enhanced due diligence to this category. This process is necessary because regulations have evolved towards trying to encompass all that could possibly generate ML danger to the regulator (and risk to obliged entities). As such, obliged entities are forced to include in the marked state of their observations an even wider set of what should be considered high risk. This necessitates applying enhanced due diligence to an even broader set of customers. Yet, at the same time, the regulation recommends performing a re-entry of the high-risk/low-risk distinction into the broader high-risk marked state that regulators have imposed onto obliged entities (with the Fourth AML Directive, such marked states now include, for instance, Fintechs, MSBs, domestic politically exposed persons, virtual currencies).

More specifically, FATF Recommendation 12 states that foreign and domestic politically exposed persons are subject to enhanced customer due diligence as are "their family members or close associates" (FATF, 2012, p. 14). However, in order to cast a wider net on the entities that require the application of enhanced customer due diligence, the FATF issued a politically exposed persons guidance manual in 2013 that defined who should be categorised as politically exposed persons. The guidance documents four politically exposed persons categories: foreign politically exposed persons, domestic politically exposed persons, international organisation politically exposed persons, family members and close associates (FATF, 2013, pp. 4–5). As one interviewee sarcastically commented "why not add neighbours, second cousins and dogs to the list?!" (Interviewee no. 16). Interestingly, however, given such a widely cast net, the same guidance states: "If the risk assessment establishes that the business relationship with the domestic/international organisation politically exposed persons presents a normal or low risk, the financial institution and Designated Non-Financial Business or Professions (DNFBP) is not required to apply enhanced due diligence measures" (FATF, 2013, p. 8). With this comment, the FATF essentially signals to obliged entities that they are not only allowed but expected to reapply the high-risk/low-risk distinction to the high-risk categories. The obliged entities are thus essentially acting as second-order observers applying a distinction onto the marked state.

However, this expectation to re-enter the high-risk/low-risk distinction to high-risk categories only applies to high-risk categories that have been selected by the regulator. If the process is performed outside of the regulator's discourse, issues arise. The literature on de-risking that has emerged over the past 5 years (explored in Chap. 4, "The FIU: boundary operationalization and attempts at bridging function systems") reflects the fact that regulators ultimately expect obliged entities to perform the RBA within parameters that they have established. Their expectations are for obliged entities to exit suspicious high-risk clients while maintaining nonsuspicious high-risk clients. The challenge, however, is for obliged entities to figure out which high-risk clients are suspicious, since no information is provided as to obliged entities regarding how they should identify suspicious high-risk clients before ML-related damages have actually occurred.

Ultimately, regulators expect high-risk categories entities (such as banks) with confirmed suspicious activity associations (refer to the literature review for a list of banking ML violations as well as interviews documented in this chapter) to perform re-entry of the high-risk/low-risk distinction on clients who have themselves been assessed as being high risk. Thus, the current AML framework depends on high-risk organisations to detect, monitor and report high-risk institutions and transactions because obliged entities such as financial institutions are in the best position to observe and identify cases of ML. However, other than by making it a regulatory requirement, the current AML framework does not *incentivise* obliged entities to detect, monitor or report suspicious transactions. Not only are obliged entities ideally positioned to observe cases of ML, they are also segments of the economic (and financial) system that bridge governmental (and regulatory) systems by means of the SAR regime. However, the current framework fails to leverage the privileged position of obliged entities further through providing better incentives to detect and report ML suspicions.

Finding 25: The current AML framework is based on the cooperation of obliged entities but fails to adequately incentivise them.

Another example of re-entry of the high-risk/low-risk distinction performed by obliged entities is generated by the review of secondary data such as the Deutsche Bank report in the aftermath of the Russian laundromat scandal (Harding, 2019). Indeed, the anti-financial crime team created a risk score matrix of what Deutsche Bank calls non-financial risks that emerged as a consequence of the Russian laundromat scandal. Similar to many risk-scoring matrices, the risk level is reached by mapping the probability of the event (marked here as likelihood) against the impact of the event (mapped here as severity). Interestingly, Deutsche Bank added a re-entry of the high-risk/low-risk distinction in the traditional low-, medium-, and high-risk categories, resulting in the following scale: minor, low, medium, high, severe and acute. This process essentially enabled Deutsche Bank's anti-financial crime team to widen the risk scale and control the risk score narrative. Clearly, the Russian laundromat risk score is still given a high grade, but it has been assigned an orange colour neatly tucked in the middle of the risk score matrix away from the red scores.

On other occasions, however, the re-entry of the high-risk/low-risk distinction has a different purpose. Review of the Bruun and Hjejle report on Danske Bank illustrates this point. The report explains that to perform the investigation and remediation of customers, the law firm had to identify and apply risk indicators to identify customers requiring review: "the portfolio investigation has developed risk indicators, which have been applied to customers subject to investigation with a view to identifying the customers with higher risk. Subsequently, the portfolio investigation grouped the risk indicators—and the customers that hit the risk indicators—and initiated a number of investigations into groups of customers" (Bruun & Hjejle, 2018, p. 16). It goes further, stating that the review adopted "a risk-based customer-by-customer approach in order to identify suspicious customers, and the investigation has used risk indicators to identify the customers with higher risks" (Bruun & Hjejle, 2018, p. 31).

In this instance, the re-entry of the high-risk/low-risk distinction into the high-risk marked state enabled a more precise risk assessment of Danske Bank's high-risk customers, which thus alleviated its workload by reducing the volume of high-risk customers in need of investigation and remediation. Banks use re-entry of the high-risk/low-risk distinction to manage or facilitate internal processes in other situations as well. For instance, if a bank wants to retain a customer despite a risky profile, they may seek to document that the high-risk customer is, in fact, of lower risk—exemplified by the Barclays bank case in which applying enhanced due diligence to high-net-worth, politically exposed Qatari clients was avoided.

In summary, the current RBA not only offers a decision tool enabling obliged entities and FIUs to observe and manage ML risks by performing high-risk/low-risk distinctions; it also allows such organisations to re-enter the high-risk/low-risk distinction into the high-risk category, essentially diluting risk, step by step, re-entry after re-entry. This thus assists obliged entities in managing another set of risks, which includes high SAR volumes, regulatory scrutiny (and thus exposure to regulatory danger), heavy remediation programmes and difficult onboarding or exiting of high-profile customers.

Finding 26: The RBA enables risk practitioners to focus their resources on high ML risk categories. It is a decision tool that enables organisations to perform the re-entry of risk onto itself through the high-risk/low-risk distinction, facilitating the observation of risk and thus its management.

3.6 Re-risking: A Consequence of De-risking

De-risking Is Risk Assessment

As discussed in Chap. 2, the FCA defines de-risking as banks removing "bank accounts/services from customers or other relationships which they associate with higher money laundering risk. (...) It has been attributed to the increasing overall cost of complying with regulatory requirements" (Artingstall et al., 2016, p. 5). The belief is that de-risking is performed in a wholesale manner with banks unwilling to truly assess the risk associated with such customers. Indeed, Interviewee no. 10 stated that "de-risking is basically about limiting business without performing any risk assessment. It is not about applying the RBA. It is about eliminating the risk, as opposed to handling it" (Interviewee no. 10).

However, the interview held with a member of the Wolfsberg Group secretariat states that "de-risking is a misnomer. It is the contagion effect of risk assessments. The cost of compliance is high, there is a lack of confidence in the regulator and fear of misinterpretations of regulatory expectations. Financial institutions simply do not have the support from the regulator" (Interviewee no. 24). This sentiment is echoed by Interviewee no. 10 who, when prompted further on the issue, stated:

> no one wants payment service providers as clients, no one wants to make dollar payments, and no one will want Ukrainian seamen on their books getting their payments through our services. When you think about it, with all that has been happening, de-risking makes sense, given the fines that financial institutions are facing. For instance, Deutsche Bank had a massive fine recently [this refers to a fine incurred between 2015 and 2016] and they had to almost be bailed out by the government. (Interviewee no. 10)

Hence, the majority of interviewees from the banking industry indicate that there is a gap between "what is codified and what is actually expected of you from regulators and how you will ultimately be assessed" (Interviewee no. 24). Such statements are actually aligned with findings documented in the FCA report on de-risking:

> Many of the banks we have spoken to have indicated that, although they take a RBA to each client relationship, they are not just building in the actual risk of a client (or its customers) acting in a damaging way—they are also building in their assessment of how the appropriate regulators, or financial institutions higher up the 'food chain' (who are almost seen to be acting in a quasi-regulatory capacity), will assess their approach. Essentially there is a certain amount of second-guessing going on. In today's environment, the vast majority of these assessments will fall on the side of caution. (Artingstall et al., 2016, p. 40)

Hence de-risking also reflects financial institutions' lack of confidence in the regulator and uncertainties in relation to regulatory expectations. In addition, de-risking concerns private sector responses to irritations from its environment (such as the regulator), communicating a willingness to forfeit a region or a sector to signal good faith based on ML scandals. This is what Deutsche Bank did when it "broke off its relationship as a correspondent bank for US dollars with Danske in Estonia in September 2015 because of concerns over non-resident customers" (Milne, 2018a). Similarly, Danske Bank announced in 2018 that "it would scale down its business in the Baltic countries to focus on the Nordic markets" (Reuters, 2018). Such an exit is, of course, not the result of a fear of misinterpreting regulatory expectations; rather it is a move that demonstrates Danske Bank's understanding of regulatory expectations. On such occasions, de-risking is a decision made by a financial institution to communicate its new risk appetite and regulate the system's exposure to ML risks and dangers.

Re-enforcing this point, the FCA report on de-risking highlights that both FATF and FCA statements on "wholesale cutting loose of entire classes of customers" (FATF, 2015) and "banks dealing generically with whole categories of customers or

3.6 Re-risking: A Consequence of De-risking   135

potential customers" (Artingstall et al., 2016) are frustrating to banks: "A bank's decision on risk assessment may be the same whether it is undertaken on a case by case basis or wholesale basis, because the factors applied will not vary too much" (Artingstall et al., 2016, p. 19). "Risk assessments will score similar customers in similar ways. Thus a set of similar customers will fall outside the FIs' risk appetite and thus be exited" (Artingstall et al., 2016, p. 24).

Finding 27: Although de-risking is perceived by the regulator as danger from its environment, it is the result of irritations triggered by the regulator itself, which in turn affect its own environment.

De-risking: Forcing the Re-entry of the Risk/Danger Distinction onto Other Systems

Another element highlighted by the empirical research is the fact that de-risking has impacted FIU1's jurisdiction and its wider region. As discussed by one of our interviewees:

> in 2015 [Anonymised bank]'s customers started looking for a new bank. They were closing down their customers without giving much of an explanation. Later, the banks that took the same customers in ended up exiting those very customers soon afterwards, probably for the same reasons as [anonymised bank], furthermore when [anonymised bank] lost [international bank], [Anonymised bank] lost its correspondent banking relationship. This is a serious thing and the awareness is such that the IMF has published an article on correspondent banking. A total of 50 countries have lost their corespondent banking relationships within two years. This has serious implications on so many levels: customers end up using Transferwise or any other payment service providers which in itself can present ML risks. (Interviewee no. 12)

Similarly, another interviewee clarified that "[international bank]'s exit from [anonymised region] will impact us. Smaller banks such as [Anonymised bank] do not have any other correspondent relationships. Banks will have to rely on payment service providers and Russian banks to do US payments and the biggest problem with such a situation will be client data and privacy protection" (Interviewee no. 10). Interviewee no. 12 also explained:

> [anonymised bank] is a new US dollar payment service provider. This institution is Russian owned, however. [International bank] used to provide that service and now it does not. Having this Russian connection represents a risk in terms of reputation and instability. It is a real country risk. Similarly my bank was approached by [Turkish owned bank] to process US dollar payments. Again this represents a risk for us and we rejected the offer. But de-risking is a new situation here in [FIU1 jurisdiction] so the regulator has not intervened in the same way as we have observed in the UK for instance. (Interviewee no. 12)

In addition, Interviewee no. 24 stated that "the de-risking wave picked up such a pace that the Committee on Payments and Market Infrastructures asked Wolfsberg to set guidance to ensure that the financial stability and the wider economy was not impacted". Former Treasury Secretary Jack Lew echoed these concerns when he noted that "financial institutions around the world have to adhere to high standards to stop the flow of illicit funds. That means anti-money laundering rules really matter. On the other hand, if the burden is so high (...) that people withdraw from the financial system or are excluded from it, it ultimately raises the risk of illicit transactions" (Clozel, 2016). Hence, policy-makers are aware of the consequences of reducing access to banking with the objective of curtailing illicit transactions. David Lewis, executive secretary of the FATF, asserted: "It's a concern to us, as it undermines transparency within the financial sector and law enforcement's ability to follow the money. (...) We are concerned about that as it reduces transparency in financial transactions, it increases the ML/TF risks we are trying to address" (Taylor, 2016).

In sum, de-risking triggers irritations that lead to a phenomenon of re-risking that was anticipated by neither obliged entities nor regulators. As such, "de-risking creates a massive role for supervisors and the public sector" (Interviewee no. 24), which is problematic because in the current AML framework, ultimate responsibility and accountability lie with financial institutions and no other entity. This represents a great source of danger for financial institutions who feel that they have no assurance from regulators and, as such, simply do not trust them. Indeed, the FCA report on de-risking highlights this concern:

> One large global bank indicated that it would prefer prescriptive regulation (and stability of regulators and regulations), giving certain Asian regulators as examples (though it also acknowledged cultural differences). The revised JMLSG guidance relating to MSBs is regarded as helpful by some, while others believe it adds nothing to their current practices and it certainly falls well short of a safe harbour, despite some (predominantly US) literature suggesting it provides one. (Artingstall et al., 2016, p. 71)

Similarly, the FATF 2015 communication on de-risking states that "the FATF recommendations do not require banks to perform, as a matter of course, normal customer due diligence on the customers of their respondent banks when establishing and maintaining correspondent banking relationships" (FATF, 2015). However, the banking industry strongly believes that should financial crime or sanctions breaches arise in the context of correspondent banking relationships, they would be held legally accountable despite the FATF's above reassurance (Artingstall et al., 2016).

Thus, the private sector perceives the regulator as having itself de-risked credibility risk by shifting responsibility and accountability of AML and regulation to the private sector through promoting and enforcing self-regulation tools such as the RBA. Unfortunately, the de-risking performed by obliged entities is re-risking the financial sector (i.e. the AML community's environment as per Luhmann's framework), thus forcing the regulator to intervene.

This is particularly interesting because other entities such as FIUs are also de-risking (by transferring SAR analysis to other systems, for instance) and therefore

3.6 Re-risking: A Consequence of De-risking

automatically re-risk their environments. FIUs, regulators and obliged entities de-risk their respective systems, triggering irritations within their environments that re-risk not only their environments but their very own systems too. Discussing current AML regulation with a member of the US Secret Services investigating international ML highlights this point. Indeed, he states that "there is a three-way tug of war between law enforcement agencies, financial institutions and the government. The failure of one impacts the others. The government makes the legislation and law enforcement agencies as well as private companies are left to strike partnerships" (Interviewee no. 14). This statement is key because it highlights that law enforcement agencies are aware that the role of financial institutions is shifting away from ML prevention towards enforcement. This mirrors Interviewee no. 10's self-justification and protestation throughout the interview: "we are not the police". Hence, when discussing the issue of risk management with Interviewee no. 24, he explained that "no matter what, risk comes back through the backdoor".

Finding 28: De-risking is performed by regulators, obliged entities and FIUs alike. It results in the re-risking of organisations, which are then faced with the decision to either accept the re-risking or reject it through re-entry of the risk/danger distinction.

This chapter aims to present the empirical findings of the fieldwork performed. This chapter began with a summary of the SAR reception, analysis and dissemination process within both FIU1 and FIU2 in order to provide the context within which both FIUs operate. The findings, identified through interviews, summary of the FIUs' internal processes and secondary data review, were then presented. The chapter uncovered the unsurprising weakness of the SARs regime, the competitive advantages that FIUs develop over others and the implication for the management of SARs and risk, the deeply problematic issues associated with the implementation of the current RBA, the ambivalent role of the regulator, futile attempts at splitting ML risk into subrisks, the communication of risk appetite and intelligence, the re-entry of risk and the risk/danger distinction and, finally, de-risking and its re-risking consequences.

This chapter is structured around 28 findings summarised for ease of reference in the Table 3.2. The following chapter analyses and discusses the findings that have been documented in this chapter. Since the findings pertain to both the AML and the ST domains, the discussion is organised across key themes which will be presented in Chap. 4.

Table 3.2 Summary of findings

	Findings
1	FIUs do not use their knowledge of financial institutions' risk profiles as intelligence in the analysis of SARs. Thus, intelligence is excluded at early stages of SAR prioritisation and analysis
2	Unlike FIs, FIUs are not required to use an RBA when analysing the SARs they receive. This means that different FIUs use different methods to prioritise and manage their SARs
3	The current AML framework focuses on identifying and punishing obliged entities executing ML, as opposed to individuals initiating ML. However, the SAR regime focuses on individuals initiating ML
4	SARs do not establish evidence of predicate offences nor money laundering. SARs rarely result in ML investigations and prosecutions, leading AML practitioners to question the efficiency of the SAR regime
5	SARs represent neither repressive nor preventive tools
6	FIUs do not analyse nor review their performances since FIUs do not need to compete in terms of SARs analysis
7	The SAR analysis performed by FIUs is limited by the poor quality of SARs information submitted to FIUs
8	The end-to-end SAR process depends on two organisations: FIUs who rely on obliged entities completely and obliged entities who, constrained by regulation, cooperate reluctantly. This creates inefficiencies
9	Although some FIUs have the ability to manage SARs quality and/or flow, they are nonetheless expected by law not to reject SARs and to analyse them, as FIUs cannot be seen as impeding the SAR reporting process
10	Some FIUs benefit from the willingness of governments and obliged entities to invest in specific software and technology, enabling FIUs to pass certain processes to other organisations, thus facilitating day-to-day operation
11	An FIU's jurisdiction and/or proximity to certain problematic jurisdictions are indicators of potential support or cooperation, as well as potential dangers or vulnerabilities that need to be internalised by the relevant FIUs
12	An FIU's geographical location, law or constitution may either facilitate FIU operations or represent a danger that FIUs need to internalise and convert into risk
13	ML scandals support the regulator's AML agenda by triggering the wider financial sector to assess and adjust its ML risk models
14	Financial institutions, despite being caught laundering money with criminal intent, as a result of incompetence or due to the sheer volume of transactions they face, are maintained by regulators at the forefront of ML prevention
15	The RBA methodology fails to capture collusion as a factor of ML risk
16	The application of a transaction monitoring software, based on the scientisation of risk, generates false positives. This hinders AML efforts, creating further dangers that require internalisation
17	The ML intelligence available across financial institutions was not adequately leveraged by the regulator and the committee in charge of completing the NRA within FIU1's jurisdiction. Thus, potentially relevant information relating to ML risks and dangers was ignored
18	The regulator needs to maintain its own credibility and reputation to preserve itself as an organisation. At times, this may conflict with its role in preserving the stability and the reputation of the economic and political systems
19	The AML framework is a tool that can be (mis)used to support and preserve a political, economic or financial system, regardless of the system's integrity and ethics

(continued)

Table 3.2 (continued)

	Findings
20	ML risk and the environment within which it evolves encompass an array of subrisks and systems that feed off, resonate and irritate one another. This generates additional risks and frictions. The current framework cannot capture this complexity
21	There is currently no framework nor standards in place for FIUs to adequately leverage existing financial institutions' ML intelligence
22	Financial institutions do not formally articulate their ML risk appetite. This makes the monitoring of their ML risk exposure extremely difficult
23	When an ML scandal occurs and associated damages and/or losses emerge, the obliged entity responsible for the decision that led to the ML scandal treats the latter as a danger and not as a risk, thus initially rejecting accountability and responsibility for the decision
24	The absence of a documented risk appetite means the absence of a decision-making audit trail. This preserves the reputations and credibility of obliged entities and regulators should losses or damages arise as a consequence of that decision-making
25	The current AML framework is based on the cooperation of obliged entities with FIUs and regulators but fails to adequately incentivise obliged entities
26	The RBA enables risk practitioners to focus their resources on high ML risk categories. It is a decision tool that enables organisations to perform the re-entry of risk onto itself through the high-risk/low-risk distinction, facilitating the observation of risk and thus its management
27	Although de-risking is perceived by the regulator as danger from its environment, it is the result of irritations triggered by the regulator itself, which in turn affect its own environment
28	De-risking is performed by regulators, obliged entities and FIUs alike. It results in the re-risking of organisations, which are then faced with the decision to either accept the re-risking or reject it through re-entry of the risk/danger distinction

References

Artingstall, D., Dove, N., Howell, J. & Levi, M. (2016). *Drivers & impacts of derisking: A study of representative views and data in the UK, by John Howell & Co. Ltd. for the Financial Conduct Authority.* [Project Report]. Surrey: John Howell & Co. Ltd. Accessed May 8, 2017, from https://www.fca.org.uk/publication/research/drivers-impacts-of-derisking.pdf

Basel Institute on Governance. (2020, February 26). *Russia's money laundering risks–what does the latest report mean in practice.* Accessed Apr 23, 2020, from https://www.baselgovernance.org/blog/russias-money-laundering-risks-what-does-latest-fatf-report-mean-practice.

Binham, C. (2019). *Danske Bank sought to discredit whistleblower, lawyer claims. The financial time* [Online]. Accessed Oct 18, 2019, from https://www.ft.com/content/32d2023c-9e6f-11e9-9c06-a4640c9feebb

Bruun and Hjejle. (2018). *Report on the Non-Resident Portfolio at Danske Bank's Estonian branch.* Accessed Feb 10, 2019, from https://danskebank.com/-/media/danske-bank-com/file-cloud/2018/9/report-on-the-non-resident-portfolio-at-danske-banks-estonian-branch-.-la=en.pdf

Chaikin, D. (2009). How effective are suspicious transaction reporting systems? *Journal of Money Laundering Control, 12*(3), 238–253.

Clozel, L. (2016, October 7). Lew on de-risking: Banks should not be penalized for engaging abroad. *American Banker* [Online]. Accessed Oct 8, 2016, from https://www.americanbanker.com/news/lew-on-de-risking-banks-should-not-be-penalized-for-engaging-abroad

Council Directive (EC). (2015). 2015/849/EC of 20 May 2015 *on the prevention of the use of the financial system for the purposes of money laundering or terrorist financing.* Accessed Aug 8, 2015, from https://op.europa.eu/en/publication-detail/-/publication/0bff31ef-0b49-11e5-8817-01aa75ed71a1

Council Directive (EC). (2018). *2018/843EC of 30 May 2018 amending Directive (EU) 2015/849 on the prevention of the use of the financial system for the purposes of money laundering or terrorist financing, and amending Directives 2009/138/EC and 2013/36/EU*. Accessed Jun 1, 2018, from https://eur-lex.europa.eu/legal-content/EN/TXT/?uri=CELEX%3A32018L0843

European Commission. (2019). *Report from the commission to the European Parliament and the Council: assessing the framework for cooperation between Financial Intelligence Units*. (24 July, COM (2019) 370 Final). Accessed July 18, 2020, from https://ec.europa.eu/info/sites/info/files/report_assessing_the_framework_for_financial_intelligence_units_fius_cooperation_with_third_countries_and_obstacles_and_opportunities_to_enhance_cooperation_between_financial_intelligence_units_with.pdf

European Union Agency for Law Enforcement Cooperation (Europol). (2017). *From suspicion to action: Converting financial intelligence into greater operational impact*. Europol. Accessed Jan 3, 2019, from https://www.europol.europa.eu/publications-documents/suspicion-to-action-converting-financial-intelligence-greater-operational-impact

FATF. (2012). *FATF steps up the fight against money laundering and terrorist financing*. FATF. Accessed Oct 19, 2015, from http://www.fatf-gafi.org/publications/fatfrecommendations/documents/fatfstepsupthefightagainstmoneylaunderingandterroristfinancing.html

FATF. (2013). *Politically exposed persons (recommendations 12 and 22)*. FATF. Accessed Sep 8, 2018, from https://www.fatf-gafi.org/media/fatf/documents/recommendations/Guidance-PEP-Rec12-22.pdf

FATF. (2014a). *Guidance for a risk based approach: The banking sector*. Accessed Jun 2, 2015, from http://www.fatf-gafi.org/media/fatf/documents/reports/Risk-Based-Approach-Banking-Sector.pdf. : FATF.

FATF. (2014b, October 23). "*FATF clarifies risk-based approach: Case-by-case, not wholesale de-risking*", conclusion from FATF Plenary on 22 October, Paris. Accessed Sep 2, 2020, from https://www.fatfgafi.org/documents/documents/rba-and-de-risking.html

FATF. (2015). *FATF takes action to tackle de-risking*. FATF. Accessed Feb 12, 2016, from http://www.fatf-gafi.org/publications/fatfrecommendations/documents/fatf-action-to-tackle-de-risking.html

FATF. (2016). *Correspondent business services*. FATF. Accessed Nov 26, 2019, from https://www.fatf-gafi.org/media/fatf/documents/reports/Guidance-Correspondent-Banking-Services.pdf

FATF. (2012b-2019). *International standards on combating money laundering and the financing of Terrorism & Proliferation, FATF*. FATF. Accessed Oct 19, 2019, from https://www.fatf-gafi.org/media/fatf/documents/recommendations/pdfs/FATF%20Recommendations%202012.pdf.

FATF. (2018). *Anti-money laundering and counter-terrorist financing measures United Kingdom mutual evaluation report*. FATF. Accessed Feb 12, 2022, from https://www.fatf-gafi.org/media/fatf/documents/reports/mer4/MER-United-Kingdom-2018.pdf

FATF. (2021). The FATF Recommendations – Updated June 2021. FATF. Accessed Feb 12, 2020. Available online: https://www.cfatf-gafic.org/home-test/english-documents/cfatf-resources/14728-fatf-recommendations-2012-updated-october-2020/file

Financial Intelligence Group. (2017). From suspicion to action: Converting financial intelligence into greater operational impact. Accessed Aug 10, 2019. Available online: https://www.europol.europa.eu/sites/default/files/documents/ql-01-17-932-en-c_pf_final.pdf

George, A. L. (1979). Case studies and theory development: The method of structured, focused comparison. In P. G. Lauren (Ed.), *Diplomacy: New approaches in history, theory, and policy* (pp. 43–68). Free Press.

George, A. L., & McKeown, T. J. (1985). Case studies and theories of organizational decision making. In R. F. Coulam & R. A. Smith (Eds.), *Advances in information processing in organizations* (Vol. 2, pp. 21–58). JAI Press.

Global Witness. (2013). *Outrage at vast HSBC profits and bonuses despite role in drug money laundering* (Press release, 4 March). Accessed May 10, 2019, from https://www.globalwitness.org/en/archive/outrage-vast-hsbc

Goldby, M. (2013). Anti-Money laundering reporting requirements imposed by English law: Measuring effectiveness and gauging the need for reform. *Journal of Business Law, 4*, 367–397.

Harding, L. (2019) Deutsche Bank faces action over $20bn Russian money-laundering scheme. *The Guardian*, 17 April [Online]. Accessed Apr 18, 2019. Available at: https://www.theguardian.com/business/2019/apr/17/deutsche-bank-faces-action-over-20bn-russian-money-laundering-scheme

IMF and World Bank. (2004). *Financial intelligence units: An overview*. Accessed Jun 21, 2017, from https://www.imf.org/external/pubs/ft/FIU/fiu.pdf

Jensen, T., & Virki, T. (2018). Danske Bank begins scaling back scandal hit Estonian Branch. *Reuters*, 12 October [Online]. Accessed May 9, 2019. Available at: https://www.reuters.com/article/us-danske-bank-moneylaundering-estonia/danske-bank-begins-scaling-back-scandalhit-estonian-branch-idUSKCN1MM10N

KPMG. (2014). *Global anti money laundering survey*. Accessed Apr 8, 2015, from https://assets.kpmg/content/dam/kpmg/pdf/2014/01/global-anti-money-laundering-survey.pdf

Lascelles, D., & Patel, K. (2014). *Banking banana skins*. Centre for the Study of Financial Innovation (CSFI). Accessed July 29, 2015. Available online: https://www.pwc.com/gx/en/banking-capital-markets/banana-skins/assets/pwc-banking-banana-skins-2014-v2-april.pdf

Law Commission. (2018). *Anti-money laundering: The SARs regime consultation paper*. Accessed Feb 8, 2019, from https://s3-eu-west-2.amazonaws.com/lawcom-prod-storage-11jsxou24uy7q/uploads/2018/07/Anti-Money-Laundering-the-SARs-Regime-Consultation-paper.pdf

Levi, M. (2002). Money laundering and its regulation. *The Annals of the American Academy of Political and Social Science, 582*, 181–194.

Megaw, N. (2019, Febryary 19). Estonian scandal forces Danske out of the Baltics and Russia. *The financial time* [Online]. Accessed Sep 16, 2019, from https://www.ft.com/content/a6881938-344c-11e9-bd3a-8b2a211d90d5

Milne, R. (2018a, September 14). Deutsche Bank warned about Danske Clients. *The financial time*, [Online]. Accessed May 9, 2019, from https://www.ft.com/content/65d1ef28-b778-11e8-bbc3-ccd7de085ffe

Milne, R. (2018b, December 19). *Estonia arrests 10 former employees of embattled Danske Bank*. The Financial Time, [Online]. Accessed Apr 9, 2019, from https://www.ft.com/content/07ec88bc-037e-11e9-9d01-cd4d49afbbe3

OCCRP. (2017, September 4). *The Azerbaijani laundromat*. [Online] Accessed Apr 14, 2020, from https://www.occrp.org/en/azerbaijanilaundromat/

Openbaar Ministerie. (2018). *Investigation Houston: Criminal investigation into ING Bank N.V., statements of facts and conclusions of the Netherlands*. Public Prosecution Service. Accessed Feb 12, 2019, from http://robscholtemuseum.nl/wp-content/uploads/2020/01/Netherlands-National-Office-Serious-Fraud-Environmental-Crime-Asset-Confiscation-National-Office-Houston-Criminal-Investigation-into-ING-Bank-N.V.-Statement-of-Facts-and-Conclusions.pdf

Power, M. (2004a). The risk Management of Everything. *The journal of risk science, 5*(3), 58–65.

Power, M. (2004b). *The risk management of everything: Rethinking the politics of uncertainty*. Demos.

Ryder, N. (2012). *Money laundering–an endless cycle?* Routledge.

Simonova, A. (2011). The risk-based approach to anti-money laundering: Problems and solutions. *Journal of Money Laundering Control, 14*(4), 346–358.

Taylor, M. (2016). *FATF chief talks de-risking dangers and correspondent banking*. Accessed May 10, 2019, from https://www.linkedin.com/pulse/fatf-chief-talks-de-risking-dangers-correspondent-banking-mark-taylor/

The New York Times. (2018). When Banks Won't Stop Money Laundering, What Can the government do? *The New York Times*, 25 September [Online]. Accessed Apr 16, 2019. Available at: https://www.nytimes.com/2018/09/25/business/dealbook/danske-bank-money-laundering.html

The Wolfsberg Group. (2014). *Wolfsberg anti-money laundering principles for correspondent banking*. The Wolfsberg Group. Accessed Dec 7, 2015, from https://www.wolfsberg-principles.com/sites/default/files/wb/pdfs/wolfsberg-standards/8.%20Wolfsberg-Correspondent-Banking-Principles-2014.pdf

Vedrenne, G. & Couvée, K. (2020, July 14). *In unprecedented move, German police raid Financial Intelligence Unit. ACAMS*, [Online] Accessed from https://www.moneylaundering.com/news/in-unprecedented-move-german-police-raid-financial-intelligence-unit/

Webb, T. (2013). Exporing system boundaries: Complexity theory and legal Autopoiesis. *Law and Critique, 24*(2), 131–151. Accessed Apr 14, 2019, from http://eprints.lancs.ac.uk/62005/1/T.E._Webb_Exploring_System_Boundaries_accepted_version_.pdf

Chapter 4
Analysis and Discussion

The findings of the case studies performed in this research were presented in the preceding chapter. The objective of Chap. 4 is to discuss and analyse those findings and their implications in order to address the issues initially presented in Chap. 1.

- What are the ways in which the risk-based approach enables (or disables) AML practitioners to observe and deconstruct ML risks and what are the challenges that they face in applying the risk-based approach?
- In what way does the application of the risk-based approach impact the handling of future/emergent ML risks and what are the broader AML systemic circumstances and challenges of such an impact?

The reader should note that the 28 findings below will not be presented in numerological order. Instead, they will be discussed thematically and combined to extract a set of key propositions. The chapter is structured as follows: Sect. 4.1 focuses on extracting key propositions arising from the 28 findings of the comparative case study, and Sect. 4.2 explores those propositions, identifies the recommendations that derive from those propositions and articulates the author's contribution to theory and the domain.

4.1 Section 1: Extracting Propositions

ML Intelligence: Using Obliged Entities' Risk Profiles

Finding 1: FIUs do not use their knowledge of financial institutions' risk profiles as intelligence in the analysis of suspicious activity reports (SARs). Thus, intelligence is excluded at early stages of SAR prioritisation and analysis.

Finding 3: The current AML framework focuses on identifying and punishing obliged entities executing ML, as opposed to individuals initiating ML. However, the SAR regime focuses on individuals initiating ML.

The author is aware that each case (based on a SAR) is unique, must be assessed in relation to a client and should be treated on its own merits. The empirical research documented in the previous chapter highlights the key fact that each of the obliged entities has a certain risk profile and hence a risk appetite in relation to ML risk. Discussion with FIU analysts highlighted the rightful reputation that some institutions have gained, confirming, for instance, that some banks have certain predilections for facilitating tax evasion, while others have a greater appetite regarding certain customers deemed to be particularly high risk. When an FIU receives a SAR, the latter is treated as an ML danger to the jurisdiction by the FIU. More specifically, even if the obliged entity *decides* to internalise a danger, transforming it into risk in exchange for financial gain, the FIU is required to assess the consequences of the obliged entity's decision and has no advantages nor gains associated with that decision. Hence, the FIU perceives the SAR as a communication of ML danger.

In such cases, the FIU must subsequently assess the magnitude of the ML danger in order to prioritise and escalate the analysis of the associated SAR. However, by ignoring the obliged entity's reputation and risk profile, the FIU essentially refuses to observe the obliged entity's responsibility and accountability in relation to the ML danger that the obliged entity has allowed to enter the financial system. This is particularly astonishing given that the current AML framework is predicated on naming, shaming and fining financial institutions that willingly or inadvertently facilitate ML. Nevertheless, obliged entities' risk profiles are typically ignored by FIU analysts when receiving and performing SAR analyses. The current SAR regime should align itself with the wider AML strategy and consider the role that obliged entities have in the facilitation of ML and the ensuing associated dangers, whether they be intentional or accidental. This is particularly relevant given that, according to Finding 22, there is currently no framework in place for acknowledging obliged entities' ML risk appetites and profiles and thus no robust avenue to leverage the intelligence that obliged entities have about themselves and others.

Finding 22: Financial institutions do not formally articulate their ML risk appetite. This makes the monitoring of their ML risk exposure extremely difficult.

Combining insights from Findings 1, 3 and 22 reveals that while obliged entities' risk profiles and appetites should not be the sole drivers of the SAR prioritisation process, they should nonetheless feed into the SAR risk-scoring mechanism, ensuring that valuable intelligence is not discarded in the SAR analysis process thus increasing the likelihood of identifying wider ML dangers that the jurisdiction may be exposed to at early stages of the analysis process.

Proposition 1: FIUs should acknowledge obliged entities' risk profiles in the SARs escalation and analysis process. This would allow FIUs to leverage their existing knowledge and/or intelligence in relation to the risk profiles of specific obliged entities.

The FIU: Externalising Danger and De-risking

Another point relating to FIUs' SAR analysis process concerns the following finding.

Finding 2: Unlike FIs, FIUs are not required to use an RBA when analysing the SARs they receive. This means that FIUs use different methods to prioritise and manage their SARs.

However, before addressing Finding 2, it is important to anchor the SAR regime and the risk-based approach in Luhmann's systems theory and risk/danger model. This will enable the reader to conceptualise the wider AML domain within Luhmann's systems theory and risk/danger model later.

Obliged entities constitute the first line of defence when it comes to ML prevention within the financial sector. Along with the empirical research documented in the previous chapter, the literature review highlights that obliged entities' infrastructures are targeted by launderers to process dirty funds and make them look legitimate. This laundering process is made easier by the fact that ML is performed through monetary transactions using the payment/non-payment code that was introduced in Chap. 2. Thus, ML operations belong to the economic function system. The payment/non-payment code and the medium of communication (i.e. money) are the operations used within obliged entities. Hence, to target dirty money and ensure it remains on the non-payment side of the distinction, AML regulations and policies created the suspicious/non-suspicious code and juxtaposed it with the payment/non-payment distinction. If money is identified as suspicious, funds are frozen and possibly confiscated. Financial institutions are thus entrusted to act as ML gatekeepers because, ultimately, they use and understand the payment/non-payment code that is operationalised by ML subsystems as well as the one mandated by the AML system, namely, that of suspicious/non-suspicious.

A suspicious activity report represents the obliged entity's decision to communicate its ML danger to an FIU. Prior to sending a SAR to the FIU, the obliged entity applies the suspicious/non-suspicious distinction to the transaction that was flagged via its internal transaction monitoring systems and processes and forwards it to the FIU if marked as suspicious. At this stage, the SAR may emanate from a danger that has been internalised by the obliged entity, i.e. a risk as per Luhmann's model, or it may be the consequence of a danger to which the obliged entity has fallen victim. However, it is important to remember that both danger and risk are manifestations of the same phenomenon. The key difference between risk and danger is that of attribution because the difference is determined by the observer. In short, the decision-maker observes the phenomenon as a *risk* while, the non-decision-maker (i.e. the victim) observes the same phenomenon as a *danger*. Nevertheless, both the victim and the decision-maker observe the same phenomenon.

Once the alert is escalated to the FIU as a SAR, the FIU sees this communication as a *danger* to the overall banking and financial sectors. The FIU is indifferent to whether the SAR was originally related to danger or a risk. Only the obliged entity has the ability to truly understand this relationship. For instance, when "Danske

Estonia filed 653 SARs based on the 10,000 high-risk portfolio customers it provided services to" (Bruun & Hjejle, 2018, p. 31), the FIU considered those SARs to be danger related and not risk related despite Danske's *decision* to bank 10,000 high-risk portfolio customers whose activities generated 653 SARs. While this could have been seen as an element of Danske's *risk*, those 653 SARs represented a *danger* to the Estonian jurisdiction in terms of Estonia's reputation and the wider stability of the Estonian financial system.

In this context, however, the reader should be reminded that the relevant FIU is a second-order observer of the SAR and does not view the SAR as a danger as it would if it were a victim or the beneficiary of the institution's decision. The function of the FIU means that it simply needs to observe the danger, i.e. the SAR, and apply the high-danger/low-danger distinction. More specifically, the FIU establishes whether the SAR represents a high-level ML danger to the jurisdiction to which it belongs. This will determine whether a case should be opened for the analysis of the specific SAR.

However, in applying the low-danger side of the (high/low) distinction, the FIU uses its internal processes to internalise the danger being communicated via the SAR and either archives the SAR or closes the case (when, e.g. a bank refuses to open an account and files a SAR for this event). At this point, the FIU internalises the danger without, however, actually converting it to risk. This is the particularity of the FIU. In such cases, it could be argued that the FIU "pauses" or "suspends" the danger until it is observed again. In contrast, when the FIU applies the high-danger distinction to a SAR, it confirms and maintains the SAR's danger status. No internalisation occurs in this scenario, and the FIU needs to find other means to manage the danger. Since, according to Luhmann, organisations support function systems and, as such, their decisions (i.e. their units of communication) are impregnated with the codes pertaining to the function systems they support, it may be argued that the function system that the FIU supports employs and understands the high-danger/low-danger distinction. This is further explored later in this chapter.

The purpose of the high-danger/low-danger distinction applied by the FIU is to identify SARs that represent a higher level of danger to the overall financial and banking sector and therefore need to be further investigated by LEAs. In essence, through its SAR analysis process, the FIU attempts to "translate" or "convert" its high-danger/low-danger observation to a distinction that the LEA will understand, namely, the illegal/legal distinction. This is performed by using the prosecutable/non-prosecutable distinction which is illustrated in Fig. 4.1.

Figure 4.1 illustrates how the SAR is observed by three different types of organisations through different distinctions that need to be converted, i.e. whose binary codes need to be converted to ensure successful communication from one function system to the next. Indeed, as discussed in Chap. 4, systems are self-referential and are incapable of deciphering the code of other systems. To bypass this issue, binary codes can be translated into a code understood by another system.

During the empirical research, the author observed that translation codes enable organisations to convert a function system's binary code. For instance, in the case of the AML domain, SARs can be adequately communicated by obliged entities that

4.1 Section 1: Extracting Propositions

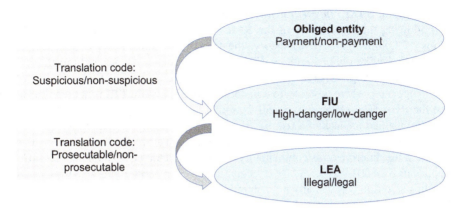

Fig. 4.1 The translation of SARs across organisations

submit them to the FIU that analyses them. Hence, provided translation codes are effective, the SAR should also be communicated to the LEA for investigation and prosecution. The SAR is therefore a tool that should communicate ML danger observed within the economic system all the way to the legal system.

Obliged entities are able to understand and easily convert their payment/non-payment code to that of suspicious/non-suspicious because of regulatory mandates. This compels obliged entities to juxtapose the suspicious/non-suspicious code with their payment/non-payment code and log a SAR with their FIU when necessary. FIUs understand the suspicious/non-suspicious code. Their challenge, however, is to pass the SAR to LEAs that do not have the same communicative logic and do not understand the suspicious/non-suspicious code. FIUs therefore convert the suspicious/non-suspicious code into the illegal/legal code via the prosecutable/non-prosecutable code. This is initiated through the FIU's high-danger/low-danger code whose operationalisation was observed during the empirical research. If a SAR is identified as high-danger, the FIU will open a case file and will investigate all the relevant elements pertaining to the SAR with the purpose of identifying key intelligence that will determine whether the case is prosecutable or not. If it is prosecutable, the FIU forwards the case to a LEA for formal investigation (in the legal function system), resulting in prosecution when appropriate.

However, the execution of such communication is not as straightforward as it seems. Indeed, the issue that has been raised by risk practitioners and documented in the previous chapter is that the prosecutable/non-prosecutable translation code is not as efficient as the suspicious/non-suspicious translation code used by obliged entities to pass their SARs to FIUs. In reality, few SARs are eventually forwarded to LEAs. The SARs system does not readily lead to prosecutions, and its role remains confined to signalling danger within the banking and financial sectors.

Finding 4: SARs do not establish evidence of predicate offences nor money laundering. They rarely result in ML investigations and prosecutions, leading AML practitioners to question the efficiency of the SAR regime.

Finding 5: SARs represent neither repressive nor preventive tools.

Following this description of the SAR regime, as operationalised by FIUs, in terms of Luhmann's systems theory, the focus now shifts to an exploration of Finding 2. Unlike obliged entities, FIUs do not internalise danger and transform it into risk in exchange for benefits or advantages. The purpose of the FIU is to observe ML danger and, where possible, to transfer it. Accordingly, the FIU is not required to use the RBA. The reader may recall from the discussion in Chap. 4 that the FIU2 director justified the lack of a risk-based approach operationalisation within FIUs in general, by stating "there is no risk-based approach on suspicion". At the time, this assertion was interpreted as contradictory since the director was explaining that FIU2 applies its own RBA to the SARs it receives. However, further interviews indicated that this assertion was actually not contradictory since it was observed that there are two separate species of the RBA: one is operationalised by obliged entities and mainly aims to internalise danger, thus converting it into risk (Findings 26, 27 and 28); the other is operationalised by FIUs and is exclusively used to transfer, or externalise, danger to another FIU (see Findings 10, 11 and 12).

However, what emerged from this realisation is that some FIUs may have developed more rigorous and standardised RBAs to assessing the SARs they receive. This enables them to swiftly differentiate between SARs that need to be externalised and SARs that can be archived because they do not require prioritisation for externalisation (e.g. suspicious but low-danger SARs). Thus, the act of developing a formal framework to operationalise the RBA allows some FIUs to facilitate clearer communication between FIU analysts, thus developing a more coherent approach for externalising ML danger to other systems.

Hence, through the application of a formalised RBA, FIUs may develop an internal means to better externalise ML danger by passing it, for instance, to other jurisdictions and/or function systems. Findings 10, 11 and 12 indicate that such danger-externalisation tools do not necessarily emerge internally. Indeed, as seen in Chap. 4, FIUs' environments also support or hinder FIUs in their ML danger externalisation efforts.

Finding 10: Some FIUs benefit from the willingness of governments and obliged entities to invest in specific software and technology, enabling FIUs to pass certain processes to other organisations, thus facilitating day-to-day operations.

Finding 11: An FIU's jurisdiction and/or proximity to certain jurisdictions are indicators of potential support or cooperation as well as potential dangers or vulnerabilities that need to be internalised by relevant FIUs.

Finding 12: FIUs' environments either facilitate FIU operations or form a danger that FIUs need to internalise and convert into risk.

Some FIUs appear to benefit from the willingness of governments and obliged entities to invest in systems, technology and infrastructures, thus potentially facilitating FIUs' handling of large volumes of SARs. Furthermore, an FIU's geographical location and proximity to certain jurisdictions indicate potential support or cooperation with other FIUs as well as potential threats or vulnerabilities, which makes it easier, or harder, for FIUs to cooperate with other FIUs and share relevant intelligence relating to SAR analysis and investigation. Finally, a jurisdiction's laws and constitution may or may not facilitate FIU minimum standards and requirements in relation to the depth and the extent to which SAR analysis and investigation must demonstrate that a predicate offence has indeed occurred. Hence, some FIUs have advantages in performing their operations of receiving, analysing and disseminating SARs. Yet according to Finding 6, FIUs do not assess their personal performance nor do they need to compete with any other organisations.

Finding 6: FIUs do not analyse nor review their performance since FIUs do not need to compete in terms of SAR analysis.

Indeed, since FIUs are required to receive, analyse and disseminate SARs, the performance of FIUs does not need to be measured or tracked. One therefore may question how the advantages or competitive edge documented in Findings 10, 11 and 12 support the operations of FIUs. The competitive advantages discussed and described in Chap. 4 are part of an FIU's environment. As systems, FIUs have environments that may or not generate perturbations or irritations that will be filtered through an FIU's operational modus. Indeed, the reader may recall that a system's environment does not have a direct input into operationally closed systems. As such, the advantages referred to above cause perturbations to FIUs, which, in turn, process such perturbations according to their own logic: "a system might create some irritations that affect another system, but this irritation is then filtered through the other system's self-steering" (Borsch, 2011, p. 122).

Some FIUs may enjoy an environment of obliged entities that invest in technology making SAR management easier or a government that supports the use of, for example, FIU.NET or GoAML, which facilitates the analysis of SARs but, more importantly, also enables FIUs to pass SARs to other systems. Indeed, the findings chapter documented that FIU2's ability to leverage FIU.NET effectively (enabling obliged entities to submit SARs to the FIU in which a transaction occurs) means that, in contrast to other FIUs, FIU2 has the capacity to transfer SARs to other FIUs and other jurisdictions. Similarly, unlike FIU1, FIU2's ability to interact with *cooperative* FIUs drives its ability to easily and effectively analyse SARs, thus improving the chance of successful dissemination to LEAs. Furthermore, the geographical location of an FIU may be an indicator that SARs received by such an FIU may be associated with high-danger transactions (as per the FIUs' high-danger/low-danger distinction) thus making the analysis process more difficult and possibly limiting the likelihood of SARs dissemination.

As the above advantages (as per Findings 10, 11 and 12) enable better and easier transfer and dissemination of SARs to other FIUs and LEAs, the next step is to discuss what this implies from a systemic perspective. As previously discussed, SARs constitute the communication of ML danger existing within the banking and financial sector to FIUs and (potentially) to LEAs. Yet, given that communication involves the tryptic of information, utterance and understanding, a SAR can communicate danger only if the LEA understands the SAR. If the final step of understanding fails to occur, then SARs communication cannot take place. If the LEA appropriately understands the SAR, ensuing communication can occur and, as such, the FIU can successfully pass the SAR to the LEA. By doing so, the FIU essentially transfers the danger to the LEA, away from its own function system (which is yet to be identified) to the legal function system, which is then in charge of internalising it or not. Through this operation, the FIU is therefore able to either transfer danger or to facilitate danger internalisation into risk. Thus, the role of the FIU, defined by the Fourth AML Directive, as receiving, analysing and disseminating SARs shifts towards transferring danger away from its jurisdiction and its own function system to other function systems: "organisations are seldom oriented to one goal. On the contrary, they tend to shift between various goals, which are often not clearly defined" (Seidl & Mormann, 2015, p. 6).

Indeed, as discussed in Chap. 4, although both FIU directors interviewed would certainly welcome higher rates of SAR conversions into prosecution cases, FIUs do not consider converting SARs into prosecution cases their raison d'être. In addition to receiving and analysing SARs, the other function of an FIU is, simply, to exist. FIUs are necessary for jurisdictions to demonstrate adherence to international AML standards because the existence and maintenance of an FIU at the national level is mandated by the FATF and the Fourth and Fifth AML Directives (Section 3 of the Fourth AML Directive and FATF Recommendation Number 29). The reader may recall Interviewee no. 17's eloquent summary: "no matter what, the FIU has to exist and as such there is no illusion to be had in relation to the overall system and its level of sophistication". Hence, FIUs do not need to compete with other organisations because no other organisations are capable of assuming the role of an existing FIU: the FIU is a monopoly at the national level. As monopoly organisations dedicated to receiving and investigating SARs, FIUs are not required to develop sophisticated key performance indicators. To legitimise its existence and performance per regulatory requirements, an FIU must simply report the number of SARs received on a monthly or yearly basis and document the number of SARs that are analysed by FIU analysts and disseminated to LEAs. The German FIU is the only institution that has failed to meet this basic requirement.

Thus, when ML scandals arise, FIUs (unlike regulators) are neither condemned nor denounced by function systems such as the media. For instance, in January 2019, the Danish FSA issued a statement documenting where it had failed as a regulator in its monitoring of Danske Bank Estonia and stated that the Estonian regulator was similarly accountable for the events that had unfolded: "the host country supervisor, the EFSA (the Estonian regulator) is responsible for the AML supervision of the Estonian branch" (DFSA, 2019, p. 2). As a response, the Estonian regulator issued the following statement on its website:

> The DFSA argues in the summary report that Finantsinspektsioon is responsible for the AML supervision of the Estonian branch. This is a simplified view of the legal circumstances. Finantsinspektsioon has repeatedly explained that AMLD3, a piece of EU legislation harmonising anti-money laundering in the EU prior to June 2015, did not have any provisions on the division of responsibilities when cross-border banking is provided and freedom of establishment is exercised. (Finantsinspektsioon, 2019)

The Estonian FIU, however, was not held accountable in the DFSA report, which actually states the following: "the Estonian FIU has continuously received a large number of reports of suspicious transactions from the branch, and the FIU has continuously requested information from the branch on a large number of customers that might be suspicious" (DFSA, 2019, pp. 2–3). Furthermore, the report elaborates on the analysis performed by the Estonian FIU: "for the approximately 10,000 customers in the International Banking Department, the Estonian branch filed 653 reports of suspicious activity in the period 2007–2015. Furthermore, in this period, the Estonian FIU made inquiries to the branch about 1,007 of the approx. 10,000 customers" (DFSA, 2019, p. 14). The only public criticism of the Estonian FIU arose from Danske's whistleblower, Howard Wilkinson during his hearing at the European Parliament. This illustrates that FIUs are merely expected to demonstrate the receipt, analysis and dissemination of SARs. Yet according to Findings 10, 11 and 12, the undocumented and possibly unacknowledged expected performance of an FIU is also to externalise ML danger to other jurisdictions and thus FIUs. As such, in relation to the Danske scandal, the Estonian FIU failed to transfer ML danger to other jurisdictions or function systems.

Proposition 2: FIUs de-risk to other FIUs and externalise ML danger when possible. The current AML framework should acknowledge this phenomenon and identify ways to leverage such mechanisms to facilitate FIUs' de-risking and ML danger externalisation mechanisms.

The Inefficiency of the Current SAR Regime: A Communication Issue

The empirical research documented in the previous chapter indicates the extent to which FIUs rely on obliged entities to fulfil their role and purpose, as per Finding 8.

Finding 8: The SAR process depends on FIUs who rely on obliged entities completely and obliged entities who, constrained by regulation, cooperate reluctantly. This creates inefficiencies.

Furthermore, the very existence of the FIU depends on a governmental body to issue AML standards and requires countries to establish an FIU (the FATF, founded by the G7 in 1989, issued Recommendation Number 29 necessitating the establishment of FIUs). In addition, the FIU needs the support of a legal body to issue relevant AML regulations (such as the European Commission and its Fourth and Fifth AML Directives). Finally, the FIU requires that obliged entities fall within the remit of AML regulations. This compels obliged entities to issue SARs, which FIUs receive, analyse and disseminate as mandated by law (Section 4 of the Fourth AML Directive). Unsurprisingly, the FIU's maintenance, or autopoiesis, is not generated through the number of SARs disseminated to LEAs. Rather, the organisational system is maintained by SARs received and the organisation's capacity to maintain and support SAR reception and analysis. The moment an FIU can no longer receive and analyse SARs, its ability to maintain its structure collapses as observed in the case of the German FIU. Since the expectation that the FIU receives, analyses and disseminates SARs is defined by governmental and legal bodies and is supported by obliged entities, the FIU's existence obviously depends on such organisations and the function systems to which they belong. Accordingly, the above may be the root cause of the issues and problems that have been raised by risk practitioners, as per Findings 4, 5 and 7:

Finding 4: SARs do not establish evidence of predicate offences nor money laundering. SARs rarely result in ML investigations and prosecutions, leading AML practitioners to question the efficiency of the SAR regime.

Finding 5: SARs are neither repressive nor preventive tools.

Finding 7: The SAR analysis performed by FIUs is limited by the poor quality of SAR information submitted to FIUs.

Indeed, the above findings indicate that although FIUs appear to successfully communicate with obliged entities, as indicated in Fig. 4.1 above, the FIU's binary code is not easily translated to the code employed by LEAs; thus, obliged entities could essentially assist FIUs with the translation process. This was discussed above. The FIU can successfully communicate with obliged entities, which are organisations that belong to the economic function system, and FIUs thus enjoy a privileged relationship with obliged entities (and therefore with the economic function system). Similarly, FIUs have the capacity to successfully communicate with LEAs, provided their SAR investigations generate sufficient ML intelligence to enable the high-danger/low-danger code to be converted into the illegal/legal code. A natural subsequent step would be to question why the suspicious/non-suspicious translation code is more effective than the prosecutable/non-prosecutable translation code, as presented in Fig. 4.1, and to ask: What are the circumstances and/or conditions that enable or facilitate the effective translation of the binary code of one function system into that of another?

To answer this question, it may be helpful to focus on a successful translation code such as the suspicious/non-suspicious code and understand how this code emerged. As already discussed, this code is used and, more importantly, understood by both organisation types—namely, FIUs and obliged entities. Suspicious/non-suspicious is a translation code that emerges within obliged entities and FIUs as a result of regulations. As such, the communication of ML danger (i.e. the SAR) between obliged entities and FIUs may be understood as imposed communication, as per Finding 9.

Finding 9: Although some FIUs have the ability to manage SAR quality and/or flow, they are nonetheless expected by law not to reject SARs and to analyse them, as FIUs cannot be seen as impeding the SAR reporting process.

In order to encourage and support SAR reporting and compliance with the relevant regulations, FIUs may not enforce overly strict rejection rules if the SAR does not contain the necessary level of information, thus avoiding impeding the understanding element of communication. The suspicious/non-suspicious translation code is therefore understood by both obliged entities and FIUs. Furthermore, FIUs are then able to subsequently apply their own code, namely, the high-danger/low-danger code, to SARs.

The FIU is then faced with the task of converting the high-danger/low-danger distinction via the prosecutable/non-prosecutable translation code into the LEA's illegal/legal code. As seen in Finding 4 above, however, this is no easy feat. According to FIU analysts, obliged entities consistently submit low-quality SARs that contain very little information, thus forcing FIU analysts to go back and forth with obliged entities in order to extract further information and intelligence in the hopes of building a case that can then be sent on to law enforcement.

Unlike existing communication between obliged entities and FIUs, regulations cannot and should not involve communication between FIUs and LEAs. Communicating the vast number of SARs to LEAs would clearly overwhelm the judicial system. Accordingly, as documented by Findings 17 and 21, FIUs and other key AML stakeholders should have an efficient framework in place to enable easy access to obliged entities' ML information and intelligence. Furthermore, an efficient framework for data and intelligence sharing would increase the success rate of the prosecutable/non-prosecutable code translation and prevent FIUs from having to solely rely on obliged entities' often reluctant cooperation, as documented in Findings 7 and 8.

Finding 17: The ML intelligence available across financial institutions was not adequately leveraged by the regulator and the committee in charge of completing the NRA within FIU1's jurisdiction. Thus, potentially relevant information relating to ML risks and dangers was ignored.

Finding 21: There is currently no framework nor standards in place for FIUs to adequately leverage existing financial institutions' ML intelligence.

Finding 7: The SAR analysis performed by FIUs is limited by the poor quality of SAR information submitted to FIUs.

Finding 8: The SAR process depends on FIUs who rely on obliged entities completely and obliged entities who, constrained by regulation, cooperate reluctantly. This creates inefficiencies.

Proposition 3: The prosecutable/non-prosecutable code should be successfully operationalised. This should be achieved through FIUs' better access and understanding of the ML intelligence held by obliged entities.

Proposition 3 essentially indicates that more should be expected from the private sector. However, as documented in Finding 14, there is a tremendous amount of pressure applied to obliged entities who, despite being perceived by FIUs and regulators alike as unreliable in the fight against ML, are expected to apply and enforce expanding and ever more stringent regulatory AML requirements. For instance, public-private partnerships such as the UK Joint Money Laundering Intelligence Taskforce (JMLIT) or the US FinCEN Exchange have "placed information sharing and collaboration across public and private sector partnership members at the centre of efforts to detect and respond to financial crime risks" (RUSI, 2020, p. 11).

Finding 14: Financial institutions, despite being caught laundering money with criminal intent, as a result of incompetence or due to the sheer volume of transactions they face, are maintained by regulators at the forefront of ML prevention.

As previously argued, this is understandable because obliged entities are essentially the gatekeepers of the financial system and are in the best position to observe

ML-related activities, given the sheer number of transactions processed by financial institutions every year. For instance, the European Central Bank estimates that "the total number of non-cash payments in the euro area, comprising all types of payment services, increased by 7.9% to 90.7 billion in 2018 compared with the previous year" (ECB, 2019). However, the misalignment between the lack of trust in obliged entities and the increasing expectation and reliance on the latter to deliver the AML agenda is striking. Even more striking is the fact that, given the validity of Finding 14, regulators have not yet developed incentive schemes, other than fines, to encourage obliged entities to act as the main ML gatekeepers.

Finding 25: The current AML framework is based on the cooperation of obliged entities with FIUs and regulators but fails to adequately incentivise obliged entities.

Rather, regulatory sanctions aim to act as disincentives to ensure adherence to the current AML framework and are intended to improve adherence in a way similar to incentives. However, as documented in Chap. 1, the list of regulatory fines incurred by the banking industry clearly suggests that these disincentives are not preventing ML infractions and scandals. As such, it could be argued that obliged entities should be given incentives, rather than merely disincentives, to deliver the AML agenda and that obliged entities should be positively acknowledged and rewarded when successfully enforcing the AML framework.

Proposition 4: The current AML framework should positively incentivise obliged entities to support the wider AML framework.

The FIU: Boundary Operationalisation and Attempts at Bridging Function Systems

The FIU's dependence on the economic function system (via obliged entities), the political function system (via the FATF, the European Commission and the state) and the legal function system (via LEAs) has been explored in previous sections. Essentially, the FIU's decision machinery and recursivity are enabled by three separate function systems whose binary codes, however, are neither used within the FIU nor comprehended by it. Indeed, FIUs use neither the economic (payment/non-payment), legal (illegal/legal) nor the political (government/opposition) binary codes.

Thus, since organisations enable the bridging of function systems and ultimately enable the empirical reality of function systems and their structuration (Nassehi, 2005), this raises the question: To which function system do FIUs belong? FIUs bridge the three systems discussed above but belong to none of them. Observing the operations performed by FIUs illuminates the above three function systems; communication within and across these systems results in the emergence of an AML framework, which, as Demetis argues, is an AML system (Demetis, 2010) in a Luhmannian sense. The FIU is thus an organisation pertaining to the AML system, and, as previously discussed, FIUs comprehend the suspicious/non-suspicious binary code (Demetis, 2010). Demetis explains how function systems with different codes, rationales and, of course, functions come together to produce a new system.

The emergence of the AML system may be attributable to structural coupling, a notion already explored and discussed in Chap. 2 and defined by Moeller as "a state in which two systems shape the environment of the other in such a way that both depend on the other for continuing their autopoiesis" (Moeller, 2006, p. 19). However, as organisations whose autopoiesis occurs through decisions, financial institutions clearly do not depend on FIUs for their existence. Their function of producing financial services would not cease in the absence of FIUs. However, the opposite scenario is not true because FIUs do depend on the decisions made by obliged entities to file SARs for their own autopoiesis. The same logic may be applied when considering FIUs' relationships with legal organisations (such as LEAs and law-making institutions) and political organisations (such as the FATF and governments). Legal and political organisations do not depend on FIUs for their existence, but FIUs would not maintain their own autopoiesis in the absence of legal or political organisations. Hence, the AML system is the manifestation of structural couplings and emerges through the communication or, as Luhmann calls it in the context of organisations, the units of decisions taking place among all three function systems.

The concept of AML system and the word "system" for that matter are such overused terms that when mentioned colloquially, the AML system is often understood by AML practitioners as the overall AML framework of institutions, regulations, processes and procedures used to address and tackle ML risk. What needs to be assessed, however, is whether the AML system is more than just a framework, i.e. whether it is an actual function system that has emerged through functional differentiation and is being supported by the economic, legal and political function systems. Demetis (2010) argues that it is indeed the case that the AML system is a function system. To establish the status of the AML system as a function system, Demetis uses the following criteria: function, code and autopoiesis (Demetis, 2010, p. 103). He argues that communication between the economic, legal and political subsystems gives rise to the AML system which "acquires the property of self-reference out of the systems that communicate for the act of its systemic formation" (Demetis, 2010, p. 107). Furthermore, Demetis argues that the "autopoiesis of the AML system comes into being out of the autopoiesis of the systems that generate it" (Demetis, 2010, p. 107). Furthermore, Demetis explains that "for the AML system, the code is the unity of the distinction between suspicious/non-suspicious" (Demetis, 2010, p. 111).

Given these considerations, FIUs would seem to be organisations pertinent to the AML system that, as posited by Nassehi (2005), enable the AML system's empirical manifestation. Indeed, it has been discussed in the previous section that FIUs use and understand the suspicious/non-suspicious code, which, as noted above, is a translation code that allows FIUs and obliged entities to communicate. Additionally, as discussed above, FIUs explicitly use the high-danger/low-danger distinction. The use of the high-danger/low-danger distinction essentially enables an FIU's autopoiesis. As documented in Chap. 2, FIUs require suspicious activity reports to fulfil their purpose and thus to exist. However, it is exclusively FIUs that perform the analysis of suspicious activity reports and collect additional intelligence held by obliged entities. Although transactions or sets of transactions first emerge as suspicious within obliged entities, FIUs are the only organisations that analyse suspicious activity reports and apply the high-danger/low-danger distinction to them.

FIUs have access to a continuous supply of suspicious activity reports and incoming ML intelligence. Furthermore, the existence of previous suspicious activity reports that were archived because of the application of the high-danger/low-danger distinction allows the FIU to combine and recombine new ML intelligence and SAR intelligence to archived suspicious activity reports marked with a low-danger status. Within their own boundaries, financial intelligence units are thus able to maintain ML intelligence in a suspended state, which allows FIUs to produce the elements needed for analysis and combine them with incoming suspicious activity reports. This allows an FIU to perform its function of analysis and maintain its existence through autopoiesis.

In addition to enable FIUs autopoiesis, the high-danger/low-danger distinction enables FIUs to operationalise the SAR regime and ensures the line of continuity extending from the obliged entity issuing a particular SAR, to the FIU performing the SAR analysis, to the LEA who receives SAR-generated cases that have been identified as potentially prosecutable. Essentially, the SAR regime is the empirical manifestation of the systemic boundary between subsystems of the economic, AML and legal function systems as well as the organisations pertaining to such function systems. Thus, the FIU as an organisation enables the AML system to stabilise its own structure, making the AML exchanges "repeatable, structured and expectable" (Nassehi, 2005, p. 188). By this very act, the FIU enables, facilitates and actualises boundary maintenance.

Luhmann (1995a, 1995b) explains that the function of a boundary is to "separate and connect system and environment" (Luhmann, 1995a, p. 28). He states that the boundary does not separate relations and, as an "abstract concept, one cannot decide whether [the boundary] belongs to system or environment" (Luhmann, 1995a, p. 29). Thus, essentially, the boundary facilitates feedback and exchange of information between system and environment. Based on the above discussion, the SAR regime may thus be considered as the empirically observable manifestation of the boundary between obliged entities, FIUs and LEAs. The SAR regime enables an obliged entity to be structurally and operationally connected to its FIU. In addition, the SAR regime ensures that the obliged entity is separate from the FIU because its function in relation to the SAR is clearly documented and delineated. Alerts are analysed and escalated to the status of a SAR within obliged entities, but no SAR analysis is actually performed within them.

The reader may recall that an organisation enables a function system to stabilise its own structure: "it takes organisations to install forms of reflexivity into the function systems" (Nassehi, 2005, p. 188) and to structure legal, economic or political exchanges. Hence, according to Luhmann, organisations support function systems, and their decisions (i.e. their units of communications) are driven by the codes of those function systems. For instance, banks support the economic system and apply the payment/non-payment code, whereas courts of justice apply the illegal/legal code. The FIU supports the AML system, understands the suspicious/non-suspicious code, uses the high-danger/low-danger code and operationalises its boundary through the SAR regime.

Some boundaries facilitate feedback between system and environment, while others do not. Indeed, boundaries make the system more or less sensitive to environmental irritations. Hence, while the SAR regime makes the AML system particularly sensitive to its environment because its function is preventing and fighting ML, the economic system is not sufficiently sensitive to the AML system as far as the latter is concerned. This is manifested, for example, by the FIUs' complaints about low-quality SARs and obliged entities that submit SARs merely to fulfil regulatory duties. Similarly, the difficulty of converting SARs into prosecutable cases that can be investigated and brought to justice by LEAs indicates that the legal system may also not be sufficiently sensitive to the AML system. Thus, the failure of a boundary to facilitate feedback mirrors the failure of an FIU to bridge different function systems, which is also linked to its failure to operationalise some translation codes effectively. While the AML system emerges from within the economic, political and legal systems, there is currently no organisation capable of bridging those three systems in an effective and credible way. The SAR regime enables the empirical manifestation and autopoiesis of the AML system, but without successful communication across relevant organisations and function systems, the fight against ML remains unsatisfactory.

Proposition 5: The current AML framework needs a mechanism that can facilitate successful communication and bridging across all the function systems that support and deliver AML efforts.

Before concluding this section, the author wishes to highlight the fact that the autopoiesis of the AML system is not only enabled by "the autopoiesis of the systems that generate it" (Demetis, 2010, p. 107). Indeed, the AML's system's autopoiesis also arises through the self-referential and reflexive nature of ML risk and danger, as documented in Findings 20, 26 and 28. Hence, the AML system is dependent on ML danger and risk not only for their very existence but also for their self-referential nature.

Finding 20: ML risk and the environment within which it evolves encompass an array of subrisks and systems that feed off, resonate and irritate one another. This generates additional risks and frictions. The current framework cannot capture this complexity.

Finding 26: The risk-based approach enables risk practitioners to focus their resources on high ML risk categories. It is a decision tool that enables organisations to perform the re-entry of risk on themselves through the high-risk/low-risk distinction, facilitating the observation of risk and thus its management.

Finding 28: De-risking is performed by regulators, obliged entities and FIUs alike. It results in the re-risking of organisations, which are then faced with the decision to either accept the re-risking or reject it through re-entry of the risk/danger distinction.

De-risking and the Recursivity of Re-risking

Section 3.3 explored the fact that risk governance has moved away from regulators (i.e. away from the political function system), towards non-governmental organisations and, more specifically, towards the private sector. Hence, as previously observed, governance mechanisms have increasingly become the responsibility of the regulated rather than the regulator, with the former being required to demonstrate transparency and justify decision-making processes. Thus, this invokes the question of why regulators and related policies fail or refuse to acknowledge the role of financial institutions in ML (as per Finding 14) while expecting the latter to abide by, monitor and enforce ever more stringent AML regulations.

Finding 14: Financial institutions, despite being caught laundering money with criminal intent, as a result of incompetence or due to the sheer volume of transactions they face, are maintained by regulators at the forefront of ML prevention.

The regulator is an organisation that supports the political system and therefore the political system's function of "making collectively binding decisions possible" (Moeller, 2006, p. 29). In addition, according to Finding 18, the function of the regulator is to protect the stability of the economic system.

Finding 18: The regulator needs to maintain its own credibility and reputation to preserve itself as an organisation. At times, this may conflict with its role in preserving the stability and the reputation of the economic and political systems.

For instance, in the case of the Danske Bank scandal, it would appear that Danish authorities including the Danish regulator were involved in protecting the institution. Indeed, Howard Wilkinson, while testifying at the European Parliament in November 2018, presented excerpts from two communication events between the Danish FSA and Danske Bank officials. The first extract states: "The FSA has helped the bank in a very critical situation. They are now very worried" (Email from [name deleted] to [names deleted], 7 April 2013). The second email states: "I don't care in the slightest what happens in Estonia. My job is to protect Danske Bank" (Comments from [name deleted-1] to [name deleted-2] shared with Howard Wilkinson by [name deleted-2] in January 2015).

As such, in order to achieve their key functions, regulators aim to manage the irritations within the environment of the economic system. The challenge, however, lies in also preserving their own credibility. Indeed, regulators need to understand that decision-making comes with accountability and responsibility regarding other organisations and function systems. Hence, as clarified by Finding 27, the regulator, in its role within the political system, needs to be aware that it is "the major decision maker of society and consequently the main source of risk" (Holmström, 2008, p. 14).

Finding 27: Although de-risking is perceived by the regulator as a danger from its own environment, de-risking is the result of irritations triggered by the regulator itself, which in turn affect its environment.

Thus, despite the above challenges, regulators pass on responsibility and accountability for decision-making to the economic system in order to perform their function of ensuring collectively binding decision-making. This process enables the regulator to limit its role as decision-maker, limit its role as a societal source of danger and limit opportunities for the private sector to become a victim (as per Luhmann's risk/ danger model) and helps to ensure that regulations are sensitive to other function systems' rationales and binary codes. Regulators achieve this by essentially transferring governance to relevant function systems via organisations that have the ability to bridge the rationales and binary codes of other function systems. In Luhmann's words: "any system can steer itself only, with the modification that other systems can regulate it not against, but exactly through its self-regulation. Politics can only create conditions that influence the program of another system and in this way the self-steering" (Luhmann, 1997, p. 53).

The above approach enables regulators to ultimately preserve their legitimacy and credibility should damages associated with their decisions arise. Indeed, as per Findings 18 and 24, the preservation of organisational legitimacy is essential to system maintenance and thus survival.

Finding 18: The regulator needs to maintain its own credibility and reputation to preserve itself as an organisation. At times, this may conflict with its role in preserving the stability and the reputation of the economic and political systems.

Finding 24: The absence of a documented risk appetite means the absence of a decision-making audit trail. This preserves the reputations and credibility of obliged entities and regulators should losses or damages arise as a consequence of that decision-making.

Indeed, as discussed in the findings chapter, and as highlighted in Finding 24, regulators aim to avoid being associated with any decisions that may prove regrettable. As Luhmann states, "the modern obsession with risk management has the practical function of teaching one how to avoid the regret of regrettable decisions" (Luhmann, 1990, p. 225). Regulators are no different from other organisations such as obliged entities or FIUs who, the reader may recall, de-risk in order to protect their respective function systems.

One of the mechanisms enabling regulators to pass regulating responsibilities to obliged entities (thus empowering the latter to self-regulate, to become the decision-makers and hence risk takers) is the risk-based approach, which allows the regulators to move away from decision-making and hence de-risk its own organisation. Indeed, while the risk-based approach was devised to allow obliged entities to handle ML risks and dangers through self-steering and self-regulation, it could be argued that this approach also enables regulators to facilitate their own de-risking efforts. As discussed in Sect. 3.3, regulators can explain any misstep from regulated entities as resulting from a misalignment in the interpretation and application of the risk-based approach (as opposed to the regulator's error). Given that the wider AML framework is used to support the political or governmental function system, this enables the regulators to manage the political system's exposure to risks and dangers associated with their own decision-making. Documentation of such practices can be found in the findings chapter, which describes the denouncement by a number of risk

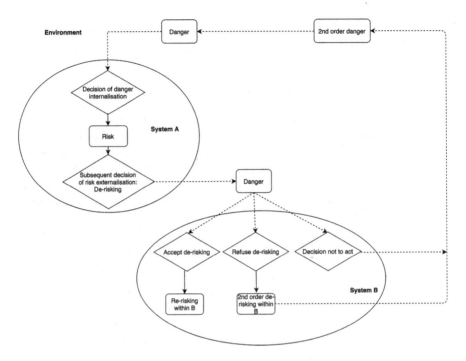

Fig. 4.2 De-risking and re-risking

practitioners of the inclusion of tax evasion within the current AML framework and recounts the case of a Russian politician who was accused of ML offences. And as Finding 28 punctuates, the main issue of importance is that de-risking has led to the re-risking of other AML stakeholders.

Finding 19: The AML framework is a tool that can be (mis)used to support and preserve a political, economic or financial system, regardless of the system's integrity and ethics.

Finding 28: De-risking is performed by regulators, obliged entities and FIUs alike. It results in the re-risking of organisations, which are then faced with the decision to either accept the re-risking or reject it through re-entry of the risk/danger distinction.

Through the de-risking process, a system signals that a particular risk is being externalised and converted back into a danger that other systems will need to internalise as a risk or leave as a danger. These other systems have the responsibility to decide whether they will or will not internalise the danger, which is illustrated in Fig. 4.2.

For illustration purposes, in Fig. 4.2, System A represents the banking sector, which has previously onboarded money service businesses and internalised the risk presented by this customer base. More specifically, onboarding money service businesses as clients is a risk that was accepted by banking institutions, and, as decision-makers, these institutions implemented adequate mitigating tools for

4.1 Section 1: Extracting Propositions 161

managing this risk. Now System A has decided to de-risk, which, for instance, entails the banking sector to now exclude money service businesses because of a new climate of close regulatory scrutiny, thus lowering ML risk tolerance for this sector.

System B represents the money service business that now faces a decision in relation to handling the danger generated by System's A decision. System B could accept System A's de-risking decision, thus internalising this irritation coming from System A or reject it (e.g. because of lack of resources for internalisation). The money service business could decide to accept the signalling from System A and implement processes to establish and maintain the existing relationship with System A, or it could secure a relationship with another financial institution. System B may thus decide to improve its own risk management system to address the banking sector's risk aversion to regulatory scrutiny. More specifically, System B may decide to implement better procedures for account monitoring, develop KYC policies, audit CDD processes and/or strengthen risk management systems. In this scenario, System B would not be the victim within Luhmann's risk/danger framework discussed in Chap. 2. Rather, in this context, System B assumes the role of a decision-maker and internalises the risk that has been externalised by System A. When this occurs, the process of re-risking happens. Such re-risking occurs in System B because System A has been de-risked.

Another scenario illustrated by Fig. 4.2 is the possibility that System B may reject System A's de-risking signalling and refuse to internalise that danger. In such a case, System B rejects System A's de-risking decision and thus does not have to re-risk its own system. Such a scenario is illustrated by Barclays Bank's decision in May 2013 to terminate its relationship with remittance companies. Barclays (System A) stated that it terminated this relationship to comply with its obligation to apply the risk-based approach. Whether this was indeed the case or not is irrelevant to this specific point. What is important is that Dahabshiil (System B), a money service business based in the UK affected by Barclays' decision, rejected this decision and took Barclays to court; Dahabshiil obtained an injunction against Barclays based on competition law and prevented Barclays from terminating their relationship. Through this process, Dahabshiil internalised the danger posed by Barclays' de-risking decision by means of taking Barclays to court. This internalisation turned that danger into risk, more specifically, the risk of having the court judging in favour of Barclays bank. However, the court's decision allowed System B to successfully de-risk its system. This is described in Fig. 4.2 with the process "Refuse de-risking" → "Second-order de-risking within B". Furthermore, the decision to reject Barclays' de-risking attempt impacted Barclays itself, as is shown in Fig. 4.2 by the arrow between the "Second-order de-risking within B" box and the "Second-order danger" box, which then leads to the "Danger" box affecting System A. This case illustrates the repurposing of System B danger into System A danger.

A final scenario is one in which System B does not reject System A's de-risking decision. However, if System B fails to internalise System A's de-risking decision into a risk and cannot transfer the danger posed by such a decision back onto System A or onto any other system for that matter, it becomes an affected party—in other words, a victim facing the dangers triggered by System A's decision. Such dangers may also subsequently expand to other systems, which then leads to second-order dangers (e.g. customers of money service businesses in remote regions without easy access to banking or institutions seeking banking services within parallel, underground and unregulated economies). The FCA report documents such dangers as follows: "It is clear from the evidence that many small money service businesses have had difficulties with their banking arrangements and more regard their situation as precarious. Many have felt pressurised to change their business model" (Artingstall et al., 2016, p.49; FCA 2015b). The report also documents the wider implications of banks de-risking money service businesses: "Given the role these sectors play in supporting developing economies, UK communities and businesses, de-risking could be having a significant socio-economic impact" (Artingstall et al., 2016, p. 5).

This scenario is documented in the figure above. System A de-risks system B, which perceives this decision as a danger (because it is not part of the decision-making process); based on the irritation imposed by System A, System B decides not to internalise the danger into risk, and it thus remains a danger. This is presented in the "Decision not to act" box. When this occurs, second-order dangers arise in the form of, for example, precarity for System B (as documented in the 2015 FCA report) or wider socioeconomic impact, should additional money service businesses be de-risked. Hence, such dangers no longer impact System B alone and can have repercussions on other systems including System A as well as others. Along with other systems, System A is then faced with new decisions to internalise the danger or not. Note that the figure above does document the process of second-order danger internalisation and externalisation for Systems A and B as well.

Something that Fig. 4.2 above does not represent, however, is the fact that organisations can re-risk self-referentially, absent of any irritation imposed by their environment. Indeed, Finding 16 illustrates this statement. As discussed with risk practitioners during the empirical research segment of this study, scientised risk assessment tools are designed to automate the decision-making process and thus the communication of risk, with the aim of reducing the complexity of decisions required to evaluate risk and provide the illusion that the ambiguity of risk can be captured by a set of key rules. These automated communication and decision-making processes seek to de-risk an obliged entity in its role of risk assessor. The risk assessment decision process thus becomes technicised (Luhmann, 2018) and enables decisions about customers or transactions to be automated and unimpeded by decisions made by human analysts.

However, based on Luhmann's concept of understanding, in the context of the triple information-utterance-understanding construct proposed by Luhmann, there is "the acceptance or rejection of the specific meaning that was communicated" (Luhmann, 1995a, p. 147). Discussion with risk practitioners indicated that there are a number of circumstances in which practitioners must reject such automated decisions. This seems almost paradoxical given that, according to Luhmann, technology as a concept should "take place automatically and is not to be interrupted by decisions" (Luhmann, 2018, p. 304). Therefore, deciding to reject such automated decisions impacts AML efforts, thus re-risking the decision-maker.

Finding 16: The application of a transaction monitoring software based on the scientisation of risk generates false positives. This hinders AML efforts, creating further dangers that require internalisation.

To summarise, by definition, all organisations aim to protect their function systems' stability. To achieve this, organisations de-risk their operations and, if successful, pass risk to other organisations and, depending on the organisation, other function systems, which allows organisations to further reduce their own complexity. This de-risking is performed by a regulator leveraging the risk-based approach—illustrated, for instance, by the regulator enabling FIU2 to leverage FIU. NET and pass SARs to other jurisdictions. Similarly, obliged entities apply the risk-based approach to unbank risky customers (Artingstall et al., 2016), and customers may litigate when they are unwilling to serve as victims of a decision-maker (as observed in the case of Dahabshiil vs. Barclays Bank case). Thus, de-risking occurs through the use of regulation, technology and law.

However, while all organisations engage in de-risking, only one organisation has the power to enforce collectively binding decisions, namely, the regulator. Accordingly, regulators need to acquire what Holmström calls a polycontextual worldview that acknowledges one's own worldview as contingent and facilitates exchanges of perspectives (Holmström, 2008). The reader should note, however, that the author is not recommending that regulators completely cease de-risking their own systems or prevent de-risking of other systems. This would generate even further risk. Indeed, de-risking essentially aims to reduce a system's complexity. By preventing this process, systems would then be exposed to a level of complexity that they may not be able to handle, thus potentially resulting in the system's instability and eventual collapse. However, what is suggested is that coupled with the right incentives motivating obliged entities to effectively deliver the AML agenda, as per Propositions 1, 3 and 4, regulators should recalibrate their own appetites to credibility risk by accepting more accountability when "things go wrong". Regulators assume that de-risking is the result of obliged entities' misperceptions of regulation but fail to recognise their responsibility in relation to the de-risking of obliged entities.

Proposition 6: The regulator needs to be mindful of its de-risking practices in order to limit irritations to its environment. As the ultimate decision-maker (because of its power to make collectively binding decisions possible), it should be willing to absorb additional complexity in order to support obliged entities in their fight against ML.

The Important Role of Risk Taker as Risk Bearer

As discussed above, decisions result in risk for decision-makers and danger for individuals or organisations that are not part of the decision-making process. Such individuals are what Luhmann refers to as "affected parties" (Luhmann, 1993a), whereas Holmström calls them "victims" (2006). The findings discussed below point towards the need to explore the way in which society manages risk takers and how the latter communicate their risks when associated damages and losses eclipse the benefits or profits generated by their risk taking. Finding 23 indicates that once the potential damage associated with a decision related to ML risk actually arises, if the damage is greater than the associated benefits, the decision-maker will communicate such risks as dangers.

Finding 23: When an ML scandal occurs and associated damages and/or losses emerge, the obliged entity responsible for the decision that led to the ML scandal treats the latter as a danger and not as a risk, thus initially rejecting accountability and responsibility for the decision.

At face value, this empirical observation challenges Luhmann's observation that: "in the case of risk, losses that may occur in the future are attributed to decisions made. They are seen as the consequences of decisions, moreover as consequences that, with regard to the advantages they bring, cannot be justified as costs" (Luhmann, 1993a, p. 101). However, the case of Danske Bank clearly contradicts Luhmann's comments. Danske's potential USD8 billion fine, coupled with its decrease in profits in 2019, the USD231.72 million lawsuit filed by a number of international investors, Aivar Rehe's suicide (CEO of Danske Bank's Estonian Branch 2006–2015), the prosecution of ten Danske Bank Estonia employees, Danske Bank's forced exit from the Estonian jurisdiction and Estonia's tainted reputation can only be described as extremely high costs. These costs were imposed not only on society at large but also on Danske Bank itself. Beyond a certain threshold, a distinction arises between consequences and regrettable consequences. While all decisions to accept high-risk non-resident customers were those of Danske Bank alone, the damages that emerged as a consequence of these decisions transformed into dangers for the decision-maker itself, indicating a re-entry of the risk/danger distinction into risk.

The fine line between consequence and regrettable consequence is ambiguous, however, and is also observer relative. Indeed, when the Estonian regulator issued a report in 2015 effectively forcing Danske to de-risk and close its non-resident portfolio, this constituted a consequence of Danske's decision-making. Likewise, the 2017 *Berlingske* article on Danske that caused its reputation to be publicly questioned was also the consequence of deciding to bank non-resident customers between 2007 and 2015. Similarly, the public scolding in the form of a GBP1.5 million fine issued by the Danish regulator in late 2017 was, again, the consequence of Danske not exiting its non-resident portfolio as promptly as the regulators would have liked. At some point, however, a shift occurred: the consequences faced by Danske became regrettable and more akin to danger, meaning that the decision-maker became the affected party as well as the risk taker. The question that arises, however, is how such a shift occurs and where, exactly, the threshold between consequence and regrettable consequence occurs.

A shift arises when there is a convergence of different function systems acting as observers. In the case of the Danske Bank scandal, the legal system (US prosecution), the economic system (JP Morgan stepping down from its correspondent banking relationship with Danske), the political system (Estonia forcing

Danske Bank out of its jurisdiction), the media (*Berlingske* and *Financial Times* publishing their ML investigations) as well as the AML system (the Danish and Estonian regulators putting pressure on Danske) all converged to observe Danske Bank, which essentially triggered the materialisation of ML damage, leading to what the media has called the greatest ML scandal to date (Garside, 2018). Indeed, ML-related damages arising from risks taken by banks only emerge when they are observed—not before. Unlike credit risk, for instance, whose associated damages arise when enough customers default on their payments, thus leading the bank to face liquidity issues, damages associated with ML risk arise only when a sufficient amount of observers converge to observe the fact that the ML risks taken were too great. Once there is information concerning actual ML, damages arise in the form of fines, reputational damage, market share loss, etc.

However—as seen in the timeline of the Danske Bank debacle, which indicates regulators' knowledge of ML risks as early as 2007—information on Danske's dealings existed prior to the convergence of observations described in the previous two paragraphs. But such information only became *relevant* information because of the convergence of the observations of many systems. Indeed, the 2018 Bruun and Hjejle report and the timeline of events published in *The Financial Times* (Milne & Winter, 2018) indicate that there were warning signs of ML as early as 2007; these sources also confirm the presence of high levels of suspicious activities in 2010, regulatory scrutiny in 2012, a damning internal audit report, refusal to scale down the non-resident business, a whistleblowing report concerning dealings with Putin's family and Russian intelligence services and further refusal to hasten the non-resident business exit strategy in 2014, eventually followed by the closure of the non-resident portfolio in 2015, after being pressed by the Danish and, more importantly, Estonian regulators. However, all this information failed to amount to the "difference that made the difference" (Bateson, 1979, p. 92). It was not until 2015–2017, when the Danish newspaper *Berlingske* (Bendtsen et al. 2019; Jung et al. 2017a, 2017b) published multiples stories relating to its investigation on the billions of euros that Danske Bank had laundered, that the Danske Bank ML scandal was born. "Information is information only if it is not just an existing difference; it is information only if it instigates a change of state in the system. This is the case whenever the perception (or any other mode of input one might have in mind) of a difference creates a difference in the system" (Luhmann, 2006, p. 40). Finding 13 states that ML scandals act as a regulating force within the financial sector, indicating that information about ML-related damages comprises the "difference that makes the difference" (Bateson, 1979, p. 92), incentivising the financial sector to self-observe when such circumstances arise.

Finding 13: *ML scandals support the regulator's AML agenda by triggering the wider financial sector to assess and adjust its ML risk models.*

The reader should thus not underestimate the power of the economic function system and its role of self-observation and self-regulation. The privatisation of risk governance and the ever-increasing role of economic systems in that sphere were discussed in Chaps. 1 and 2, but this needs to be further explored, especially in the context of Luhmann's risk/danger model which currently offers only a limited explanation of these factors.

Luhmann states that since dangers injure affected parties, compensation mechanisms are required to ensure social equality between decision-makers, beneficiaries (who often are decision-makers) and affected parties (Luhmann, 1993a, 1993b). Such compensation mechanisms, he argues, are provided by the legal system. For instance, the French authorities started prosecuting Danske Bank in relation to the Magnitsky case involving Danske Bank in a case of "tax fraud and corruption amounting to USD230 million in Russia" (Danske Bank, 2017). Similarly, a group of institutional investors are launching a EUR 358 million lawsuit against Thomas Borgen (ex-Danske CEO) for misleading investors. What Luhmann fails to explore, however, is the importance of the risk taker or the regulatory body emerging as the provider of credible social compensation. The role of risk bearer is fundamental to negotiating the right to continue taking future risks. Many scholars interchangeably refer to risk bearers and affected parties (Renn, 2008), which is misleading: affected parties bear dangers, and when regrettable consequences arise, risk takers (or any other *credible* entity) bear risks.

The process of becoming a risk bearer is, unsurprisingly, not straightforward. Indeed, as previously discussed, the risk taker does not automatically adopt the role of risk bearer. Review of the ING report as well as the Danske Bank report and the Deutsche Bank presentation indicates that the risk taker needs to first minimise responsibility in relation to the risks and dangers generated by its decisions. Minimising responsibility is achieved through a careful narrative evidencing that there were no decisions made to internalise dangers to begin with, i.e. no risk taking decisions per se. Again, review of the ING report, the Danske Bank report and the Deutsche Bank presentation indicates that obliged entities carefully document the root causes of such scandals as a weak AML framework, lack of procedures, different operating language or systems and/or customer legacy. Such attributions suggest that no acceptance of ML risk per se ever took place. Yet obliged entities' regrettable consequences generally reflect their ML risk appetite and tolerance. As Luhmann explains:

> When risks are attributed to decisions that have been made, this leads to the taking of a number of consequent decisions, to a series (or a decision tree) of bifurcations each in its turn offering risk decision making options. The first distinction is whether the loss remains within the usual cost bounds (...) or whether it brings about a situation in which one retrospectively regrets having made the decision. (Luhmann, 1993a, 1993b, p. 23)

Furthermore, as interviews with regulators, FIUs and risk practitioners indicate, ML scandals associated with the ML risk internalisation of obliged entities are never within what Luhmann refers to as "cost bounds"—in other words, risk appetite—which the reader may recall is never documented by obliged entities anyway.

Indeed, Luhmann argues that "risk is the hopefully avoidable causal link between decision and damage. In other words, it is the prospect of post-decisional regret. In fact the modern obsession with risk management has the practical function of teaching one how to avoid the regret of regrettable decisions" (Luhmann, 1990

p. 225). However, when post-decisional regrets arise, not only does the obliged entity need to deal with the associated loss; it also needs to take into account the element of time difference and repurpose this internalised danger, i.e. risk, for the future in order to avoid future losses associated with this internalised danger. In addition, whatever new decision is made in order to repurpose this internalised danger, the obliged entity must take time into account and must assess the possibility that, should future losses arise as a consequence of that decision, the organisation must be able to affirm that it made the right decision given the situation. In such circumstances, the use of the risk-based approach enables obliged entities to observe their risks and communicate them to relevant stakeholders such as the regulator.

Finding 26: The risk-based approach enables risk practitioners to focus their resources on high-ML-risk categories. It is a decision tool that enables organisations to perform the re-entry of risk on itself through the high-risk/low-risk distinction, facilitating the observation of risk and thus its management.

According to Finding 26, the moment an obliged entity is identified as having exceeded the acceptable level of ML risk, the use of a further distinction, i.e. an observation, is necessary to enact what AML practitioners call remediation. The risk-based approach enables this process by facilitating the observation of risk and, through re-entry, allowing the observer to make further distinctions in marking one side of the high-risk/low-risk distinction. The high-risk side requires further distinction to make it observable to the observer. Luhmann states "a risk gains in precision and definability only when we determine what a risk is to be distinguished from" (Luhmann, 1993a, 1993b, p. 219). Indeed, review of the 2018 Bruun and Hjejle report on the Danske Bank scandal highlights that the law firm's remediation methodology consisted in identifying:

> All customers with non-resident characteristics, such as address, contact data or ownership outside Estonia, that were active during the period between 1 January 2007 and 31 January 2016 (with one or more transactions) to make sure that all potentially suspicious activity on the part of non-resident customers is examined. (Bruun and Hjejle, 2018, p. 16)

In essence, the portfolio investigation identified high-risk customers within Danske Estonia, based on their non-resident status. Once this distinction was made, another distinction was performed on the marked state (i.e. the high-risk customers). As the report explains, the remediation team "developed risk indicators, which have been applied to customers subject to investigation with a view to identifying the customers with higher risk" (Bruun & Hjejle, 2018, p. 16). Thus, the remediation team performed a re-entry of the high-risk/low-risk distinction into the high-risk marked state. Through a re-entry of the high-risk/low-risk distinction, a risk practitioner can artificially preserve the contingency of risk. Essentially, the risk practitioner then narrows the fixed contingency to limit the obliged entity's exposure to risk and thus its responsibilities with regard to managing a high-risk business. The process of high-risk/low-risk re-entry is documented in Fig. 4.3.

This figure demonstrates the incredible versatility of the risk-based approach. It is used by key ML risk practitioners such as FIUs, regulators and obliged entities for a variety of purposes including de-risking and risk remediation programmes. While, as

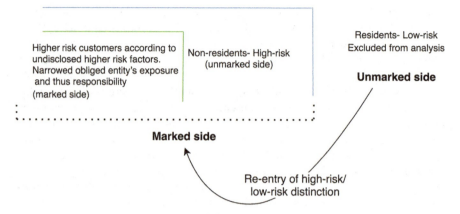

Fig. 4.3 High-risk/low-risk re-entry [adapted from Åkerstrøm Anderson (2001)]

indicated by Findings 15 and 20, the risk-based approach may not have fully demonstrated its capacity for capturing the complexity of risk, it is nevertheless a tool that helps obliged entities perform observations and, more importantly, communicate risk and risk-related decisions.

Finding 15: The risk-based approach methodology fails to capture collusion as a factor of ML risk.

Finding 20: ML risk and the environment within which it evolves encompass an array of subrisks and systems that feed off, resonate and irritate one another. This generates additional risks and frictions. The current framework cannot capture this complexity.

In circumstances of post-decisional regret, once the above exercise of re-entry of the high-risk/low-risk distinction is completed, the risk taker will willingly assume the role of risk bearer and assist regulators in investigations, paying regulatory fines, investing in relevant compliance and financial crime departments, setting up integrity committees and, if necessary, replacing senior executives. Such initiatives are always criticised by the media for being "too little too late", but they serve a very important purpose. Accepting culpability in the process of self-attribution ensures that the affected party retains the role of victim while the risk taker preserves its right to make decisions. When affected parties reject the role of victim, protest movements arise and create a destabilising force. Recent events such as Black Lives Matter, Greta Thunberg-inspired climate change rallies, "gilets jaunes" protests in France and the Occupy Wall Street initiative in the wake of the 2008 credit crisis constitute "communications addressed to others calling on their sense of responsibility" (Luhmann, 1993a, p. 125) and illustrate consequences of affected parties' unwillingness to accept the dangers stemming from the decisions of others. As such, to ensure a system's survival, a credible entity, such as the regulator or the risk taker, must assume the role of risk bearer when the fine line between consequences and regrettable consequences is crossed. This is essential for enabling future decision-making and risk taking and is fundamental to organisations that support the materialisation of function systems, "reproduce themselves by means of decisions, and which have to incorporate the results of decisions into further decisions. In these circumstances, there can certainly be no question of a calculable balance between opportunity and risk" (Luhmann, 1993a, p. 197). Thus, the regulator (who is also an affected party at times) must ensure that the risk-bearing role (assumed by the risk taker or the regulator itself) does not create a positive feedback loop, destabilising the system or, worse, the function system to which it belongs. In the negotiation framework between risk takers and affected parties, affected parties must assume the role of victim so that society can continue to take the risks necessary for societal evolution.

Proposition 7: The role of risk bearer is fundamental to the risk/danger model, ensuring society's sustainability and evolution by preserving organisations' abilities to make future decisions and take risks despite past or present regrettable consequences.

The systems theoretical deconstruction of the 28 findings documented in Chap. 3 derived seven propositions that must be considered in order to improve and enhance the AML domain. The following section summarises those seven propositions and explores the theoretical and domain contributions arising from them.

4.2 Section 2: Theoretical and Domain Contributions

Table 4.1 summarises the seven propositions that have emerged from the empirical research and the discussion relating to the findings documented in Chap. 3 The propositions will be further explored in order to demonstrate the extensions this research makes to Luhmann's risk/danger model and to create a conceptual model for enhanced ML risk communication process and a more robust AML framework.

Contributions and Recommendations

Three themes emerge from the propositions presented in Table 4.1: de-risking and re-risking (Propositions 2 and 6), the central role of the risk bearer (Proposition 7) and ML risk communication (Propositions 1, 3, 4 and 5). Each of those themes will be discussed in turn.

Re-risking: The Inevitability of De-risking

Proposition 2: FIUs de-risk to other FIUs and externalise ML danger when possible. The current AML framework should acknowledge this phenomenon and identify ways to leverage such mechanisms to facilitate FIUs' de-risking and ML danger externalisation mechanisms.

Table 4.1 Summary of propositions

	Proposition	Supporting findings as documented in Sect. 4.1
1	*FIUs should acknowledge obliged entities' risk profiles in the SAR escalation and analysis process. This would allow FIUs to leverage their existing knowledge and/or intelligence in relation to specific obliged entities' risk profiles. This would therefore increase the likelihood of identifying the wider ML dangers that the jurisdiction may be exposed to at an early stage of the analysis process*	1, 3, 22
2	*FIUs de-risk to other FIUs and externalise ML danger when possible. The current AML framework should acknowledge this phenomenon and encourage and facilitate FIUs' de-risking and ML danger externalisation efforts*	2, 4, 5, 6, 10, 11, 12
3	*The prosecutable/non-prosecutable code needs to be successfully operationalised. This should be achieved through better access and understanding of the unleveraged ML intelligence held by obliged entities*	4, 5, 7, 8, 9, 17, 21
4	*The current AML framework needs to positively incentivise obliged entities to share their ML intelligence in a more cooperative manner, thus further supporting the wider AML framework*	14, 25
5	*The current AML framework needs an organisation that can successfully bridge function systems that support and deliver AML efforts*	Proposition 3, Findings 4, 5, 8
6	*The regulator needs to be mindful of its de-risking practices in order to limit irritations to its environment. As the ultimate decision-maker (because of its power to make collectively binding decisions possible), it should accept absorbing additional complexity in order to support obliged entities in their fight against ML*	14, 16, 18, 20, 24, 26, 27, 28
7	*The role of the risk bearer is fundamental to the risk/danger model, ensuring society's sustainability and evolution by preserving organisations' abilities to make future decisions and take risks despite potentially regrettable consequences*	13, 15, 20, 23, 27

As illustrated in Fig. 4.2, this research identified and discussed the proposal that all institutions de-risk, with FIUs and regulators being no exception, because organisations, as the empirical manifestations of function systems, work towards reducing their own complexity. Accordingly, preventing de-risking is not recommended, as doing so would essentially force an organisation to retain a degree of complexity that it no longer feels it can manage or adequately handle. De-risking has been generally demonised in the academic and AML literature (Ramachandran et al., 2018; Rose, 2019; FCA, 2015a, 2015b), but it is a phenomenon that is essential to the sustainability of any organisation and hence function system. Organisations work towards reducing their own complexity and thus that of the function systems they belong to. Proposition 2 documents the fact that FIUs need to be supported in their de-risking initiative and ML danger externalisation efforts. Not all FIUs are created equal, and some have a superior infrastructure, analyst headcount, budget, level of technology access or quality of stakeholders than others, thus facilitating ML danger externalisation. "National differences in information collection, analysis, and dissemination reflect a variety of financial intelligence uses and purposes as well as the roles, powers, and responsibilities associated with FIUs" (Scherrer, 2017, p. 80). For example, the UK 2018 Mutual Evaluation Report states that "the UK has made a deliberate policy decision to limit the role of the UK Financial Intelligence Unit (UKFIU) in undertaking operational and strategic analysis" (FATF, 2018, p. 4). Thus, one could argue that unable to adequately fulfil the second of FIUs' three functions (receipt, analysis and dissemination), the UK FIU has focused on achieving high dissemination rates. "The SARs database is made available to 4 825 accredited financial investigators or administrators. This distributed model of SARs dissemination enables LEAs to access SARs directly and apply their own resources to their analysis without waiting for a dissemination from the UKFIU" (ibid. p. 43). UKFIU has a mechanism in place to de-risk and externalise ML danger.

In order to address such imbalances, relevant governing bodies should aim to homogenise the environments of FIUs, where possible, to facilitate the ability of FIUs to pass SARs to LEAs and other FIUs and/or jurisdictions where pertinent. While the 2021 AML and CFT legislative package focuses on improving the operationalisation of the prosecutable/non-prosecutable translation code, it fails to consider SARs dissemination as a de-risking and ML danger externalisation tool that supports FIUs in managing their complexity as an organisation. As previously discussed, this phenomenon can be observed in jurisdictions such as that of FIU2 or UKFIU.

Recommendation 1: The EU Platform of FIU experts should review dissemination practices and processes across EU FIUs to identify cases where mechanisms have been implemented to facilitate SARs dissemination to other function systems and/or jurisdictions thus enabling de-risking and ML danger externalisation.

Such research could be performed with the support of the Egmont Group and would enable to identify cases across potential jurisdictions where de-risking and ML danger externalisation mechanisms have been implemented. Once identified, root causes and rationale for such mechanisms would be discussed and shared with relevant stakeholders to assess whether similar mechanisms can be implemented in relevant jurisdictions to facilitate dissemination and thus support FIUs in their de-risking and ML danger externalisation efforts. Figure 4.4 illustrates such a mechanism.

Proposition 6: The regulator needs to be mindful of its de-risking practices in order to limit irritations to its environment. As the ultimate decision-maker (because of its power to make collectively binding decisions possible), it should be willing to absorb additional complexity in order to support obliged entities in their fight against ML.

Before discussing Proposition 6, the phenomenon of de-risking and re-risking will be explained through Luhmann's concepts of irritation and resonance. A system's de-risking (in Fig. 4.5 it is presented as System A) will result in irritations

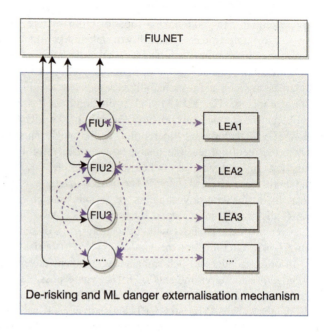

Fig. 4.4 De-risking and ML danger externalisation mechanism

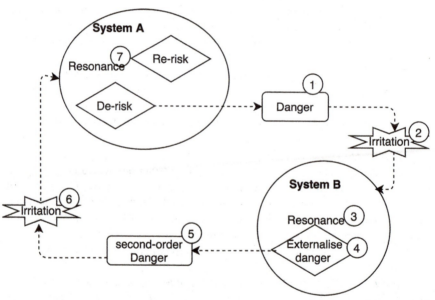

Fig. 4.5 Irritation and resonance; de-risking and re-risking

to another system (System B in Fig. 4.5), which will then resonate according to these irritations. The system will not directly respond to such irritations because it is operationally closed. Rather, the resonance will be filtered through System B's operations, but the system will nonetheless be irritated by System A. This resonance may, in turn, create irritations to System A, which will in turn resonate within that system, potentially irritating System B again. The phenomenon of irritation and resonance through de-risking and re-risking is illustrated in Fig. 4.5.

When System A makes the decision to de-risk, it generates danger for System B (1). This creates an irritation for system B (2); the irritation crosses the boundary of System B and, through System B's operations, resonates (3) within system B. This resonance implies that System B is irritated by System A. System B will therefore make the decision to either accept this danger or not. In the context of Fig. 4.5, System B rejects this danger and externalises it (4), which generates a second-order danger (5) and irritates System A (6). Filtered through System A's operations, this irritation resonates (7) within system A which is observed through the re-risking phenomenon.

Now that irritation and resonance through de-risking and re-risking have been illustrated, Proposition 6 can be discussed. This proposition acknowledges that the regulator also de-risks because it is an organisation. However, the regulator's de-risking creates second-order dangers to obliged entities, which, because of the regulator's collectively binding decisions, cannot easily externalise them. This phenomenon is illustrated in Fig. 4.6.

The regulator makes a decision (1) that generates a risk to the regulator (2) and danger to victims (3). An example of this would be the decision to change regulatory requirements in relation to correspondent banking relationships. This causes an irritation (4), which, filtered through obliged entities' operations, resonates (5) within their systems (here represented by System B). Obliged entities may then take the decision not to accept this danger by unbanking correspondent banking relationships (6). This creates an irritation to the regulator (7) and generates a danger. Through its power as a collectively binding decision-maker, the regulator can de-risk and avoid resonance (8). This, however, creates a second-order danger to obliged entities (9) and an irritation (10) that obliged entities will need to internalise (11). This will likely create ripples across the financial sector, as obliged entities not only must then contend with new regulations relating to correspondent banking relationships (in the case of the above scenario); they also need to handle a regulator who controls their response to new regulation. Thus, in controlling irritations to its own system, the regulator adds further complexity to obliged entities (System B in Fig. 4.6). To limit second-order irritations and dangers faced by obliged entities, the regulator therefore needs to be mindful of its de-risking practices and its wider repercussions. As such, the recommendation arising from Proposition 6 is as follows.

Recommendation 2: The regulator needs to be aware of the repercussions of its de-risking practices. To limit the latter, the FATF should set up a working group with regulators and banking associations to identify "hot spots" of regulation that could be more rules-based, thus giving regulators more accountability in relation to governance and obliged entities clearer guidance as to what is expected of them.

A potential de-risking hot spot may indeed be correspondent banking relationships. In Chap. 4, a number of interviewees mentioned regulations relating to

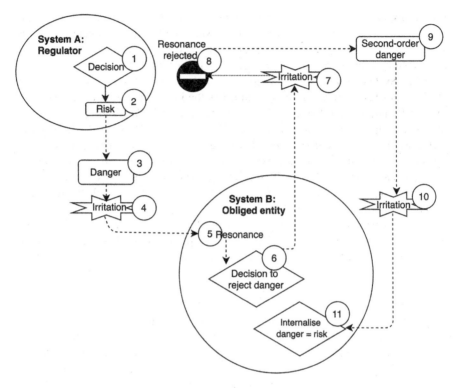

Fig. 4.6 Regulator's de-risking decisions

correspondent banking relationships as being exceedingly ambiguous in terms of regulatory expectations. Furthermore, interviewees strongly suggested that regulators offer very little support, leaving obliged entities guessing. Should the relevant regulator be willing to absorb the risk of being held accountable should something "go wrong", obliged entities would have fewer irritations to contend with and a less complex system to manage. This would align with the regulator's remit which, as discussed in Chap. 3 and Section 1 of Chap. 4 is to protect the stability and credibility of the wider financial system.

The Role of the Risk Bearer

Proposition 7: The role of risk bearer is fundamental to the risk/danger model, ensuring society's sustainability and evolution by preserving organisations' abilities to make future decisions and take risks despite past or present regrettable consequences.

As documented in Chap. 3, Sect. 4.1, and Fig. 4.2, generally successful de-risking decision programmes of obliged entities, FIUs and regulators lead to re-risking.

However, it has not yet been discussed what happens when the victim, affected by a third party's decision, faces a danger that is simply too big. This section explores the wider implications of a decision's regrettable consequences.

As of September 2020, the Danish regulator has still not issued a fine against Danske Bank. However, the economic function system has taken matters into its own hands in the meantime, with a group of institutional investors seeking restitution damages of EUR 358 million in a lawsuit against ex-Danske Bank CEO Thomas Bergen (Monroe, 2020). This is an illustration of the re-risking phenomenon under the specific circumstances of regrettable consequences and post-decisional regret.

The risk bearer is the recipient of re-risking when the risk taker and/or other parties face a danger that is so great that post-decisional regret arises. However, this role is not featured in Luhmann's risk sociology (1993a), where Luhmann explains that "the law and economy are compensation mechanisms" (p. 102) but describes such compensation mechanisms as "protection against danger" (p. 102) engendering "a climate of rights" (p. 103). The role of accountable party is indeed protection, but not against danger in the way that Luhmann appears to imply. If credibly and adequately rewarded for their danger acceptance initiatives, victims that have been affected by a decision-maker's decision signal that other victims can also reasonably accept the role of victim. They indicate to future victims that beyond the threshold of regrettable consequences, decision-makers will be held accountable, or beyond the threshold of acceptable dangers, victims will be compensated, and they too can therefore accept the role of victim in the future. This social contract enables decision-makers to make decisions, take risks and generate dangers for others. However, should it become apparent that dangers are beyond an acceptable threshold; the risk taker needs to assume the role of risk bearer. This is observed in the case of the Danske scandal, for instance.

Just like the re-risking scenarios presented in Fig. 4.2, the risk-bearer scenario is an empirical manifestation of risk's self-referential nature. The difference, however, is that the risk bearer role is required only when post-decisional regret arises. Luhmann's risk/danger framework presented in Fig. 4.7 (Chap. 2) and replicated below fails to capture those two re-risking scenarios. It does not illustrate the possibility that (a) past a certain threshold leading to post-decisional regret, the role of "risk bearer" becomes essential, re-risking whoever assumes this role. Likewise, it does not acknowledge that (b) the victim may reject the role of victim and force the decision-maker to re-risk. Figure 4.8 proposes extensions to the framework illustrated in Fig. 4.7 (and first introduced in Chap. 2) that accommodate points a and b.

Figure 4.8 presents Luhmann's risk/danger framework extended with the risk bearer, de-risking and re-risking phenomena observed in this research (Findings 10, 27, 28 and Propositions 2 and 6). New elements are given in purple for ease of reference, and references to the numbers in Fig. 4.8 are given in the following summary describing the two re-risking scenarios observed in this research: the first scenario (point a, as per the previous paragraph) entails a decision to internalise a risk whose associated consequences (as observed with the Danske scandal) are regrettable (1), leading to post-decisional regret (2). The threshold of what

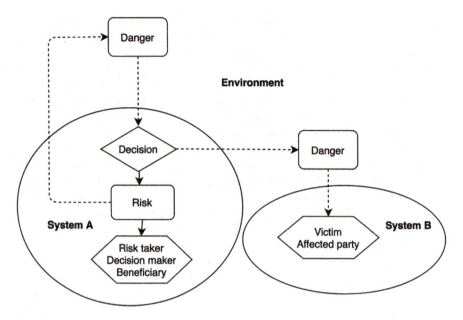

Fig. 4.7 Luhmann's risk/danger model

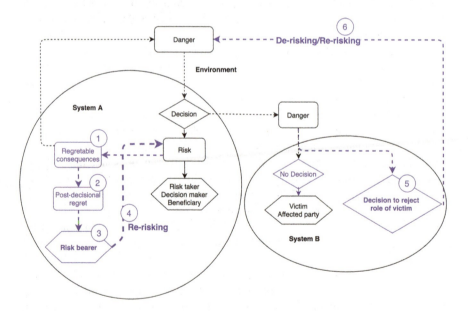

Fig. 4.8 Luhmann's extended risk/danger model

constitutes regrettable consequences is not defined here, but the circumstances surrounding the Danske scandal qualify as regrettable consequences. Under such circumstances, compensation and/or accountability is required, and the entity must adopt the role of risk bearer (3). The risk bearer can be the risk taker (or the regulator). For simplicity, Fig. 4.8 depicts the risk taker as the risk bearer. By adopting the role of risk bearer, System A internalises additional danger and thus re-risks itself (4). If this is successful, System A will be allowed to pursue future decision-making along with other systems that belong to the same industry (for instance, the banking industry).

The second scenario (point b in the previous paragraph) aims to present what was discussed in Fig. 4.2 but in the context of Luhmann's risk/danger model. It involves the victim of System A's decision, i.e. system B. In this case, the victim rejects the role of victim (5) and makes the decision to hold the risk taker accountable for the dangers the victim faces, as observed in the Dahabshiil vs. Barclays case. The de-risking performed by System B is observed as danger for System A who then needs to internalise it and re-risk (6). Although Fig. 4.8 successfully captures de-risking, re-risking and the role of the risk bearer in the self-referential re-risking process, it does not illustrate how the risk bearer enables and facilitates future decision-making.

The extended framework presented in Fig. 4.9 acknowledges the risk taker's responsibility towards future risk takers. More specifically, the risk taker's accountability as a risk bearer in the present (or *period t*) drives the risk taker's ability to take risks in the future (*period t + 1*). If the risk taker does not fulfil its responsibility as risk bearer in *period t,* under circumstances of post-decisional regret, victims in *period t + 1* may de facto reject their roles as victims and therefore the danger generated by the decisions of future risk takers. In this case, the decision-maker would not be able to take risks and its role as a decision-maker would become uncertain. On the other hand, if the risk taker (or any relevant and/or credible party such as the regulator) acts as risk bearer in *period t*, future victims will understand that future decision-makers can act as risk bearers (again, under circumstances of post-decisional regret). As such, future victims will be comfortable with allowing future decision-makers to take risks and therefore accept being affected by future dangers. Essentially, the risk bearer stabilises the decision-maker/victim social contract and facilitates the sustainability of the risk/danger model. Essentially, the affected party/decision-maker distinction is a social contract for present as well as future decision-making.

This is illustrated in Fig. 4.9. It replicates Fig. 4.8 but also demonstrates how the risk bearer in *period t* is essential to decision-making in *period t + 1*. As seen in Fig. 4.8, the risk bearer must be credible, take accountability for the decision leading to regrettable consequences and address those regrettable consequences. Essentially, the risk bearer in the present, or *period t*, signals that future victims are likely to be compensated should regrettable consequences arise. As such, they can therefore confidently accept the decisions of future decision-makers. The blue dotted arrow between risk bearer in *period t* and decision in *period t + 1* illustrates this. Of course, there should be a similar blue arrow linking the risk bearer in *period t + 1* to the decision in *period t + 2* which will be left to the reader's imagination.

To ensure the stability of the risk/danger model and guarantee that society can make decisions in the future and thus evolve, there must be an accountable party or

178   4 Analysis and Discussion

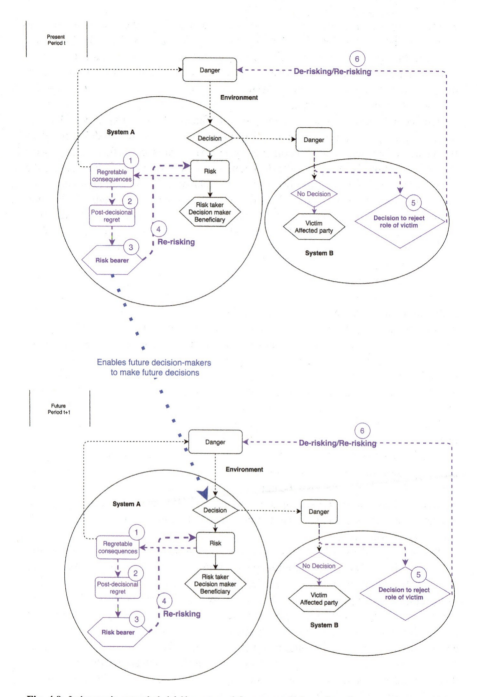

Fig. 4.9 Luhmann's extended risk/danger model across period t and $t + 1$

"risk bearer". This process is fundamental not only to organisations that "reproduce themselves by means of decisions, and have to incorporate consequences of decisions into further decisions" (Luhmann, 1993a, p. 197) but to society itself. Traditionally, one would expect the risk taker or the regulator to assume the role of risk bearer.

As previously discussed, regulators have been de-risking, privatising regulatory governance and, as such, increasingly stepping away from the role of risk bearer. This is illustrated by the back-and-forth documented between the Estonian and Danish regulators regarding who should be held accountable for the Danske scandal (see Sect. 3.3). Hence, influenced by regulators' de-risking initiatives, the risk-bearing role has increasingly been assigned to obliged entities that also happen to be the beneficiaries of their risk taking decisions. Hence, current international AML legislation assigns accountability to the private sector through the legal and political function systems. Article 4 of the EU's Fourth AML Directive requires administrative and criminal sanctions for obliged entities in breach of AML regulation. The role of risk bearer is acknowledged and documented in AML legislation. However, as discussed in Chap. 1 "Are fines adequate indicators of AML effectiveness?", the media function system has observed that banks benefit from impunity and that certain institutions are "too big to jail" (Greenwald, 2012). In sum, the amount of financial fines imposed on banking institutions when breaching AML regulations does not reinforce the role of obliged entities as credible risk bearers. In the case of the Danske scandal, for instance, as of July 2020, the Danish regulator has still not issued a fine. Despite a group of institutional investors seeking restitution damages of EUR 358 million in a lawsuit against ex-Danske Bank CEO Thomas Bergen (Monroe, 2020), there is uncertainty as to whether Danske will credibly act as the risk bearer, hence putting their future risk taking at risk (as observed in Estonia whose regulator has told Danske Bank to close its Estonian branch).

Recommendation 3: To ensure that obliged entities assume their risk-bearer roles (thus protecting the ability of future decision-makers to take risks), the FATF should identify and facilitate additional avenues through which the role of risk bearer can be attributed and enforced. For instance, in addition to administrative fines and criminal sanctions, a fast-track framework facilitating investors' initiatives to seek compensation from decision-makers should be developed to reenforce the risk-bearer role. Similarly, a clear threshold relating to potentially regrettable consequences should be defined to ensure that beyond this threshold, the regulator also assumes the role of risk bearer.

Translation Codes

Proposition 3: The prosecutable/non-prosecutable code should be successfully operationalised. This should be achieved through FIUs' better access and understanding of the ML intelligence held by obliged entities.

Proposition 5: The current AML framework needs a mechanism that can facilitate successful communication and bridging across all the function systems that support and deliver AML efforts.

The empirical research documented and discussed in Chap. 3 and Sect. 4.1, indicates that the current AML framework assumes that the FIU represents a smooth and effortless conduit of information between LEAs and obliged entities. In Luhmannian terms, the framework assumes that FIUs bridge the economic and legal systems. The bridging of economic and legal systems via the FIU is illustrated in Fig. 4.10.

However, the bridging of function systems is only successful when the bridging organisation successfully translates one function system's binary code into another's. As discussed in Chap. 4, the FIU cannot translate its own high-danger/low-danger binary code to the illegal/legal code because it cannot successfully operationalise the suspicious/non-suspicious and prosecutable/non-prosecutable translation codes. This is shown in Fig. 4.11.

Proposition 4: The current AML framework should positively incentivise obliged entities to support the wider AML framework.

To improve the chance of successful suspicious/non-suspicious and prosecutable/non-prosecutable translation codes operationalisation, obliged entities must share their data with FIUs but also across other obliged entities. This would allow obliged entities to share their ML intelligence and recognise typologies across the industry's customer base, patterns of transactions and account closures. This would also enable obliged entities to look into alerts that had previously been discarded as unworthy of

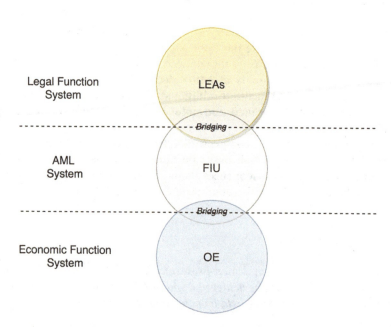

Fig. 4.10 FIUs and the bridging of the economic and legal function systems

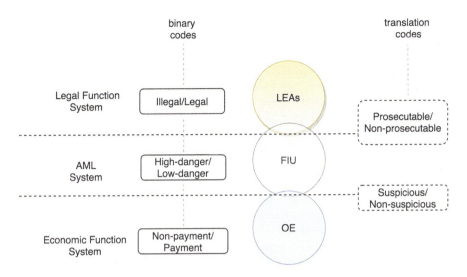

Fig. 4.11 FIUs' operationalisation of translation codes

a SAR, for instance, and use data sharing to identify relevant beneficial owners consistently associated with alerts, thus building stronger SARs with better data quality.

Recommendation 4: The European Commission should develop a tool similar to FIU.NET for obliged entities to enable them to share, access and leverage ML intelligence currently held across financial institutions.

As seen in Chap. 3, FIU.NET allows FIUs to share information multilaterally as well as bilaterally. FIUs contact other FIUs to assess whether a SAR-related individual or organisation is known or unknown to others and, if known, request further information. An equivalent tool (called OE.NET perhaps) could be developed to support obliged entities in a similar way. Current legislation on banking secrecy and privacy laws would initially present an obstacle, but if the data were to be anonymised in the same way it has been for the use of Ma^{3}tch, obliged entities would be able to use "OE.NET" while complying with such regulations. Initiatives such as TMNL in the Netherlands or AML Bridge in Estonia demonstrate that this is possible.

Proposition 4 also explains that there is a real need for incentivisation as supported by Findings 14 and 25. Proposition 1 essentially builds towards a formalised incentivisation process because it highlights the need to acknowledge the respective risk profiles of obliged entities. A process that takes into account an institution's known reputation in terms of risk appetite (as observed through its risk profile), as well as the quality of the SARs it submits, would incentivise obliged entities to strive for robust processes.

Proposition 1: FIUs should acknowledge obliged entities' risk profiles in the SARs escalation and analysis process. This would allow FIUs to leverage their existing knowledge and/or intelligence in relation to the risk profiles of specific obliged entities.

Recommendation 5: A scoresheet should be developed for obliged entities tracking their risk profile as well as SAR submission quality. The institution's risk profile could feed into the SAR risk-scoring analysis increasing the likelihood of identifying wider ML dangers that the jurisdiction may be exposed to at an early stage of the SAR analysis process.

Recommendation 6: The SAR quality scoresheet along with obliged entity risk profile should be formally communicated to the regulator so it can incorporate this intelligence into its supervision strategy.

In addition to further incentivising obliged entities in supporting the AML framework, Recommendations 5 and 6 enable the regulator to support the FIU in bridging the economic and legal function systems by operationalising both translation codes documented in Chap. 3—namely, suspicious/non-suspicious and prosecutable/non-prosecutable. Figure 4.13 illustrates Propositions 4 and 1.

The reader may recall a striking comment made by Interviewee 12: "there is no point in sending account details because it will not be analysed by the FIU and it will be archived". Hopefully, the above framework presented in Fig. 4.13 addresses this issue. Better intelligence means better SAR quality, which would lead to improved analysis and a better chance at prosecution. This, in turn, means that obliged entities would have confidence that the information they send will actually be analysed, thus motivating them to submit better quality SARs and creating a virtuous cycle.

To conclude, Fig. 4.14 consolidates Figs. 4.10, 4.11, 4.12, and 4.13 and illustrates the suggested AML communication framework. Recommendations 1, 4, 5 and 6 indicate that current AML communication should be enhanced by (a) the FIU being supported in its role of code translator and function system bridging, (b) an EU FIU de-risking and re-risking on behalf of national FIUs, (c) obliged entities being able to share and leverage their ML intelligence as well as that of others and (d) obliged entities being incentivised to support AML efforts through a SAR quality and risk profile scoring mechanism.

The research's three contributions have been discussed, documented and illustrated in Figs 4.8, 4.9 and 4.14 In summary, the contributions are as follows.

The role of the risk bearer is essential to Luhmann's risk/danger model, which should be extended accordingly. The role of risk bearer highlights the fundamental nature of the social contract between decision-makers and victims who decide to accept, or not, the role of victim now and in the future. The acceptance of such a role pivots on credible and adequate risk bearers in case regrettable consequences arise from risk takers' decisions.

Re-risking is the by-product of de-risking, and both are unavoidable and necessary because systems aim to minimise their own complexity, which in turn impacts the complexity of other systems. Regulators and policy-makers must not only account for de-risking and re-risking behaviour but also facilitate such behaviour to support the wider AML framework.

4.2 Section 2: Theoretical and Domain Contributions

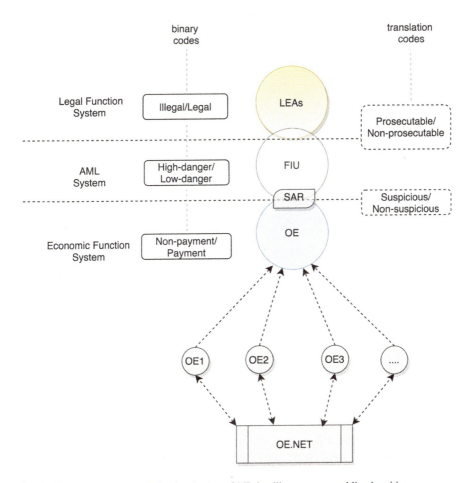

Fig. 4.12 A suggested model for the sharing of ML intelligence across obliged entities

Finally, there are translation codes that are more or less successfully operationalised by organisations. Successful operationalisation enables one function system's binary code to be translated into another function system's code. Without the successful application of translation codes, organisations cannot bridge function systems, communication across function systems fails and the AML framework cannot deliver effective ML prevention.

The following discussion presents the ML risk and communication framework informed by the contributions and recommendations of this research documented in Chap. 5. For ease of reference, Table 4.2 summarises Recommendations 1–6, mapping them against relevant propositions and findings.

Based on the above, Fig. 4.15 presents the proposed ML risk communication framework informed by the extended risk/danger model (illustrated in Fig. 4.9), the need for successful translation code operationalisation (illustrated in Fig. 4.14) and the inevitability of de-risking and re-risking behaviour (illustrated in Fig. 4.2).

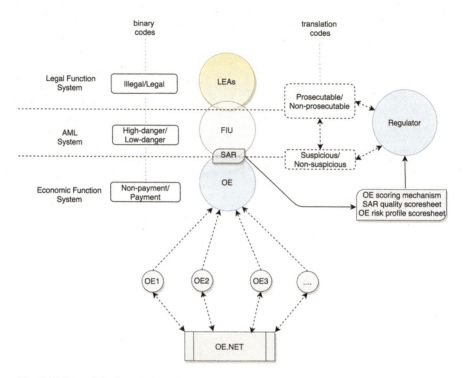

Fig. 4.13 Incentivisation of obliged entities

Figure 4.15 depicts two periods, *period t* (the present) and *period t + 1* (the future). As seen in Fig. 4.9, the regulator and obliged entities are expected to act as credible risk bearers under circumstances of post-decisional regret arising from a risk taker's decision. The blue dotted lines in Fig. 4.15 indicate that the risk bearer in *period t* enables decision-makers (Systems D, and F) to make decisions and take risks in *period t + 1*. The reader should also note that by potentially being risk bearers, Systems D and F also enable decision-makers to make decisions and take risks in *period t + 2*. For simplicity, *period t + 2* is not depicted in Fig. 4.15. Furthermore, the reader will recognise the extended risk/danger model represented by systems D, E, F and G, as per Figs. 23 and 24. In addition, the reader should bear in mind that Systems G and E's de-risking/re-risking efforts may impact dangers faced by Systems D and/or F as well as potentially themselves.

According to Recommendation 4, the framework documents the proposed OE. NET, which would enable obliged entities to share and leverage their ML intelligence. A database such as this, made available to FIUs, would support SAR analysis and dissemination. In addition, Recommendation 1 proposes the creation of an interorganisational European FIU (as previously illustrated in Fig. 4.4) to identify the FIU that would be best suited to adopt and lead specific case files. This would essentially enable FIUs to de-risk and re-risk regardless of whether they have the same competitive advantages as other FIUs.

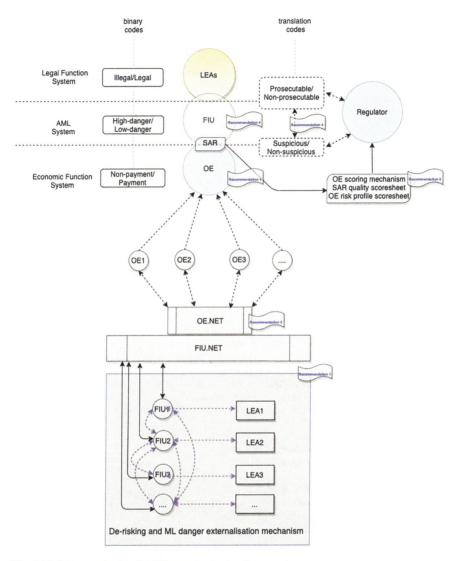

Fig. 4.14 Interorganisational AML communication framework

Recommendations 2 and 3 state that the regulator should be cognisant of its own de-risking decisions in order to limit the incentives of obliged entities to de-risk and thus re-risk the wider AML system. The risk-bearer role assigned to the regulator in Fig. 4.15 would also inhibit the regulator's de-risking initiatives. Finally, Recommendation 5 and 6 demonstrate that to incentivise obliged entities to further support AML efforts, a profile for each obliged entity that is informed by the quality of their SAR submissions and their risk profiles should be communicated to the regulator to feed into the latter's supervisory strategy.

Table 4.2 Summary of recommendations mapped against propositions and relevant findings

Recommendations	Propositions	Findings
Recommendation 1: The EU Platform of FIU experts should review dissemination practices and processes across EU FIUs to identify cases where mechanisms have been implemented to facilitate SARs dissemination to other function systems and/or jurisdictions thus enabling de-risking and ML danger externalisation	*Proposition 2: FIUs de-risk to other FIUs and externalise ML danger when possible. The current AML framework should acknowledge this phenomenon and identify ways to leverage such mechanisms to facilitate FIUs' de-risking and ML danger externalisation mechanisms*	2, 4, 5, 6, 10, 11, 12
Recommendation 2: The regulator needs to be aware of the repercussions of its de-risking practices. To limit the latter, the FATF should set up a working group with regulators and banking associations to identify "hot spots" of regulation that could be more rules-based, thus giving regulators more accountability in relation to governance and obliged entities clearer guidance as to what is expected of them	*Proposition 6: The regulator needs to be mindful of its de-risking practices in order to limit irritations to its environment. As the ultimate decision-maker (because of its power to make collectively binding decisions possible), it should be willing to absorb additional complexity in order to support obliged entities in their fight against ML*	14, 16, 18, 20, 24, 26, 27, 28
Recommendation 3: To ensure that obliged entities assume their risk-bearer roles, (thus protecting the ability of future decision-makers to take risks), the FATF should identify and facilitate additional avenues through which the role of risk bearer can be attributed and enforced. For instance, in addition to administrative fines and criminal sanctions, a fast-track framework facilitating investors' initiatives to seek compensation from decision-makers should be developed to reenforce the risk-bearer role. Similarly, a clear threshold relating to regrettable consequences should be defined to ensure that beyond the threshold, the regulator would also assume the role of risk bearer	*Proposition 7: The role of the risk bearer is fundamental to the risk/danger model, ensuring society's sustainability and evolution by preserving organisations' abilities to make future decisions and take risks despite past or present regrettable consequences*	13, 15, 20, 23, 26
Recommendation 4: The European Commission should develop a tool similar to FIU.NET for obliged entities to enable them to share, access and leverage ML intelligence currently held across financial institutions	*Proposition 3: The prosecutable/non-prosecutable code must be successfully operationalised. This should be achieved through better access and understanding of the unleveraged ML intelligence held by obliged entities*	4, 5, 7, 8, 9, 17, 21
	Proposition 4: The current AML framework should positively incentivise obliged entities to share their ML intelligence in a more cooperative	14, 25

(continued)

4.2 Section 2: Theoretical and Domain Contributions

Table 4.2 (continued)

Recommendations	Propositions	Findings
	manner, thus further supporting the wider AML framework	
	Proposition 5: *The current AML framework needs a mechanism that can facilitate bridging of all the function systems that support and deliver AML efforts*	Proposition 3, Findings 4, 5, 8
Recommendation 5: A scoresheet should be developed for obliged entities tracking their risk profile as well as SAR submission quality. The institution's risk profile could feed into the SAR risk-scoring analysis, increasing the likelihood of identifying wider ML dangers the jurisdiction may be exposed to at an early stage of the SAR analysis process **Recommendation 6:** The SAR quality scoresheet along with obliged entity risk profile should be formally communicated to the regulator so it can incorporate this intelligence into its supervision strategy	***Proposition 1:*** *FIUs should acknowledge obliged entities' risk profiles in the SARs escalation and analysis process. This would allow FIUs to leverage their existing knowledge and/or intelligence in relation to the risk profiles of specific obliged entities* *This would also increase the likelihood of identifying the wider ML dangers that the jurisdiction may be exposed to at an early stage of the analysis process*	1, 3, 22

188   4 Analysis and Discussion

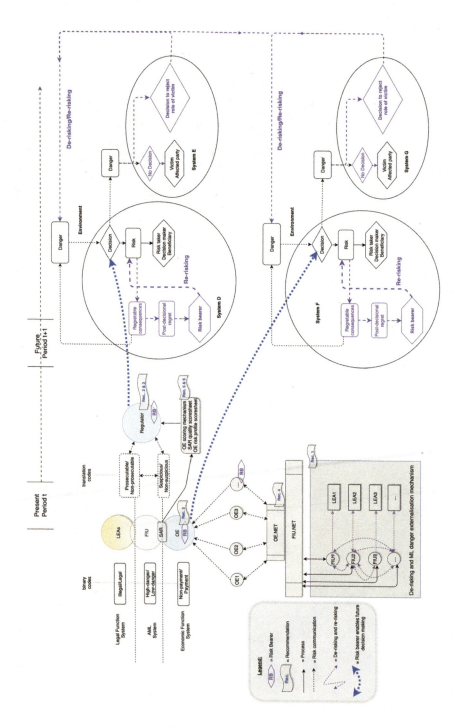

Fig. 4.15 Consolidated framework for ML risk communication

References

Åkerstrøm Anderson, N. (2001). *The Undecidability of decision* (Copenhagen Business School Working Paper No. 12/2001). Accessed Feb 24, 2016, from https://research-api.cbs.dk/ws/portalfiles/portal/58900668/wp122001.pdf

Artingstall, D., Dove, N., Howell, J. & Levi, M. (2016). *Drivers & impacts of derisking: A study of representative views and data in the UK, by John Howell & Co. Ltd. for the Financial Conduct Authority.* [Project Report]. Surrey: John Howell & Co. Ltd. Accessed May 8, 2017, from https://www.fca.org.uk/publication/research/drivers-impacts-of-derisking.pdf

Bateson, G. (1979). *Mind and nature: A necessary Unity*. E.P. Dutton.

Bendtsen, S., Lund, M., & Jung, E. (2019). An overview of the Danske Bank money laundering scandal. Berlingske, 19 March [Online]. Accessed Jan 10, 2020. Available at: https://www.berlingske.dk/samfund/english-versionan-overview-of-the-danske-bank-money-laundering-scandal

Borsch, C. (2011). *Niklas Luhmann*. Routledge.

Bruun and Hjejle. (2018). *Report on the Non-Resident Portfolio at Danske Bank's Estonian branch.* Accessed Feb 10, 2019, from https://danskebank.com/-/media/danske-bank-com/file-cloud/2018/9/report-on-the-non-resident-portfolio-at-danske-banks-estonian-branch-.-la=en.pdf

Danske Bank. (2017, October 11). *Danske Bank placed under AML investigation in France* [Company announcement]. Accessed Jan 23, 2020, from https://danskebank.com/news-and-insights/news-archive/company-announcements/2017/ca11102017

Demetis, D. (2010). *Technology and anti-money laundering: A systems theory and risk-based approach*. Edward Elgar.

European Central Bank. (2019, July 26). *Payment statistics*: 2018. Accessed Jan 23, 2020, from https://www.ecb.europa.eu/press/pr/stats/paysec/html/ecb.pis2018~c758d7e773.en.html

FATF. (2018). *Anti-money laundering and counter-terrorist financing measures United Kingdom mutual evaluation report*. FATF. Accessed Feb 12, 2022, from https://www.fatf-gafi.org/media/fatf/documents/reports/mer4/MER-United-Kingdom-2018.pdf

Financial Conduct Authority. (2015a). *Final notice 2015: Barclays Bank PLC–November 2015.* Accessed Dec 5, 2015, from https://www.fca.org.uk/publication/final-notices/barclays-bank-nov-2015.pdf

Financial Conduct Authority. (2015b). *FCA fines Barclays £72 million for poor handling of financial crime risks*. (Press release 26 November) Accessed Dec 5, 2015, from http://www.fca.org.uk/news/fca-fines-barclays-72-million-for-poor-handling-of-financial-crime-risks

Finanstilsynet. (2019). *Report on the Danish FSA's supervision of Danske Bank as regards the Estonia case.* Accessed Nov 2, 2019, from https://www.dfsa.dk/~/media/Nyhedscenter/2019/Report_on_the_Danish_FSAs_supervision_of_Danske-Bank_as_regards_the_Estonia_case-pdf.pdf?la=en

Finantsinspektsioon (2019). *Response to the report on the Danish FSA's supervision of Danske Bank.* Accessed Nov 2, 2019, from https://www.fi.ee/en/news/response-report-danish-fsas-supervision-danske-bank

Garside, J. (2018, September 21). Is money-laundering scandal at Danske bank the largest in history? *The guardian*. [Online] Available at: Accessed Nov 7, 2019, from https://www.theguardian.com/business/2018/sep/21/is-money-laundering-scandal-at-danske-bank-the-largest-in-history

Greenwald, G. (2012, December 12). *HSBC, too big to jail, is the new poster child for US two-tiered justice system. The guardian* [Online]. Accessed Oct 9, 2015, from http://www.theguardian.com/commentisfree/2012/dec/12/hsbc-prosecution-fine-money-laundering

Holmström, S. (2006). The reflective paradigm in theory and practice. In S. Holmström (Ed.), *Organizational legitimacy and the public sphere* (Vol. 1, pp. 54–72). Roskilde University.

Holmström, S. (2008). Reflection: Legitimising late modernity. In A. Zerfass, B. V. Ruler, & K. Shriramesh (Eds.), *Public relations research: European and international perspectives and innovations* (pp. 235–250). Westdeutscher Verlag.

Jung, E., Lund, M., & Bendtsen, S. (2017a). Dictatorship sent billions through Denmark's biggest bank. Berlingske, 5 September [Online]. Accessed Oct 25, 2018. Available at: https://www.berlingske.dk/virksomheder/dictatorship-sent-billions-through-denmarks-biggest-bank

Jung, E., Lund, M., & Bendtsen, S. (2017b). Links to dead Russian lawyer behind French money laundering probe against Danske Bank. Berlingske, 13 October [Online]. Accessed Dec 22, 2019. Available at: https://www.berlingske.dk/business/english-links-to-dead-russian-lawyer-behind-french-money-laundering-probe

Luhmann, N. (1990). Technology, environment and social risk: A systems perspective. *Industrial Crisis Quarterly, 4*, 223–231.

Luhmann, N. (1993a). *Risk: A sociological theory*. Transaction Publishers.

Luhmann, N. (1993b). Observing re-entries. *Graduate Faculty Philosophy Journal, 16*(2), 485–498.

Luhmann, N. (1995a). *Social systems*. Stanford University Press.

Luhmann, N. (1995b). The paradoxy of observing systems. *Cultural Critique, 31*, 37–55.

Luhmann, N. (1997). Limits of steering. *Theory, Culture & Society, 14*(1), 41–57.

Luhmann, N. (2006). System as difference. *Organization, 13*(1), 37–57.

Luhmann, N. (2018). *Organization and decision*. Edited by Baecker, D. Translated by Barrett, R. Cambridge University Press.

Milne, R., & Winter, D. (2018, February 19). *Danske: Anatomy of a money laundering scandal. The Financial Time*, [Online]. Accessed Oct 24, 2019, from https://www.ft.com/content/519ad6ae-bcd8-11e8-94b2-17176fbf93f5

Moeller, H.-G. (2006). *Luhmann explained*. Open Court.

Monroe, B. (2020, February 28). *Ousted Danske bank CEO faces nearly $400 million lawsuit tied to historic money laundering scandal*, acfcs, [Online] Accessed from https://www.acfcs.org/ousted-danske-bank-ceo-faces-nearly-400-million-lawsuit-tied-to-historic-money-laundering-scandal/

Nassehi, A. (2005). Organizations as decision machines: Niklas Luhmann's theory of organized social systems. *The Sociological Review, 53*, 178–191.

Scherrer, A. (2017). *Fighting tax crimes–cooperation between financial intelligence units, Ex-post impact assessment, European parliamentary research Service* [Online]. Accessed Mar 25, 2022, from https://www.europarl.europa.eu/RegData/etudes/STUD/2017/598603/EPRS_STU%282017%29598603_EN.pdf

Ramachandran, V., Collin, C., Juden, M., & Walker, C. (2018). De-risking: An unintended consequence of AML/CFT regulation. In J. Gurulé (Ed.), *The Palgrave handbook of criminal and terrorism financing law* (Vol. 1). Springer International Publishing AG.

Renn, O. (2008). *Risk governance: Coping with uncertainty in a complex world*. Earthscan.

Rose, K. J. (2019). *De-risking or re-contracting the way around money laundering risks*, (Copenhagen Business School, CBS Law Research Paper No. 19–37). Accessed Sep 2, 2020, from https://papers.ssrn.com/sol3/papers.cfm?abstract_id=3474298

RUSI. (2020). *Future of Financial Intelligence Sharing–survey report: Five years of growth in public-private financial information–sharing partnerships to tackle crime*. Accessed Mar 31, 2022, from https://www.future-fis.com/uploads/3/7/9/4/3794525/five_years_of_growth_of_public-private_partnerships_to_fight_financial_crime_-_18_aug_2020.pdf

Seidl, D., & Mormann, R. (2015). Niklas Luhmann as organization theorist. In P. Adler, P. du Gay, & M. Reed (Eds.), *Oxford handbook of sociology, social theory and organization studies: Contemporary currents*. Oxford University Press.

Chapter 5
Conclusion

5.1 Propositions' Overview

As previously discussed, the research and its 28 findings have been distilled in seven core propositions. These propositions will be presented here in order to not only provide an overview of the findings of the comparative case study, but to offer the context essential to answering the questions documented in the introduction.

Although de-risking is traditionally associated with obliged entities as per the current AML literature (Bukola, 2014; Artingstall et al., 2016; Chatain et al., 2018), this research indicates that the majority of AML stakeholders, i.e. obliged entities, FIUs and regulators, engage in one form or another of de-risking or, in the case of the FIU, in ML danger externalisation. They all transfer risks to other systems. This is a perfectly normal behaviour in a functionally differentiated society, as each function system and organisation seeks to transfer risk and danger to another entity with the aim of minimising its own complexity and protecting its own organisation and function system. Another element discussed in Chap. 3 and Sect. 4.1 is the fact that each de-risking or ML danger externalisation initiative has a re-risking effect. This re-risking phenomenon, although observed, is currently not accounted for by wider AML policy-making initiatives. Like de-risking, the re-risking phenomenon is not anticipated by stakeholders, and the systemic circumstances are misunderstood; thus, when they emerge, they are typically addressed through disincentives such as fines.

Propositions 2 and 6 essentially address the de-risking point and indicate that de-risking initiatives should not be prevented. De-risking initiatives enable each function system to leverage their organisations' decision units, to adjust the risk or, in the case of an FIU, the danger it can comfortably handle without risking (!) destabilisation or, worse, system atrophy. Regulators perform de-risking through the use of power and regulations; obliged entities and FIUs perform de-risking by means of the RBA and the SAR regime and, in the case of FIUs, occasionally through technology use under very specific circumstances, as described in Chap. 4. The SAR regime thus emerges as a flexible and versatile tool that enables de-risking between obliged entities and FIUs and between FIUs and LEAs and communicates ML danger between obliged entities, FIUs and LEAs. However, as per Proposition 3, while the economic and AML systems achieve successful communication through operationalising the suspicious/non-suspicious code, the AML system fails to operationalise the prosecutable/non-prosecutable code and needs to successfully bridge function systems that support the AML agenda (Proposition 5). This is manifested not only by low SAR conversion rates but also by FIU complaints that SARs are often of low quality and that obliged entities generally submit SARs merely to perform their regulatory duties. Since current AML efforts rely on obliged entities being the first line of defence, the current AML framework needs to positively incentivise obliged entities to share their ML intelligence in a more cooperative manner (Proposition 4).

Proposition 1 describes the way that the current AML system handles the responsibility and accountability of obliged entities regarding their ML activities. Indeed, the current AML system targets what obliged entities need to do to perform AML but does not account for obliged entities' facilitation of ML, whether intentional or not. Hence, Proposition 1 would allow the current framework to openly acknowledge that an institution's risk profile and risk appetite determine a system's exposure to ML risk and danger. Accordingly, if FIUs were to include the risk profiles of obliged entities in their risk-scoring mechanisms, it would account for exposure to reputational or regulatory risks associated with obliged entities. This would also prevent regulators from having to formally document and validate the risk appetite of specific obliged entities. In addition, it would enable FIUs to leverage their knowledge and expertise regarding the relative risk profiles and appetites of each obliged entity. It would also indicate to obliged entities that their risk culture is being observed and accounted for, which would essentially signal how the AML market perceives the profiles of individual obliged entities.

Finally, Proposition 7 addresses the fact that the current AML framework fails to acknowledge and, more importantly, fails to formalise the accountability of obliged entities for laundering money. As discussed in Chap. 4 the role of the risk bearer is fundamental to the risk/danger model, as it essentially enables the model to stabilise itself by ensuring that victims, or affected parties, continue to accept dangers associated with the decisions made by others. Indeed, if there is no accountability for the risks one takes and the dangers one forces onto others, the model ceases to function. Victims would reject their danger-bearing duties, which would threaten widespread societal decision-making processes. As such, the accountability of a risk bearer is essential. Having summarised the seven core propositions, the following section aims to address the questions presented in the introduction.

5.2 Answering Key Issues

The two questions proposed in the introduction are:

- What are the ways in which the risk-based approach enables (or disables) AML practitioners to observe and deconstruct ML risks and what are the challenges that they face in applying the risk-based approach?
- In what way does the application of the risk-based approach impact the handling of future/emergent ML risks and what are the broader AML systemic circumstances and challenges of such an impact?

The research presented here demonstrates that AML practitioners interpret ML risk as an entity that can be contained. However, AML practitioners tend to be unaware of ML risk's self-referential and autopoietic nature or do not acknowledge it, perceiving it instead as an entity that disappears the moment the consequences of risk taking have been observed and relevant fines have been paid. The experience faced by respondents and documented in Chap. 4 along with the Danske Bank scandal, for instance, demonstrates this to be incorrect. Indeed, as of September 2020, the impact and consequences of the decisions made by Danske to bank high-risk non-resident customers are still being felt, despite the fact that the non-resident portfolio was closed in 2015. For example, in late January 2020, the Danish Business Authority, Denmark's business watchdog, announced that two Ernst and Young auditors were being brought before the Danish Disciplinary Board of Auditors for failing to meet auditing standards when providing services for Danske Bank in 2014. Thus, 6 years later, the scandal continues to reverberate beyond the immediate environment expected for the observation of ML risk.

This complex phenomenon of feedback and irritation is not and cannot be accounted for by the current AML framework, which aims to deconstruct ML risk into subrisks using the risk-based approach ignoring ML risk's autopoietic nature. As seen in Chap. 3, in their attempts to deconstruct risk, some obliged entities have created additional prisms through which to observe ML risk—namely, regulatory risk, reputational risk, market risk, correspondent banking risk, risk of poorly integrated IT systems, failed internal AML procedures, staff complacency and internal collusion—which have been superimposed onto the traditional categories of customers, countries, geographic areas and product categories (defined through the FATF's risk-based approach). Attempts to capture the globality of ML risk through an ever-expanding list of risk categories evolve each time knowledge emerges pursuant to the latest ML scandal. Such attempts indicate that ML risk has no boundaries, travels across a multitude of environments and systems and is thus observable to countless observers, such as fraud risk specialists, operational risk practitioners, journalists, investors, shareholders, the media, laypeople, etc. Thus, ML risk is not only autopoietic; it evolves through the eyes of multiple observers and environments, creating further risk and enhancing ML risk's interconnectedness and systemicity. Accordingly, one must question where ML risk starts and where it ends. The RBA cannot address such a question.

An additional element is that of risk communication. There is an important distinction between ML risk and ML danger. As discussed in earlier chapters, ML danger and ML risk are both based on the same observed phenomenon; their fundamental difference lies in who the observer is. The decision-maker observes

ML risk, whereas the victim observes ML danger. ML risk and ML danger are, respectively, communicated through the risk-based approach and the SAR regime. The risk-based approach operationalises the high-risk/low-risk distinction, thus enabling obliged entities to communicate their internalised ML risk. The SAR regime, on the other hand, communicates ML danger and operationalises the suspicious/non-suspicious distinction within both obliged entities and FIUs, as well as the high-danger/low-danger distinction within FIUs. The SAR regime also operationalises the prosecutable/non-prosecutable distinction (as discussed in Sect. 5.2) but with less success. Both the SAR regime and the risk-based approach enable ML danger and ML risk to be communicated within systems and, more importantly, across systems and thus across AML stakeholders.

In addition, the risk-based approach enables obliged entities to apply the high-risk/low-risk distinction to ensure that their controls, processes and procedures are commensurate with not only the ML risks they decide to internalise but also with their risk appetites, which lack formal documentation and formalisation. In the FIU context, the risk-based approach enables applying the high-danger/low-danger distinction to SARs. SARs identified as low-danger are archived, thus enabling the FIU to suspend judgement regarding ML danger until information or knowledge emerges that justifies removing the SARs from its suspended state. The ability to suspend danger is unique to FIUs in the AML domain.

In this respect, the phenomenon of re-entry is particularly interesting. Indeed, the re-entry of the high-risk/low-risk distinction into categories that have been previously identified as high-risk support obliged entities in their externalisation of ML risk, i.e. de-risking. Obliged entities have been observed performing de-risking by leveraging the risk-based approach and exiting customers that are deemed to be high-risk within high-risk categories. Although de-risking is pejoratively associated with mass customer exiting strategies and risk avoidance, de-risking properly describes a process whereby risk is simply transferred to another system. In the case of obliged entities, it entails high-risk customers being identified through a risk-based methodology and exited when the risks associated with these customers can no longer be managed by the relevant organisation.

The risk-based approach also enables organisations to control what they observe. Specifically, the risk-based approach determines which risks an organisation decides to observe and which risks it decides to set aside, which can help organisations to control their risk narrative. For instance, regarding the Deutsche Bank case discussed previously, in the aftermath of the Russian Laundromat scandal, the institution diluted ML risk categories by performing a re-entry of the high-risk/low-risk distinction into each of the three traditional risk categories, namely, low, medium and high. This gave rise to a more precisely graduated scale of impact, documented as minor, low, medium, high, severe and acute, which allowed Deutsche Bank to control the narrative of the risk it was facing. Similarly, but with different objectives in mind, Danske Bank performed a re-entry of the high-risk/low-risk distinction into its high-risk customer category in order to minimise the volume of high-risk customers it would have to investigate in the context of its non-resident portfolio review and remediation exercise. This essentially enabled Danske Bank to focus its resources on a narrower segment of its high-risk customers, thus allowing Danske to more effectively manage its workload.

In terms of the wider consequences associated with the use of the risk-based approach, the author does not believe that de-risking initiatives among organisations represent such a consequence. While it has been claimed that de-risking is the result of obliged entities misunderstanding and misapplying the RBA (FCA, 2016), the risk-based approach is merely a tool that facilitates de-risking. Organisations will seek to de-risk in order to manage their systems' complexity regardless of the existence of a risk-based approach to do so; the RBA simply makes the de-risking and re-risking processes more fluid—exemplified, for instance, by regulators fully leveraging the risk-based approach to privatise ML risk governance and thus limit their own liabilities and hence risk.

Finally, the risk-based approach operationalises the risk/danger model. It facilitates future decision-makers' risk internalisation through which danger is generated. It is then the future victim's decision to either face such danger or transfer it back to the decision-maker or any other entity, whereby re-risking its environment. As discussed in Chap. 4, the credibility and robustness of the risk-bearer influences future decision-makers' decision-making process and future victims' danger acceptance. On a broader systemic level, risk practitioners' application of the RBA could enable supervisory authorities to predict who future decision-makers and victims may be. Regulators and policy-makers could therefore leverage the intelligence generated by financial institutions' RBA and implement mechanisms that account for or perhaps predict future de-risking and re-risking initiatives, facilitated by the use of the risk-based approach. Such mechanisms should aim to support re-risking while creating incentives to channel further de-risking and re-risking initiatives thus minimising adverse de-risking consequences documented in the AML literature (Artingstall et al., 2016; Durner & Shetret, 2015; Ramachandran et al., 2018). Having addressed both key issues laid out in the introduction, the following section aims to summarise the implications for future research.

5.3 Applicability and Implications for Future Research

This work opens up several avenues for future research. First, future research should further examine the way in which organisations operationalise translation codes to seek successful bridging of function systems. Such research might focus on identifying key criteria common to successful and poor translation code operationalisation. This would facilitate the development of communication processes in which multiple function systems and thus organisations work together to deliver public policies. Similarly it would enable institutions to understand the root cause of conflicting responses to risk and danger (for instance, the current pandemic). Another area of research might evaluate the role of the risk bearer within industries that manage risk. Such research could address how the enforcement of the risk-bearer role (or lack thereof) may, for example, accelerate the de-risking or re-risking phenomena whose root causes and systemic circumstances have not been identified or adequately assessed. Finally, examining the European Commission's 2020 action plan for ML and TF prevention would also represent a fruitful research avenue. In light of the current research, the European Commission's proposal for a single EU supervisory authority as well as a mechanism for FIUs' cooperation should be evaluated.

References

Artingstall, D., Dove, N., Howell, J. & Levi, M. (2016). *Drivers & impacts of derisking: A study of representative views and data in the UK, by John Howell & Co. Ltd. for the Financial Conduct Authority.* [Project Report]. Surrey: John Howell & Co. Ltd. Accessed May 8, 2017, from https://www.fca.org.uk/publication/research/drivers-impacts-of-derisking.pdf

Bukola, A. (2014). *AML de-risking: An effective method of plugging AML control failures?* ACAMS. Accessed Feb 12, 2016. Available online: http://www.acams.org/wp-content/uploads/2015/08/AML-De-Risking-An-effective-method-of-plugging-AML-controlfailures-B-Adisa.pdf

Chatain, P-L., Van Der Does De Willebois, E. J. M., Gonzalez Del Mazo, I., Valencia, R. D., Aviles, A. M., Karpinski, K., Goyal, S., Corazza, C. Priyani, M., Endo, I., Eckert, S. E., & Abel, D. (2018). *The decline in access to correspondent banking services in emerging markets: Trends, impacts, and solutions–lessons learned from eight country case studies.* FCI Insight. World Bank Group. Accessed Dec 17, 2018, from http://documents.worldbank.org/curated/en/552411525105603327/The-decline-in-access-to-correspondent-banking-services-in-emerging-markets-trends-impacts-and-solutions-lessons-learned-from-eight-country-case-studies

Durner, T., & Shetret, L. (2015). *Understanding Bank De-risking and its effects on financial inclusion.* Oxfam. Accessed Feb 3, 2016, from https://www.globalcenter.org/wp-content/uploads/2015/11/rr-bank-de-risking-181115-en.pdf

Financial Conduct Authority. (2016). *Derisking banks' management of money-laundering risk – FCA expectations.* 24 February [Company announcement]. Accessed Feb 12, 2016. Available online: https://www.fca.org.uk/about/what/enforcing/money-laundering/derisking

Ramachandran, V., Collin, C., Juden, M., & Walker, C. (2018). De-risking: An unintended consequence of AML/CFT regulation. In J. Gurulé (Ed.), *The Palgrave handbook of criminal and terrorism financing law* (Vol. 1). Springer International Publishing AG.